The New Testament Pattern:
God's Blueprint for Christians and Their Churches

By Chad Sychtysz

© 2023 Spiritbuilding Publishers.
All rights reserved. No part of this book may be reproduced in any form without the written permission of the publisher.

Published by
Spiritbuilding Publishers
9700 Ferry Road, Waynesville, Ohio 45068

THE NEW TESTAMENT PATTERN:
God's Blueprint for Christians and Their Churches
By Chad Sychtysz

ISBN: 978-1955285-60-5

Spiritbuilding
PUBLISHERS

spiritbuilding.com

Table of Contents

Author's Preface 1

Introduction 3

Part One: God Has Given Us a Pattern to Follow

Chapter One: What Does It Mean to Be a "Christian"? 12

Chapter Two: Why Do Christians Need Churches? 23

Chapter Three: "According to the Pattern" 34

Chapter Four: Why Many People Do Not Follow the Pattern 49

Part Two: The New Testament Pattern

Chapter Five: The Pattern for Fellowship with Christ 61

Chapter Six: The Pattern for Becoming a Christian 71

Chapter Seven: The Pattern for Church Organization 84

Chapter Eight: The Pattern for Collective Worship 97

Part Three: Policies, Expedients and Departures

Chapter Nine: Human Policies within a Church 109

Chapter Ten: What Expediency Is and Is Not 121

Chapter Eleven: The Danger of Unwarranted Interpretations . . . 139

Chapter Twelve: Departures from the Pattern 153

Chapter Thirteen: Denominationalism 164

Endnotes 178

Sources Used 208

Author's Preface

There is a great need for a book like this. Whether I was the right person to have written it, time will tell. But the need is present, and it is an urgent one. The modern assault against Christianity—ironically, from people who claim to be "Christian"—needs to be exposed for what it is: a departure from God's blueprint. Nothing less than a return to the New Testament pattern of teaching, conversion, and church organization is desperately needed.

A mind-numbing, heart-dulling, and soul-blinding *spirit of deception* has been cast upon the religious world. The wide path of least resistance has never looked so much like the seemingly noble path of sincerity and "God knows my heart" religion as it does today. This deception can be difficult to resist since, on the surface, it appears to be good, loving, and harmless. Yet, feelings are being put on par with divine truth; personal convictions are posing as heavenly doctrine; and people are doing whatever seems right in their own eyes, despite the clear instruction otherwise. As a result, many are being duped into thinking they are pleasing to God even as they trample underfoot His pattern and dismiss His apostles' teaching.

The assault of religious error is not new, of course, nor are those who have spoken out against it. I have been reading for decades the writings of Christian ministers, historians, and apologists who have exposed the errors of those who use the Bible as a prop rather than a blueprint. Through my own in-depth studies of the Scriptures, I have come to many of the same conclusions as these writers did. Yet, it seemed time for a fresh approach, a different style, and a new voice to identify modern errors as well as a biblical response to them. I don't believe that I am "the" new voice of reason, for I am hardly alone in my endeavor, but I certainly am "a" voice.

In my opinion, this message is not limited only to those caught up in systematic religious error. The errors of drifting away from the pattern are diverse and widespread: anyone who claims to be a Christian can succumb to them. In other words, it's not just people "out there" in their religious beliefs who have drifted, but it can be members of churches that have for many decades been stalwart defenders of the faith—or even my own congregation. Because of this, I would strongly recommend this book to anyone who is *already* a Christian, *thinks* he is already a Christian, or is seeking to *become* a Christian. The intention of this book is not to stand on its own merit, but to lead the reader to *God's* book (the Bible). The better we are armed with God's word, the better we can expose any errors we might have and practice His truth.

This book has its roots in a series of lessons I wrote in 2013 on promoting the New Testament of the Bible as a divinely revealed pattern rather than a humanly amendable document (as it is often treated). The core "pattern" chapters herein are derived from lessons in that series. Other chapters are based on lessons or classes that came later. A few chapters were written from scratch, so to speak, because I felt they were needed for further explanation or clarification. My intended approach is a "Come, let us reason together"-kind of narration, but I will let you judge how well that worked. It is always my intention not to appeal to one's emotion, tradition, or religion, but to that person's intellect. God's word is consistent and reasonable regarding fellowship with Him; therefore, it will always appeal to those seeking consistency, reason, and His fellowship.

I would like to thank Matthew Allen, owner of Spiritbuilding Publishers, for his great support for this book. Upon receiving the manuscript, he was eager to publish it—and I am deeply grateful for his enthusiasm. I would also like to thank my son, Logan (who has a bachelor-of-arts degree specializing in English and literature) for editing the original manuscript and calling attention to my grammatical flaws. I also appreciate my fellow preacher, Darrell Beane, for reading the manuscript and offering his response to it. And many thanks, as always, to my wife, Honey, for her unfailing love and concern for me and my passion for writing.

I also thank all of you who have supported my "other ministry" through your genuine interest, personal encouragement, and purchasing my books. Hopefully, over time, much good will come from all of this.

Chad Sychtysz

November 24, 2022

Introduction

This book is both a biblical and critical-thinking approach to the New Testament pattern for Christians and their churches. The numerous biblical references provided within are meant to underscore the need to rely upon the Bible as the highest and final source of all matters pertaining to God, salvation of the human soul, and the future disposition of *all* human souls. This book is not meant to equal or replace the Bible. It is meant only to expound upon what it teaches for the purpose of understanding, clarity, and explanation of topics or terminology.

A proper respect for the Bible is necessary to engage in a study of it. The Bible should not be regarded as merely a book on religion, since this undersells and misrepresents its original intent. Instead, it should be taken as God's revealed message to all of humankind. Since every person is made in God's "own image" (Gen. 1:27), He wants every person to hear what his Creator has to say to him. Because of this innate connection between Him and every human soul, God's message to *all* souls is a sacred book of *relationships*. In this revealed word, He explains what ruins this relationship, what is needed to restore it, what is required from those who are in it, and its ultimate outcome.

The Bible was written over a 1,500-year span of time by more than forty authors from all walks of life—prophets, priests, scribes, psalmists, kings, a tax-collector, a doctor, a rabbi-turned-Christian, etc. It is a compilation of sixty-six books, letters, prophetic oracles, legal documents, historical records, genealogies, character studies, homiletics (sermons), doctrinal treatises, psalms, moral philosophies, and visions. Despite such diversity in factors and subjects, the Bible has one consistent and united message: God's redeeming love for "the world" (John 3:16), meaning, all of humankind. With no central earthly committee, human planner, or single human editor, the Bible is united and completely interconnected.

The Bible is a book of history as well as sacred religion. It is a book of literature—all *kinds* of literature: historical narrative, poetry, artful rhetoric, formal documentation, prophetic writing, elaborate discourses, collections of proverbs and philosophic perspectives, and formal writing. It is a book of law, containing codified, organized collections of legal ordinances. It is a book of prophecy and revelation:

it is the record of predictions and promises both given and fulfilled. It is also a book of origins, life, love, grace, hope, and promise.

The Bible has consistently been proven to be authentic through archaeology, history, science, and eyewitness accounts. It has had every opportunity to be ridiculed, distorted, corrupted, and destroyed—yet it has survived all of this, its text amazingly preserved and its message perfectly intact. Noted biblical scholar R. K. Harrison writes:

> No book has ever been so minutely studied, has had so many books written on it, has founded so vast a literature of hymns, liturgies, devotional writings, sermons, has been so keenly assailed, has evoked such splendid defenses, as the Bible. Its spiritual influence cannot be estimated. To tell all the Bible has been and done for the world would be to rewrite in large part the history of modern civilization.[1]

The Bible is divided into two major parts: Old Testament and New Testament. "Testament" is usually a word associated with the written will of one who has died (e.g., "The last will and testament of ..."), but God the Father has not died and *cannot* die. Its second meaning, and the one that applies in this case, is that of a covenant relationship between God and certain people.[2] The Old Testament focuses upon God's covenant relationship with Israel, a nation descended from Abraham, his son Isaac, and *his* son Jacob (whose name God changed to "Israel"—Gen. 32:24–29). God made a personal covenant with Abraham that would eventually affect all of humankind (Gen. 12:1–3). He made a separate covenant with the nation of Israel, however, that was limited in scope and duration (Deut. 5:1–3).

The New Testament describes God's fulfillment of His covenant with Israel *and* the establishment of a new covenant with all who seek His fellowship (regardless of race or nationality). God's Son, Jesus Christ, accomplished all this: He fulfilled the first covenant by His perfect obedience to it, and His blood ratified (or, brought to life) the second covenant that God has with each follower of Christ. The first covenant emphasized God's authority, human sin, and the process of atonement *for* sin through literal blood sacrifices. The second covenant emphasizes God's love (as expressed through the giving of His Son—1 John 4:9), the redemption of sinners, and the once-for-all blood sacrifice that Christ provided for that redemption. Having died as a sacrifice for our sin, then raised from that death, and then ascended into heaven, Christ now sits at the right hand of God, having received "all authority" over all that has begun to exist (Mat. 28:18).

To say that the Bible is important in our understanding of God, human souls, and the future destination of all souls is an immense understatement. We could know nothing about *any of these things* unless God (through the Bible) had revealed them to us. We are completely dependent upon the Bible for any factual knowledge of these subjects. While we could know that God existed through deductive reasoning, based upon the design, complexity, engineering, and massive scope of the physical creation (as the apostle Paul argues in Rom. 1:18–20), we could not know anything *personally* about Him. We could know by deduction that God is all-knowing and all-powerful, but we could not know that He is loving, merciful, forgiving, patient, kind, and longing for our fellowship unless He had disclosed this information to us.

Now that we *know* these things—or at least have access to this knowledge—we can enter a relationship with Him through His Son. "In Christ" is a phrase repeatedly used in the New Testament to refer to a covenant relationship with God through Christ. All those who have agreed to the terms of this covenant (as revealed by Christ's apostles) are disciples of Christ, or "Christians," which means "followers of Christ." Such people enjoy all the blessings and privileges of this new relationship, if they remain faithful to what they first agreed to and continue to grow in their faith in God and His Son. Collectively, these followers are all brought into the same spiritual sanctuary, Christ's church ("the body" of Christ—Col. 1:18). Thus, once people are Christians, they are "fellow heirs and fellow members of the body, and fellow partakers of the promise in Christ Jesus through the gospel" (Eph. 3:6). "Gospel" means "good news": it refers to the good news of God's grace and forgiveness offered to all humankind. Yet only those who are "in Christ" receive this grace and forgiveness.

The Bible reveals but also magnifies God's authority (and the authority He has delegated to His Son) and our subordination to that authority. We have no *right* or *ability* to fix the problem of our own sin once it has been committed; we become completely reliant upon God's authority and power to rectify this. If we choose to decline God's help, for any reason, we remain condemned by God and separated from

His fellowship because of our sins. In the hereafter, we will experience condemnation in the form of punishment, inconsolable regret, and awful misery. God, because of His love for us, wants to *spare* us from all of this and has thus invited us into fellowship with Him through His Son, Jesus Christ, and the mediation that He (Christ) provides for us. This *good news* is all spelled out in the New Testament of the Bible.

Citing the Sacred Record

Yet today, what passes for "Christian religion" has been steadily drifting and sometimes even aggressively speeding away from the Bible. This is bizarre since every "Christian" group claims to derive its identity and belief system *from* the Bible. So then, the Bible is honored for establishing credibility and legitimacy, but is almost immediately dismissed as being out of touch, outdated, antiquated, irrelevant, and in need of updating and modernizing. This is not only contradictory but holds God and His word in contempt. In Acts 13:45, while Paul and Barnabas were preaching in Antioch of Pisidia, some of the Jews there "began contradicting the things spoken by Paul, and were blaspheming." To blaspheme is to speak evil of what God says is holy. The Holy Spirit was speaking through Paul—an apostle appointed by Jesus Christ—and the allegedly God-fearing Jews were rejecting it. Today, some men are preaching exactly what Paul wrote to Christians, and allegedly God-fearing Christians are rejecting it. This, too, is blasphemy.[3]

It is impossible to claim allegiance to God while at the same time resisting, in any manner, what He has said in His word (the Bible). This is especially true of those who identify as Christians: of all people, Christians should be defending the Bible's authority more passionately and simply *better* than anyone else. Yet today, a great deal of those who call themselves Christians are turning aside from biblical authority and stepping out into the unknown.

Genuine Christians do not only *sometimes* use the Bible for their authority to act in God's name. They do not claim that "all Scripture is inspired by God [lit., God-breathed] and profitable for teaching, for reproof, for correction, for training in righteousness," but then deem it out of touch, outdated, in need of revision, etc.[4] Christ has already made His decision as to what will be the blueprint for His church; we cannot make any different decision and still claim allegiance to Him.

This means we either accept the entire New Testament at face value or we reject it altogether. It is an all-or-nothing package. If we accept it, then this means we let *it*—not conventional wisdom, social pressure, technology, or modern expectations—have the final say. We let *it* determine who Christians are, what they believe, what they do collectively (as churches), and how they are to respond to internal and external threats to all these things. If we will not accept this position, then the only thing left to do (without contradicting our claim) is to reject its authority, strike out on our own, and hope that we will somehow win Christ's favor in the process—a hopeless and guaranteed-to-fail plan if there ever was one.

Christ's "Plan A" is for us to accept biblical authority as our *only* authority for all things related to God and salvation. He has no "Plan B" for His people or their churches. Will this be popular? Hardly. Worldly thinking has made serious inroads into all religious thinking; it is not going to just evaporate in the event of a noble decision. Will this be easy? Likely, no. Years, decades, even centuries of traditions, rituals, deeply ingrained doctrines, etc., are part of our collection of baggage that must be left behind. Many churchgoers are simply not going to do this; many church leaders, who make their living from and pride themselves on their elevated positions in the "Christian religion," will balk at the very idea. Will this be doable? Absolutely, if we trust in Christ's leadership and the Holy Spirit's instruction. But this requires great faith, a lot of work, time, and sacrifice—things that are typically not expected of or seen in the typical contemporary churchgoer.

Getting back to the Bible—I'm speaking to any of us who have indeed *left* the Bible behind for any reason—is exactly what God wants us to do. I know this confidently because: 1) He never wanted us to leave it behind in the first place; 2) the New Testament is His revealed instructions to His people and their churches; 3) there is no better, higher, or more important source of information for such people; and 4) there are serious consequences—namely, divine curses—for anyone who sets aside His commandments. Let the world mock, ridicule, stereotype ("Fundamentalists!"), and criticize all it wants; this is irrelevant to the Christian's allegiance to Christ. Let all the pseudo-Christians mock, roll their eyes, spew bitter condemnations, and walk away from us all they want; they, too, are not our master, but Christ is. Such people "went out from us [i.e., the apostles], but they were not really of us; for if they had been of us, they would have remained with us; but they went out, so that it would be shown that they all are not of us" (1 John 2:19, bracketed words are mine).

"Back to the Bible!"

When people get off-track from an original cause, movement, teaching, or discussion, someone will likely say, "Let's go back to the drawing board." The "drawing board" represents where the cause, movement, etc., began, and what the original ideas, intentions, and direction for this were first defined and put down on paper, so to speak. The Bible serves as the "drawing board" for all those who humbly and earnestly are seeking God by faith (Heb. 11:6). To seek Him properly requires a return to what *He* said and leaving behind whatever conflicts with this. In effect, we must return to the blueprint of what it means to be a Christian and how groups of Christians are to work together. "Back to the Bible" is not a call to *move* backward but just the opposite: we are always to be moving *forward* according to the pattern given to us (Phil. 3:13–17). No one can move forward with a plan who does not *know* what the plan is supposed to be.

This is not a new call, however. For the last five hundred years, groups of Christians (and those who thought themselves to be Christians) have been issuing a "Back to the Bible!" proclamation. Some of these groups have done this better than others; some have had good intentions but not great follow-through. Some groups, under the banner of "conservatism," have meticulously studied the New Testament with such rigidity and legalistic fervor that they have allowed for no other conclusions other than their own.[5] Other groups, under the pretense of "liberalism," have viewed the New Testament as a moral guide, or a loosely prescribed general code of ethics and basic procedure, but not to be taken too seriously.[6]

The Reformation (16th century) provided a watershed of long-lost information, ideas, and access to God's word.[7] For the first time in over a thousand years, men had the entire text of the Bible in its original languages (Hebrew and Aramaic for the Old Testament; Greek for the New Testament), which allowed for translation into predominant languages—English being the first. The invention of the printing press (15th century) made duplication of these translations available to more people than ever before in human history. Before this, for a thousand years, virtually the only ones who had access to the Bible were Catholic priests, monks, and theologians. They purposely kept the New Testament in Latin (translated by Jerome, early 5th century), which was no longer a viable language, so that they alone could read it. This, as well as a high rate of illiteracy, kept the masses in the dark as to what God's word said. This also allowed for a considerable number of customized interpretations, creative explanations of biblical passages, and outright abuses of power and authority.

The Reformers, as they have come to be known, challenged many of the Roman (Catholic) Church's unbiblical teachings. Sadly, the Reformation also produced new *versions* of Christianity, each with its own slant on the New Testament, and its own doctrines, creeds, chains of command, and church organization. Some of these were close to what the New Testament teaches; others were just tangents from Roman Catholicism. These different religions—defined as "denominations"—all claimed "unity" with God, legitimacy for their existence, and (of course) a "Back to the Bible!" rally cry. Yet, their plea for Christian unity was immediately undermined by their having divided into separate groups, each with their own distinctive name, doctrine, and practice. Most denominations in existence today are the products of the Reformation experience.

In the 19th century, an undertaking began in the eastern United States to abandon all denominationalism and get "back to the Bible." Many good men and women devoted a great deal of time, energy, and sacrifice to it. This became known as the Restoration Movement, with the idea that Christ's church had to be restored, true Bible study had to be restored, or that Christians and their churches needed to be restored to the genuine teachings of the Bible. By this time, the Bible was well-known, particularly the King James Version (1611), also known as the Authorized Version (AV) because its production and publication were authorized and commissioned by King James I of England. Therefore, people in the United States (mid-19th century) were quite familiar with the Bible in general, but not necessarily how to study it or implement its teachings.

The American Restoration Movement accomplished two major things. First, it exposed denominationalism for what it is—a humanly-manufactured system of church organization rather than a Christ-ordained one. Second, it brought great attention to the need to *study the Bible* to know what Christ wants for His people (*the* church) and their congregations. In all this, however, it is important to keep in mind exactly *what* needs restored. People can be restored, and individual congregations can be restored. But Christ's church—the sanctuary of genuine believers in Him and His authority—has *never fallen away from Him* and needs no human restoration efforts. To say that Christ's *church* has apostatized [lit., departed from the truth] is to speak derisively about His ability to govern, protect, and preserve it. The best that the Restoration Movement did was to bring people back to the pattern of authority for Christians and their churches: the written instructions of Christ's hand-picked apostles.[8] These apostles were guided not by other men, earthly circumstances, or the times in which they lived, but by the Holy Spirit Himself (1 Cor. 2:10, Gal. 1:11–12, Eph. 3:5, and 2 Peter 1:21).

The Restoration Movement produced a tremendous amount of writing on numerous biblical subjects. These writings were not limited to preachers but were intentionally made available to Christians everywhere. The mid-19th century was also a time of great stress, as the country entered a bloody Civil War (1861—1865) just as this movement was gaining momentum. And, despite a strong emphasis on New Testament doctrine, social innovations and human teachings began creeping into the churches and had to be addressed. Often, divisions occurred as some members tried hard to maintain the purity of doctrinal teaching, as they understood it, while others embraced a more permissive view of the Scriptures.

Every generation of Christians has faced the "issues" of its day, whether doctrinal or social, and this is no less true today. Sadly, the greatest issue faced today is not over which church doctrine to believe, or which human innovation to reject, but a widespread *indifference* to biblical and spiritual concerns altogether. Indifference (an "either way works for me" attitude) often gives way to apathy (an "I just don't care anymore" attitude). I am not talking about attitudes found among non-Christians, but among Christians (and those who claim to be Christians but are not) and their churches. During the Reformation, striving to draw near to God was supremely important to most people; during the Restoration, striving to learn and understand God's word was paramount. But now, many "Christians" are often not striving for anything except their own customized, creative, and emotional "take" on the Christian religion in general.

The erosion of respect for New Testament authority is the reason for this indifference and apathy. When people do not respect what Christ *said*, it becomes easy not to respect who Christ *is* or why anyone should do anything *for* Him. The emphasis turns inward: "What am *I* getting out of this?" "How can this 'Christian religion' make *me* feel better about *myself*?" "What will the church do for *me* (regardless of whether *I* do anything for the church)?" "I already have *my* beliefs; I just need someone—preferably an entire congregation—to validate them." Such sentiments are increasingly common. As a result, modern "Christian religion" wants to dabble in what it calls "Bible study" but largely caters to the modern churchgoer's insatiable desire for entertainment, self-worship, and feel-good therapy.

It is impossible to develop a sincere and accurate love for God when fixated on ourselves, our families, our culture, social concerns, or even technology. Surrendering ourselves to God, worshiping His Son, proclaiming the "word of the cross" (1 Cor. 1:18), and working together with fellow Christians with a Christ-like attitude (Phil. 2:1–5) are decisions and lifestyles that do not come easily and need regular reinforcement. The instruction Christ has given us has not changed, has no need to change, and will not tolerate changes. We are forced to choose between faithful compliance and preferential customization: we cannot do them both equally.

Thankfully, not every person who wants to be saved by God has succumbed to the siren call of contemporary religion. There are those of us—and I'm including you in this "us," since you are reading this book—who desire to worship God "in spirit and truth" (John 4:24). We choose to honor Christ as the head of His church and follow the recorded instructions of God's Holy Spirit. This means we need to know what the New Testament says for Christians and our churches. We also need to have the courage to study, internalize, and practice this information, even to our own hurt. And we need to make strenuous effort to teach these things to others (2 Tim. 2:2), so that they, too, will "understand what the will of the Lord is" (Eph. 5:17).

It is with this perspective that this book has been written.

Part One: God Has Given Us a Pattern to Follow
Chapter One: What Does It Mean to Be a "Christian"?

Before we can start examining objectively what the New Testament (NT) says about Christians and their churches, we need to identify who "Christians" are. A socially generated or popularly held definition will not work, since society and popular wisdom have little regard for divine authority or biblical teaching. To know how *Christ* defines a Christian, we need to investigate His word and let it speak naturally, objectively, and conclusively.

The word "Christian" occurs only three times in the NT: Acts 11:26, 26:28, and 1 Peter 4:16. However, the *definition* of a Christian is the subject of most of the NT letters to individuals or churches. "Christian" is from the Greek word *Christianos*, which literally means "follower of Christ."[9] (The word "Christ" is the Greek counterpart to the Hebrew word "Messiah," both of which mean "anointed"—or, in the case of Jesus, "*the* Anointed."[10]) A Christian, then, is not merely someone who believes that Jesus is the Christ. Instead, it identifies someone as a Christ-*follower*. To "follow" Christ means to be fully devoted to Him as His disciple, as He Himself says: "If anyone wishes to come after Me, he must deny himself, and take up his cross and follow Me" (Mat. 16:24).

A Christian is one who has entered a covenant relationship with God through the mediation of His Son, Jesus Christ. The terms and conditions of this covenant are, in effect, the teachings and commandments of the NT. The agreement to this covenant is determined through one's personal agreement to (or faith in) these teachings and his obedience to these commandments. Upon demonstrating this agreement (by acting in obedient faith), the person no longer lives for himself, but for Christ. The apostle Paul expresses this: "I have been crucified with Christ; and it is no longer I who live, but Christ lives in me; and the life which I now live in the flesh I live by faith in the Son of God, who loved me and gave Himself up for me" (Gal. 2:20).

To *live* for Christ requires that one *dies* to the world. This "death" is symbolized by one's burial in water (i.e., baptism). While being symbolic in nature (since this is not a literal death), this "death" is both real and necessary. Teachings and commandments having to do with *becoming* a Christian are just as important as those having to do with *living* as one. When a person is "buried with Him [Christ] through baptism into death," he is "united with Him in the likeness of His [own] death." The "old self" had given its allegiance to sin; in dying to that allegiance, which is what baptism symbolizes, one gives a new allegiance to Christ. As a result, he no longer lives under divine condemnation for being a sinner, but in "newness of life" as a child of God (Rom. 6:3–7). This process is also identified as being "born again" (John 3:3, 5, 1 Peter 1:3) or being "born of God" (John 1:12–13). Thus, a Christian is one who has died to sin—thus severing his allegiance to its mastery—and now lives as an obedient servant of Jesus Christ.

Misconceptions and Clarifications

Unfortunately, "Christian" is one of the most abused, misunderstood, and hijacked words in the religious world today. People identify as "Christians" even when their beliefs, lifestyles, and worship of God bear little resemblance to those described in the NT. The term is sometimes so loosely applied that it defines only a God-fearing person rather than a loyal and duty-bound follower of Jesus Christ.

The NT speaks of God-fearing people as a separate group from Christians (or "disciples"). Cornelius was identified as a "God-fearing" man (Acts 10:22) before he became a Christian. In Antioch of Pisidia, the apostle Paul was warmly received by "many of the Jews and God-fearing proselytes [i.e., converts to the Jewish religion]" (Acts 13:43, bracketed words are mine). He met a similar group in both Thessalonica and Athens (Acts 17:4, 17). These people had not yet obeyed the gospel of Christ but were certainly interested in hearing about it, and (we assume) were considering whether to respond to it. God-fearing people are those who revere God, respect His people, and are receptive of His word, but have not (yet) decided to become permanently identified with Him. While all Christians fear God, "God-fearing" people are not yet Christians until they *obey* Him.

The term "Christian" is also commonly applied to a "good person" who exhibits godly virtues. Yet, calling someone a "good person" is not the same as identifying him as a "Christian." Good people can exist regardless of, or even apart from, the Christian belief system. Atheists, for example, may be considered "good people" by their families, friends, and peers, but they remain what they are—unbelievers. Moralists are people who have a fairly solid values system that is, most often, based upon NT teaching, but they have not committed themselves to its obligations.[11] Those who often self-identify as a "good person," even if they know some Scriptures and have a general idea of the gospel of Christ, are in fact moralists at best. If they were genuine Christians, they would conform to the image of Christ Himself, since He is the point of reference for all morality.

When I talk to people who visit our congregation's assemblies, I often ask, "Are you a Christian?" A common response is, "I'm a Catholic [or, Methodist, Baptist, Presbyterian, etc.]." This tells me several things. First, they put their denominational status *ahead* of any identification with Christ. While likely they did this unconsciously, it still reflects their priorities. Second, they obviously assume that being part of a denomination is equivalent to having an identity with Christ. (Even "non-denominational" people do this regarding their church membership.) Third, they probably know very little of the Bible, otherwise they would not be making these first two assumptions. I'm not saying this in ridicule or with reproach but with concern. People never benefit from spiritual ignorance, and it is my strong desire that they would turn to God's word to become enlightened.

Others will freely use the word "Christian" as an adjective rather than a noun. In some cases, this is nearly inescapable, as I did earlier in referring to the "Christian belief system." I don't know what else to call it so that everyone will know what I'm talking about. But in so many contemporary cases, the word "Christian" is applied to things that have nothing to do with God, Christians, or the gospel of Christ. A "Christian college," for example, leads one to believe that every Christian (and Christ Himself) endorses everything taught at that college, and that every person who teaches or attends there is also a genuine Christian. A "Christian bookstore" leads one to assume that every book sold there is accurately based upon and promotes the genuine gospel of Christ. In my decades of experience in visiting these stores, this has never been the case. A "Christian radio station" leads one to believe that every song proclaims the gospel, every singer (and disc jockey) is a Christian, and the sole aim of that station is to lead people to Christ. This, too, is not the case. All radio stations are in business to make money; when the money stops coming in, the station disappears. The same can be said for most performers of so-called "contemporary Christian music" or CCM, for short.

Colleges, bookstores, and radio stations cannot become Christians. Putting the "Christian" adjective in front of these businesses does not make their participants, supporters, or material right with God. Even a belief system, simply because it claims to honor Christ, cites verses from His gospel, and loosely adheres to His teachings, is not necessarily a "*Christian* belief system." The only way for a belief system to be "Christian" in its design, content, and objective is for it to follow the NT teachings completely, not just partially or by giving a token nod to it. No doubt every "Christian denomination" (a self-refuting phrase, if you just think about it) makes a claim to teach the "Christian belief system." Yet, this is impossible to maintain because if its followers did teach this, they would cease to identify and operate as a denomination. (Denominational systems are devoted to *separatism*, not unity; see chapter 13, "Denominationalism.") Instead, they would simply teach Christ and His message of salvation apart from their own brand of religion.

I have so far repeatedly used the word "identify" or "identity" to describe where people are at regarding their beliefs. People identify with other people by shared values, convictions, conclusions, and (in some cases) delusions. People who identify with each other also can have fellowship with one another. "Fellowship" can be defined across the board—in religious and non-religious circles—by those who have common goals, a shared effort toward achieving those goals, and their own individual devotion to that shared effort. This is true in business, sports, and marriage as in religion. People cannot have fellowship who do not have commonality. I cannot have *spiritual* fellowship with someone whose spiritual goals and efforts are not common to my own. On the other hand, just because we *do* have fellowship does not mean we are right with God. Just because two people enjoy spiritual fellowship does not necessarily mean that they are Christians.

For us to have fellowship with Christ, we must properly be identified with Him. (I will explain this in detail in future chapters.) I cannot choose *how* or to what *extent* I will identify with Him; He has the authority to define these things, not me. All I can do is either agree with His terms or reject them; I have no right to modify or re-write them. (This does not stop people from doing this, but human modifications cannot change divine truth.) If you and I are going to have mutual fellowship in Christ, it is necessary that we both subscribe to the belief system which He has authorized. If we belong to Christ, then we cannot belong to someone who opposes Him. This "belonging" refers to spiritual fellowship, as Paul means it in 2 Cor. 4:14–16:

> Do not be bound together with unbelievers; for what partnership have righteousness and lawlessness, or what fellowship has light with darkness? Or what harmony has Christ with Belial, or what has a believer in common with an unbeliever? Or what agreement has the temple of God with idols? For we are the temple of the living God; just as God said, "I will dwell in them and walk among them; and I will be their God, and they shall be My people."

Paul says: a Christian cannot walk with Christ *and* be in league (spiritually) with someone or something that opposes Him. This is biblically untenable: Christ will not approve of this unholy union. People might *think* they can make this work, but this does not change the truth of the matter. A genuine Christian cannot and will not enter spiritual fellowship with an enemy of God. This would be like a groom having a mistress while professing fidelity to his new wife, or a person carrying a pagan idol into the temple of God, all the while claiming "loyalty" to Him.

No one can identify with Christ by any means that He did not prescribe. No one can have fellowship with Christ who has not properly identified with Him. And no one can call himself a Christian who refuses, for any reason, to do these things. Jesus asked rhetorically, "Why do you call Me, 'Lord, Lord,' and do not do what I say?" (Luke 6:46). This makes sense: a person is not making Jesus Christ his Lord (or Master) who refuses to listen to Him. No one truly "follows" Christ who does not give his allegiance to Him; no one truly *loves* Christ who refuses to obey Him (John 14:15).

Who is in the Christian family? Jesus already answered this: it is "whoever does the will of My Father who is in heaven" (Mat. 7:21, 12:46–50). The One who sanctifies and those sanctified "are all from one Father," which makes them "brethren" (Heb. 2:11). ("Sanctify" means "make holy," or to be separated or consecrated for a sacred work.) In other words, there is no gray area surrounding the question of who belongs to Christ and who does not. Those who belong to Him are obedient to His word, cleansed by His blood, and sanctified by God's Spirit (1 Peter 1:2). "By this we know that we have come to know Him, if we keep His commandments," John says. "The one who says, 'I have come to know Him,' and does not keep His commandments, is a liar, and the truth is not in him" (1 John 2:3–4). A contemporary author says:

> What we tend to forget is that it is God, not we, who determines the boundaries of "in Christ" fellowship. Neither "in Christ" fellowship nor "in Christ" unity is something we ourselves can define, limit, or regulate, since being "in Christ" involves the forgiveness of sins and reconciliation with God.[12]

In other words, regardless of what we think, have come to believe, or even *want* to believe, it is not our place to define what a Christian (Christ-follower) is, but Christ's. We do not have the authority, ability, or wisdom to decide for everyone else—much less for ourselves—what constitutes fellowship with God through the mediation of His Son.

Disciples and the "Called-out"

The earliest Christians called themselves and each other "disciples." It was not until years later that they were known as "Christians" (Acts 11:26). A "disciple" is a student, pupil, and follower of a teacher or master. Disciples will not challenge the teacher but seek to become *like* him, to conform to his teachings. Jesus said, "A disciple is not above his teacher, nor a slave above his master. It is enough for the disciple that he become like his teacher, and the slave like his master" (Mat. 10:24–25a). Only those who are true followers of Christ can be His disciples (Mat. 16:24). Those who resist, rebel against, or reject the teachings of their master can hardly be his "disciples."

So it is with Christians, in the genuine sense of the word: No Christian—no *Christ-follower*—will resist the Master's influence, rebel against His authority, or reject His teachings. If he does, then he is something other than a Christian, regardless of what he thinks of himself or how others regard him. Christians are never defined by peer approval or church status. Rather, they are defined by the One whom they follow—the Lord Jesus Himself. No person can be identified as a Christian indeed who has not already discipled himself after Christ.

I am convinced that if the religious world stopped using the much-diluted and -abused word "Christian" and started using the word *disciple*, things might immediately become much clearer. "Christian" today can mean nothing more than a churchgoer, a member of a known congregation, or someone who merely dabbles in the Christian faith but is not committed to it. A "disciple," however, forces the issue: this demands that he be a student of the Master, devoted to His teachings, and conformed to His will. Christ's church—the *real* church, not the ambiguous, loosely-defined, and multi-faith mass of churchgoers—is comprised of those who no longer live for themselves but instead are completely devoted to Him and His cause. Real disciples do not rewrite, redefine, or reinvent Christ's NT pattern; they strive to live according to it, even to their own hurt.

Genuine Christians are also known as "the called of Jesus Christ" (Rom. 1:6), having been "called [by God] according to His purpose" (Rom. 8:28, bracketed words added).[13] They are "called into fellowship with His Son, Jesus Christ our Lord" (1 Cor. 1:9). As such, they are "to walk in a manner worthy of the calling by which [they] have been called" (Eph. 4:1). The Greek word often translated as "church" in the NT (over 100 times) is *ekklesia*, which literally means "the out-called" or "the called out."[14] God's people are called *out* of the world and simultaneously *into* Christ. One cannot be "in Christ" who remains in the world; one who is "in Christ" has promised to sever all ties with the world's sinful behavior.

To be "called" means, in the most basic sense, to be invited by someone who has the authority to do the inviting. No one can come to God who has not been invited to do so; no one can come to Christ unless the Father has invited him first (John 6:44, 65). The gospel of Christ serves as a formal invitation to *every* person to come to Christ. We are called through this gospel by God's Spirit (2 Thess. 2:13–14): a divine Personage offers us a heavenly invitation. This is extraordinary, yet it is often overlooked by many people and may be undervalued even by those who have responded to the call.

Like with many formal invitations, certain conditions must be met first. No one can impose himself upon God or His Son. This is an altogether improper thing to do toward those of great authority; God Himself will not permit it. To become a Christian—to accept properly the invitation offered him—a person must fulfill whatever obligations are required of him.[15] All such obligations fall under the umbrella of "faith," but faith itself must be defined by God and exercised according to His will. Not just any "faith" is acceptable to Him; I cannot choose my own brand of "faith" and assume that God will (or should) be happy with it. God is the possessor of salvation, not me, us, our churches, or human religion; we are the ones in need of salvation, not Him. So then, we are not able to barter, negotiate, or act presumptuously with the One who is offering to save us.

God offers the invitation—He calls people to Him through His Son's sacrifice and His Spirit's revealed truth—and those who respond rightly to this invitation become "the called." Such people are not merely in pursuit of salvation itself—although, this too—but they are in pursuit of the *God* of salvation. God has gone well out of His way to provide us with a means of salvation. More importantly, He has done everything in His power to grant us fellowship with Him in this life and in the life to come. He has revealed to us how we can identify with Him and His Son now and forever. This is all part of the invitation: He lays out exactly what our problem is and how He—and He alone—is willing and able to rescue us from it.

But no one is forced to be rescued just because he has been called. In giving you the invitation to be saved, God also gives you the ability to decline it. You can spurn the invitation and turn your back on Him if you want to. So far, billions of people have done this; billions more may do so in the future. Or you can counteroffer with your own terms and assume that God accepts your proposal and grants you fellowship with Him based upon this. Or you can rewrite His offer and create your own customized "invitation" and assume that God will approve of it. Or you can be one of those people who thinks that God *owes* you salvation just because He loves you: you do not have to do much of anything in the way of obedience and God will save you "anyway."

You can believe whatever you want—people do this all the time—but it does not change the original invitation and its terms. God is happy to offer you salvation; you and I—sinners, all of us—should be extremely happy to receive such an offer. Christians, as the Bible portrays them, are to be "overflowing with gratitude" (Col. 2:7) for the privilege of walking in fellowship with God. The apostle Peter says that Christians "are a chosen race, a royal priesthood, a holy nation, a people for God's own possession, so that you may proclaim the excellencies of

Him who has called you out of darkness into His marvelous light" (1 Peter 2:9). This is not the picture of people doomed to "going to church" and listening to sermons for the rest of their lives. This is the picture of those who are happy to be saved by a God who is happy to save them. These people have willingly and even sacrificially changed their beliefs, modified their behavior, and altered their lives for the sake of their new Lord and Savior, Jesus Christ.

Those who are "called" by God ideally will not resist that into which they have been called. They will not say to God, "Thank you for saving me, but I'm upset that You expect anything from me in return." Instead, they are happy to love, happy to serve, and happy to proclaim His name to those who remain lost. Even so, discipleship to Christ remains difficult, to say the least. Jesus likens it to carrying a cross in His name *every day* (Luke 9:23). In the ancient world, people who carried their own crosses were not mere spectators of an impending death: they were the ones about to die. So it is with Christians: we are not those who merely wear crosses around our necks like costume jewelry or put "Jesus Is the Answer" bumper stickers on our cars. We are those who manifest our death to the world *every day* in our allegiance to Christ. And even if literal death is the result of that allegiance, we have already made up our minds to accept it.

The difficulty of discipleship is daunting, intimidating, and sacrificial. Therefore, many people are quick to identify as "Christians" (mere churchgoers or church members) rather than *disciples* of the Master. Yet, the rewards—personally, mentally, and spiritually—of discipleship to Christ are incalculable. Paul wrote that "the sufferings [as a follower of Christ—MY WORDS] of this present time are not worthy to be compared with the glory that is to be revealed to us" (Rom. 8:18). James wrote: "Blessed is a man [i.e., a Christian] who perseveres under trial [for his faith]; for once he has been approved, he will receive the crown of life which the Lord has promised to those who love Him" (James 1:12, bracketed words are mine). For this reason, such people willfully, joyfully, and obediently accept the challenges, sorrows, and losses that come with discipleship to Christ. They know that, in the end, they will be more than compensated for whatever they sacrificed up front.

Those who respond to God's invitation to be saved are made "a new creature" in Christ (2 Cor. 5:17). They are not awarded new *souls*, for this is impossible and unnecessary; rather, a new, covenant-bound relationship is formed between them and God. In this new union, fellowship with God is restored; the relationship between the Creator and those created "in His own image" (Gen. 1:27) is reconciled. Things are not the same as before they fell from innocence; in fact, they are far better. In their innocence as literal children, these people were ignorant, naïve, and uneducated about God. However, "in Christ," they are enlightened, responsible, and acting on divinely revealed knowledge. As a result of their having accepted God's call, they were added to a group of people distinctly known as "*the* called," a spiritual sanctuary so closely and intimately identified with Christ that it is referred to as "His body" (Col. 1:18). We are speaking here, of course, of His church—a subject further defined and expounded upon in the next chapter.

Not only did God call these people but they also called upon Him. He called them by proclaiming to them His gospel; they called upon Him by showing faith in His willingness and ability to save them from their spiritual condemnation.[16] Compare, for example, what Peter said to the Jews in Jerusalem on the day of Pentecost: "and it shall be that everyone who calls upon the name of the Lord will be saved"; "For the promise [of salvation] is for you and ... as many as the Lord our God will call to Himself" (Acts 2:21, 39, bracketed words are mine). God called them through the preaching of His gospel; they called God through their faithful obedience to whatever He required of them (Acts 2:38).

Summary Thoughts

The gospel's invitation to walk in fellowship with God is priceless and incomparable with any other invitation. Sadly, millions of people have chosen to believe in some people's "take" on the gospel teaching rather than the teaching itself. In fact, entire "Christian denominations"—again, an oxymoron—have been established on the premise of one person's "take" over another's.

Because of such human inventions, the real meaning of "Christian" has been redefined or altogether lost. Instead of deferring to God's authority on the matter, we have allowed people—some, well-intentioned; others, with ulterior motives—to become the authorities. "Christian" has been assigned multiple meanings but with little biblical substance. The result is not a united, consistent, and submissive community of followers of Christ, but a deformed, disfigured, and fractured group of people. While all these people claim to have the same "Lord," relatively few are paying attention to what He said.

Christians are to separate themselves from the godless world, not from each other. Jesus said, explicitly,

> For their sakes I sanctify Myself, that they themselves also may be sanctified in truth. I do not ask on behalf of these alone, but for those also who believe in Me through their word; that they may all be one; even as You, Father, are in Me and I in You, that they also may be in Us, so that the world may believe that You sent Me. (John 17:20–22)

Unity—not in human opinions, but in His doctrine—is one of the genuine characteristics of His people. (Godly love—for Him and fellow disciples—is another: see John 13:34–35.) Real Christians do not divide over descriptors, subjective "interpretations," or humanly defined "faiths." Rather, they are "diligent to preserve the unity of the Spirit in the bond of peace" (Eph. 4:3). In other words, they are bound together in unity under Christ's headship, according to a doctrine revealed by God's Spirit.

How do we get back to what Christ originally meant for His people to be? How can we learn how to be Christians indeed—not just in name, and not presumptuously, but genuinely and biblically? The solution is amazingly simple: we need to go back to the blueprint of the revealed word of God. Christ gave us everything we need to have unity with Him and (thus) peace with God. All those who are genuinely united with Christ will be—indeed, *must* be—united in fellowship with one another.

This blueprint, when followed diligently, will produce only one kind of people: *Christians*. It never produces denominational Christians, casual Christians, or Christians who separate and divide over human teachings that pose as biblical doctrines. Instead, it only produces *Christ-followers* of the highest caliber, which is what God calls anyone to be who desires to have fellowship with Him.

This is what *you* need to be if you wish to receive God's generous invitation to eternal life. If you have already done this, then this is what you must *continue* to be, to the point of your dying breath.

Chapter Two: Why Do Christians Need Churches?

Before discussing the NT *pattern* for churches, it is important to establish the *need* for churches in the first place. By "churches," there is meant no reference to a system of churches, such as a denominational or otherwise-linked group of churches.[17] There is no NT pattern for these. Instead, the reference is to individual, standalone, and autonomous congregations of Christians.[18] These are the only physical "churches" mentioned, established, and addressed in the NT. Before defining physical churches, however, it is necessary first to define the spiritual church, or simply "the church." And before defining "the church," it is necessary to recognize the individual members of it, which are Christians.

In the previous chapter, we allowed the Bible to define what it means to be a "Christian." The decision to become a Christian—to enter a covenant relationship with God through Christ—is most certainly an *individual* decision, action, and commitment. *The church* is not deciding for anyone; *the church* does not enter a covenant with God collectively. One's salvation begins as, and will always be, an extremely personal and intimate relationship with God through the mediation of Jesus Christ.

On the other hand, Christians are not identified only individually but also collectively. Once a person obeys Christ's gospel and becomes one of His disciples, he is added to the group of all other human souls that have done the same thing. This collective group of saved people has numerous designations in the NT: "disciples"; "believers"; "brethren"; "fellow heirs," "fellow members," and "fellow partakers" of the promises of Christ (Eph. 3:6); followers of "the Way" (Acts 9:2); "the bride" of Christ (Rev. 19:7); "the church" (nearly 60 times); "the church of God" (1 Cor. 10:32, and several other times); etc.

But the most intimate designation of this group is the body of Christ. The apostle Paul wrote that God has "put all things in subjection under [Christ's] feet, and gave Him as head over all things to the church, which is His body, the fullness of Him who fills all in all" (Eph. 1:22–23). Similarly, he wrote, "[Christ] is also head of the body, the church; and He is the beginning, the firstborn from the dead, so that He Himself will come to have first place in everything" (Col. 1:18). There cannot be any closer union to Christ than to be part of His "body." For example, there are billions of arms and legs in the world, but none so intimate to me as *my own*. There are billions of women in the world, but none so intimate to me as *my wife*. There are billions of children in the world, but none so intimate to me as *mine*. In like manner, there are several billions of people on the planet, but none so intimate to Christ as *His own blood-bought people*. These have a relationship with Him that supersedes all other relationships. It is the relationship factor that changes everything.

The context of Christ's "body" as the church is spiritual, not physical. His church, in its full meaning, includes all souls, both living and dead—all who *are* faithful to Him or *had been* faithful to Him until death (Rev. 2:10b). It even includes all those who lived faithfully to God *prior to* Jesus' death on the cross, since they, too, have been redeemed by His blood and are justified according to divine grace (Rom. 3:21–26). Whoever has fellowship with God through Christ's redemption—because "without the shedding of blood there is no forgiveness" (Heb. 9:22b)—is made a part of Christ's spiritual body of ransomed souls.

Christ's Mission for His Church

Christ is the *head* of this body, which means that He has full, absolute, and unquestionable control over it. His church is not an organization that defines its own mission, makes its own rules, votes on its own doctrines, or acts independently of its head. His church—*His* body, not ours—gives its full allegiance to Him. The church never tells Christ what to do, or even what it will do, but always receives its instruction, direction, and doctrine from Him. Any religious group or church claiming to be God's people that does not honor Christ as its supreme source of authority is an impostor group. God only recognizes one group of people: His Son's "body," which is "the heavenly Jerusalem" and "the general assembly [of believers] and church of the firstborn [see 1 Cor. 15:20–22] who are enrolled in heaven" (Heb. 12:22, bracketed words are mine).

The mission of Christ's church is not spelled out in any one verse in the NT. On the other hand, anyone who reads the NT comes away with exactly what His church is all about: **discipleship to Christ**. The NT explains how disciples:

- are made (Mat. 28:19, Luke 24:47).
- are grounded in apostolic teaching and instruction (Eph. 4:11–16, Col. 2:6–7).
- encourage and edify fellow disciples, especially in their assemblies (1 Cor. 14:26, 1 Thess. 5:14–15).
- carry the gospel message out to the unconverted world (Col. 1:25–27, 1 Tim. 2:3–6).

The NT instruction also focuses on the individual disciple himself: first, how he came to become a disciple; then, what he is supposed to do as a disciple (as he himself matures, increases in knowledge, and gains experience); and finally, his role as a model example for other disciples to follow (1 Cor. 11:1). Even so, it is in the context of the spiritual church that all these actions are carried out once the person has been converted to Christ.

The works of the church and the work of the individual believer do overlap but are not interchangeable. For example, while the church (as a whole) is most certainly involved in promoting evangelism in the NT, it is always individual Christians *doing* the evangelizing. The church is never told to take upon itself the roles for which individual Christians are responsible. Likewise, individual Christians (except Christ's apostles) are never told to exercise authority over the entire church. Instead, it is Christ—through the agency of the Holy Spirit and His own hand-picked apostles—that provides all the instruction His church needs to operate in His name.

To see how far contemporary Christendom has drifted from this simple and straightforward mission, consider some of the typical practices of and social expectations for modern churches. The "Christian" church today is expected to:

- Accept all people who choose to identify as "Christians"—even in the most passive sense, even those whose beliefs and practices contradict Scripture.

- Accept all lifestyles, sexual orientations, gender choices, and liberal-minded opinions because God loves everyone, and allegedly no one is allowed to question anyone for fear of "judging" them. (The crime of perceived "judging" is apparently far more severe than sexual deviation or moral confusion.)
- Support certain political issues, particularly in moral demonstrations, and endorse political candidates that most closely identify with "Christian values."
- Feed the hungry, house the homeless, pay utility bills, allow "tent cities" to be erected on church property, and offer social programs for the troubled, lonely, divorced, single parents, and socially challenged.
- Provide sponsoring, counseling, and other care for those embroiled in substance abuse and other addictive behaviors.
- Cater to children, even to the point of creating a separate church entity, especially for children and teens (often under the guise of a "youth ministry"). Children are expected to be treated like mini-adults and are encouraged to commit to a lifelong and difficult conversion to Christ at young ages. Churches are expected to provide (and fund) youth groups, field trips, movie nights, teen workshops, homeschooling programs, and Bible camps.
- Raise money for God's work by soliciting unbelievers through car washes, bake sales, rummage sales, firework stands, and any other lucrative commercial enterprise.
- Use its buildings and property as a kind of community center and neighborhood recreational gathering point. For this, they are to provide fellowship halls, kitchens, sporting venues, big-screen TVs (for Superbowl Sunday), music and musical equipment, video presentations, and other forms of entertainment.
- Observe Christmas and Easter as holy days, often with a special service, "sacred" traditions, and possibly dramatic presentations or reenactments.

The two "missions"—that of the NT church that Christ established, and today's entertainment-driven, feel-good, and socially-acceptable "Christian church"—are not compatible. Instead, they stand in sharp contrast to each other. The issue here is not whether all these things are good works in themselves, for some of them certainly are. Rather: are these things the reason why Christ established His church? Are these identified as the *mission* of His church? No one can defend this biblically.

Again, the work of the church (or churches) will be different than the work of individual Christians. An individual Christian can engage in, support, and finance activities that the church has no right to do. Churches operate as a collective unit; individual believers are not bound to the collective responsibilities or limitations of that collective unit. These are related but not interchangeable areas of work. On the other hand, Christ has the final say over what His church does *and* what individual believers do. In neither case can human decisions conflict with nor override Christ's instructions.

Sadly, Christ's church *system*—not the actual body of believers but the earthly organization of those believers (both real and imagined)—has been hijacked. "Hijacking" is the right word here. Self-serving groups of men and women have taken illicit and illegal control of the church system outlined in the NT. In the process, entire generations of people have been led to believe that modern uses and expectations of all contemporary churches are normal, acceptable to God, and good for society. This is not true. Nothing that stands opposed to Christ will ever be acceptable or good.

Because the mission of Christ's church is defined by Christ, it **cannot** be:

- **Defined by those within the church.** You and I may belong to His church, but it remains *His* "body" and we are merely members of it. We have no authority to redefine or change its purpose.
- **Defined by those outside of His church.** Social expectations, cultural movements, racial campaigns, pseudo-Christians (i.e., those who only wear the name), government officials, or politics have no right to tell Christians how to function in Christ's church.
- **A social institution.** Christ's church is a privately-owned, privately-held, transcendent entity that neither caters to social agendas nor tends to social ills. Christ never told His church to accept moral responsibility for secular society—and we have no right to do otherwise.
- **A provider of entertainment.** While individual Christians may pursue such interests on their own time, this is not the objective, purpose, or mission of Christ's church.

Of course, none of this sits well with the modern churchgoer, or even with those who stand outside of Christian churches and critique them. In the modern era, "the church" is a social welfare agent first and a body of worshipers second. Yet, to many, it appears that "we have reached the point where 'interpretation of the Scripture must be repositioned to provide more help' for personal and social concerns."[19] Yet, who decided this? Who has the authority to "reposition" apostolic teachings in one direction or another? What should this "repositioning" look like? And, most of all, why *"must"* we do this?

Such logic is based upon how the world *wants* to use Christ's church rather than how Christ *intended* for it to be used. People should not become Christians to address "personal and social concerns." People should become Christians to address their sins through the blood of Christ, commit to a discipleship *to* Christ, and proclaim the gospel of this forgiveness and this discipleship. The NT never instructs Christ's church to be an active agent of social reform. Such reform will be addressed one disciple at a time as more and more people conform to Christ rather than to a sin-polluted world.

The Biblical Plan for Churches

While Christians habitually do participate in collective worship of God in church services, they are not to be mere churchgoers. Anyone can attend a church service—even unbelievers, agnostics, and atheists if they want to. Christians are not mere attendees of a religious function; they understand their responsibility to God, fellow believers, and those who yet remain outside of Christ. Going to church—i.e., attending a church service—is one thing; being an active member of a church is quite another.

One of the apostle Paul's regular objectives during his so-called "missionary journeys" throughout the ancient world was to establish churches everywhere he went.[20] "The church was never meant to be exclusively universal. By God's own design, the church was meant to be gathered into smaller units of fellowship through which His work on earth could be accomplished."[21] Paul also appointed elders—spiritual leadership—over every church that had been established (Acts 14:21–23). In churches that he did not establish, he instructed elders to be appointed over them as well (Titus 1:5).

Established churches with capable spiritual leadership were not exceptional things in the first century but were an *intended* objective in the preaching of the gospel. Just as the spiritual body of Christ was built upon a solid foundation (Eph. 2:20), so congregations were each built upon a solid foundation (Rom. 15:20, 1 Cor. 3:10). The foundation for every congregation is Christ Himself (1 Cor. 3:11), which is consistent with the divine truth that He revealed through the Holy Spirit. A congregation that teaches or practices anything that opposes Christ, or the written word of God, contradicts the foundation upon which it allegedly was built.

Churches are not separate entities from the people that comprise them. Churches *are* people, not buildings, programs, services, or classes. They provide an extremely important context for nurturing, training, and exercising Christians of every level of spiritual maturity. They provide a family environment in which mutual encouragement (1 Thess. 5:14), edification (1 Cor. 14:12, in principle), and submission (Eph. 5:21) are practiced. In this family structure, there are young and old, married and unmarried, families with children and families with no children, new Christians and veteran Christians, those who are very capable (spiritually and otherwise) and those who are very limited in what they can offer. Some of the men will serve as deacons or appointed servants; a few will serve as elders. Some will teach and preach publicly, some will teach privately, and all will *be* taught and receive instruction from God's word.

All members of a church are considered "family," regardless of what their roles might be. Just as importantly, everyone *has* a role—a particular function within that family that contributes to the overall forward-moving direction of the entire group. Paul uses the human body as an analogy to the collective work of any given congregation: while some members are more responsible or capable than others, *every* member has a place and thus something to contribute (Rom. 12:4–8, 1 Cor. 12:14–27). It is not the church leadership that assigns all these roles or functions (although this may be necessary and appropriate at times); ultimately, it is God who imparts various talents, abilities, skill sets, and other "gifts" to His people.[22] In fact, many of the "gifts" given to the church—the body of Christ as well as (by extension) every congregation—are in the form of *people themselves*, not only what people can do (Eph. 4:11–13).

Churches need strong Christians to function as they should. At the same time, all Christians benefit from strong churches that have much to offer in the way of teaching and spiritual support. While no one is required to be a member of a congregation to visit and even profit from it, congregations cannot operate as a bunch of uncommitted and random visitors. Membership is important, spiritually healthy, and mutually beneficial because it provides a fixed context in which Christians can learn, grow, and serve together. It is both a service and a privilege; it requires a commitment and an investment from every member, but it also provides a great return for those who are sincerely dedicated to its cause.

Christians need churches—organized groups of people working in concert for the cause of Christ—and churches are always in need of more people. God never intended for Christians to "go it alone" in their walks of faith. Churches are needed because:

- People, by nature, need to be governed. Every group of people, no matter how large or small, needs leadership and direction. Just as nature abhors a vacuum, groups of Christians will gravitate to any dominant leader(s) in pursuit of leadership. Even bad leaders, they might reason, are better than no leaders at all. However, randomly selected or default leadership is never wise or profitable. For this reason, God wants qualified leaders to be appointed in each congregation to provide leadership to that group of Christians.
- Christians, like all people, need structure, stability, and consistency to perform well and remain focused on a given objective. Churches provide these things, giving all their members a foundation to build upon and a family structure in which to participate. "The church is not pictured in the New Testament as an unorganized mass of floating members, without local church membership and responsibilities to its program of work."[23] Just as all people need *other* people, so Christians need each other to grow in knowledge, bear "fruit," and "walk" *together* in the Lord (Col. 1:9-10). In many cases, the church provides a far superior supportive "family" than one's own biological family (i.e., parents, siblings, and other relatives). In some cases, the church "family" is the *only* family some Christians have at all.
- Christians are not only to worship God and follow Christ individually but also *together*. "Active membership in a local

congregation is God's plan for the assistance and spiritual growth of every one of God's children."[24] While, ultimately, each Christian answers personally to the Lord, much of the NT instruction is directed at what entire churches are to do in a collective effort of service to Christ. Preaching the word is a group effort: there must be a preacher *and* an audience. Singing is to be done together as a form of worship to God *and* mutual edification (Eph. 5:19, Col. 3:16–17). Sharing—of money (2 Cor. 8:13–15), material goods (Gal. 6:6), emotional support (Rom. 12:15-16, 1 Cor. 12:20-26), and even the disclosure of sins (James 5:16)—is a collective action, not an individual one. Prayers may be said alone, but they are also supposed to be said together. Even the work of restoring fallen Christians requires the help and involvement of "one another" (Gal. 6:1–2).

- The "one another" principle is strong and consistent throughout the NT, and almost always refers to what *Christians* do for each other rather than having any reference to unbelievers. Christians are to love, serve, encourage, pray for, share with, and even submit to one another. Churches provide a natural and ideal context in which these actions can be carried out. This thought is not limited to a worship *service*; rather, the church provides a specific group of people that can both give and receive in these "one another" actions on any day of the week. God is putting us together for a reason: He wants us to take care of one another, and to practice our good works "especially" to those who are "of the household of the faith." This "household" refers to Christians generally and fellow members of one's own congregation specifically (Gal. 6:9–10; see Col. 3:12–15). This kind of work cannot be done remotely, virtually, or by proxy. It requires person-to-person involvement—something which no form of technology can duplicate or replace.
- Churches provide a kind of training ground for Christians to exercise their godly virtues on "one another," as was just said. But this training is to prepare us for a much larger group of people outside of the churches themselves: the world of unconverted people. If we cannot love, serve, and "do good" to one another (fellow Christians), then we are wholly unprepared to do good to those who are *not* Christians. What this means is: genuine Christianity begins at home, both literally and figuratively. Virtues we practice in our private homes are expected to carry into our

congregations (our second "home"), and virtues we practice in our assemblies must be the "salt" and "light" we share in the realm of non-Christians (Mat. 5:13–16, Phil. 2:14–15, Col. 4:5–6, and 1 Peter 2:12).

- Churches provide an excellent environment for the word of God to be taught effectively, efficiently, and emphatically to those who are new to the faith. It is critical to have such people grounded in the practice of coming together with fellow believers, building a trusting relationship among many of these believers, and engaging in the work of the church. Teaching a person to become a Christian is one thing; having them firmly established in how Christians live and what Christians do is quite another. Conversions are always a source of joy and celebration; retention, however, is even better. Many new converts—a frighteningly high percentage—may easily slip away from the church and back into their old lives. In part, this may be due to a failure of the church system to educate them, nurture them through their spiritual renewal, and hold them accountable to those who can lead them closer to Christ. Ed Wharton speaks to this:

> New converts are not left to wander aimlessly. Local churches are organized units of God's people into which new Christians are to be lovingly guided into worship, work, and spiritual growth. A local church is a unit of the divine family with brothers and sisters in a home congregation serving each other's needs and at the same time reaching out to the lost.[25]

Ideally, a congregation's preacher(s) and teachers offer excellent education from the Scriptures, and this teaching further unites and strengthens the group and supports its overall ministry. "Sound doctrine" (1 Tim. 4:6) is critical to the health, integrity, and perpetuation (for the next generation) of any congregation. Churches that have poor teaching, weak preachers/teachers, and little understanding of or respect for the word of God have no right to represent Christ. Instead, they will be gullible to embrace worldly teachings that pose as doctrine and slowly morph into thinly disguised community centers rather than "a city set on a hill" (Mat. 5:14) that radiates God's truth to a lost and dying world.

Summary Thoughts

Christ's church is just that: *His* church. The spiritual body of all those who belong to Him has always been, and remains to this day, under His full control. No one can become part of His church without fulfilling what He says is necessary for this. Likewise, no one can be removed from that "body" by any lesser authority than His. While many people have hijacked the church *system* that is detailed in the NT, no one can hijack Christ's own "body." It is impossible for Christ's own body to fall away from its own head.[26]

Many churches that were once founded by faithful Christian men and women have since succumbed to a secularized version of what they used to be. The world has, sadly, done a very good job at infiltrating, reconditioning, and indoctrinating modern Christians to think far more as *it* thinks than how *Christ* has taught us to think. The world wants to neuter churches of their power, their influence, and their courage to stand up against the "empty deception" of human philosophy and "the tradition of men" (Col. 2:8). Many churches that once claimed to boldly stand for the truth now are plastic façades of true religion, having forsaken their allegiance to Christ in pursuit of membership, money, and/or popularity.

Churches were never meant to promote a worldly version of Christianity. Rather, Christians are to stand together *as* churches to promote discipleship to Christ. No one is genuinely drawing near to God who subscribes to the modern church system. However, *everyone* draws near to God by coming together with fellow believers to be "conformed to the image of His Son" (Rom. 8:29). While self-described "contemporary" or "progressive" churches seek to win the hearts of the masses, Christ's churches seek to follow the will of the Master. This latter pursuit is by far the more difficult of the two but is also the far nobler, better, and more rewarding.

God wants Christians to form congregations, and these congregations are to be organized and function in a certain way. The instruction for all of this comes to us from the same source material from which we get the instruction for how to become a Christian: the NT pattern. Now that we have examined what "Christian" means and why Christians need to organize themselves into churches, it is time to take a deeper look into the pattern itself.

Chapter Three: "According to the Pattern"

People do not just build things without knowing *what* they are building and *why* they are building it. Buildings are meant to be definable structures that serve a given purpose. To achieve their form and function, people all begin the same way: with a plan. This plan may be very detailed and complex, such as a blueprint for a high-rise apartment or medical facility. Or it may be very primitive and even crude, such as a penciled sketch with measurements for a backyard tool shed or a small barn. Even if nothing is literally written down on paper, the plan for what is being built will be in the mind of the one who builds it.

Since this is true for earthly structures built by mere human beings, it is far truer for a spiritual structure built by a divine being. Since this spiritual structure is not a brick-and-mortar design but comprised of human souls, the specifications must first deal with these souls individually, and then collectively. In other words, the souls themselves must first be fit to be a part of this structure, and then the structure itself must conform to a heavenly design.

This refers, of course, to Christ's church (the structure, so to speak) and those individuals who belong to it (Christians). Consider the following passages:

- "Or what agreement has the temple of God with idols? For we are the temple of the living God; just as God said, 'I will dwell in them and walk among them; and I will be their God, and they shall be My people.'" (2 Cor. 6:16)
- "So then you are no longer strangers and aliens, but you are fellow citizens with the saints, and are of God's household, having been built on the foundation of the apostles and prophets, Christ Jesus Himself being the corner stone, in whom the whole building, being fitted together, is growing into a holy temple in the Lord, in whom you also are being built together into a dwelling of God in the Spirit." (Eph. 2:19–22)
- "And coming to Him as to a living stone which has been rejected by men, but is choice and precious in the sight of God, you also, as living stones, are being built up as a spiritual house for a holy priesthood, to offer up spiritual sacrifices acceptable to God through Jesus Christ." (1 Peter 2:4–5)

Clearly, a heavenly temple requires a heavenly design, just as each "living stone" within that temple needs to conform to a heavenly expectation. Patterns, blueprints, designs, etc. are not the work of chance; they do not simply "happen"; they will not just appear out of nowhere. If there is a pattern to follow, there must by necessity be a pattern-maker—a designer who came up with the pattern and has the authority and ability to say what is needed and the purpose being served.[27]

The Pattern Concept

God, in His wisdom, knew we needed a pattern to follow. Left to ourselves, we tend to wander aimlessly, gravitate to base desires, or follow the impulses of our hearts. (Watch a toddler, for example, in a home environment: he does not have a plan, but simply moves toward and wants to touch whatever catches his eye.) We cannot serve a living God by acting like self-guided, self-gratifying, and self-defined people. Instead, God equips believers to carry out His will and provide Him with appropriate worship. His gospel message has outlined this plan for both His people and their collective identities as churches.

Since God *has* provided a pattern, it is necessary that this pattern be followed. God did not give us a pattern for no reason, and we cannot honor Him or His Son by refusing to follow this heavenly plan. All that is meant by using the word "pattern" is "that human beings are obligated to go to the Bible and learn what God wants them to know and practice. If the Bible is not a 'pattern' in this sense, then the Bible is completely irrelevant when it comes to how people choose to live life."[28] Wharton adds:

> A pattern may be thought of as a mold, cast, or form into which some substance such as concrete, lead, or wax is poured, and each time the same image in reproduced. Doctrinally speaking, the pattern concept should produce the idea of doctrinal identity. Consequently, modern church builders should search the scripture for and attempt to conform to the same pattern of teaching that the apostles delivered to the first-century churches. This pattern of teaching gives the church her distinct identity of nature and form.[29]

The apostle Paul told the Roman Christians that "you became obedient to that form of teaching to which you were committed" (Rom. 6:17).

The word "form" here is from the Greek word *tupos*, which is the same word from which we get our English word "type" and is translated "pattern" elsewhere in the NT. In other words, Paul wrote that there is a specific *type* or *pattern of teaching* that must be obeyed to be "freed from sin" and produce "slaves of righteousness" (6:18). It stands to reason that if that pattern is not followed, then neither will one be freed from sin, nor can he become one of God's righteous servants. This illustrates how important and necessary it is that we adhere to divine patterns. Wharton continues:

> The pattern principle means no more than going to the Bible to discover what God wants His people to believe, to be and to do until Jesus returns. The pattern embraces what men are to believe and do in order to be saved, it embraces the worship in the church's assemblies as well as an individual's daily worship for God's glory and our spiritual benefit, it embraces the work of the church and the organizational structure of both the universal church and of the local congregations. The pattern principle implies that what God revealed to the apostles to be preached, believed, and obeyed in the apostolic age can be identified in the New Testament, and that God intentionally made that clear in the New Testament writings so that this same message would be reproduced in proclamation and practice throughout history until Christ returns. The New Testament pattern principle insures [sic] the identity of the body of Christ as God purposed it from eternity.[30]

Any intentional departure *from* this pattern constitutes not obedience, but disobedience since we ought to know the plan and are held accountable to it. This is not an imposition upon us but is necessary to bring us into fellowship with God and then to serve Him in such a way that befits a divine Being.[31] We do not know how to be heavenly people unless a heavenly Being showed us the way. And, once told, we are expected to listen to and obey this way rather than choose a course of our own making.

Churches and church systems that practice and promote doctrines that do not come from God mislead people into thinking that they are "saved" even though they have not conformed to God's pattern *for* salvation. Likewise, many people think themselves to be "Christians" based upon their own sincerity and good intentions rather than the specific instructions of God's pattern. But no church is justified by God just because it cites the Bible or invokes Christ's name in its sermons and liturgies (worship services). And no person is saved based upon sincerity or good intentions.[32]

The written NT pattern is not meant to be an ornamental fixture for pews and pulpits; it is God's blueprint for believers everywhere. It is not open to subjective interpretation: it is not a negotiable design that can be amended or modified at human will. Rather, it is of utmost importance since it gives us the only acceptable information that prepares us for the life to come.[33] It is required since we are unable to prepare ourselves for this according to our own designs. And it is binding, which means that God is not merely suggesting what we are to do but is *commanding* these things. He is in the position of authority, and we are to be subject to His will. All this works in His best interest as well as our own.

An overall pattern is more important than the individual rules that within it. For example, an army unit needs to have rules by which to conduct itself, even down to the most mundane tasks (camping, fixing meals, shaving, etc.). But the overall pattern for any army is not to produce glorified campouts but to fight battles. This requires an overarching plan or strategy that does need individual rules but is not defined by any one of them. Similarly, there are rules to baking, cooking, and food preparation, but producing meals is the real objective, not cooking rules. We need rules to produce good meals, but the rules are subordinate to the overarching plan: the finished product.[34]

The pattern is the context for its rules, not the other way around. In the same manner, the NT pattern is why we have specific commandments, not the other way around. The pattern is not merely a collection of commandments but is an overarching blueprint of what God says is our ultimate objective as His people. When we follow the NT pattern, we transform into something different than what we were. This does not happen without divine help (the work of the Holy Spirit within our hearts), but part of the divine help is the pattern itself (what the Holy Spirit has revealed, recorded, and preserved for us). We are not to assume that the pattern is all about "rule-keeping," for then we would just have to follow rules without transformation. And, if we follow those rules well enough, then we will be saved. (This is the mindset of every legalistic churchgoer.) Instead, the rules or commandments within the pattern are there to fulfill the objective of the pattern itself—namely, to become increasingly conformed to Christ rather than remain what we were when we started the process.

What we commonly see today, however, is people pitching aside (in one way or another) God's rules yet wanting the same result that His pattern is meant to produce. The word that best describes this mentality is "liberalism," a humanly manufactured philosophy (or "-ism") that treats God's word as a general or moral guideline rather than an authoritative prescription for Christians everywhere. Adaptation, customization, and fluidity are its objectives; obedience, conformity, and attention to detail are deemed constrictive, legalistic, and unnecessary. As one writer put it, "Liberalism, whether in politics or religion, relies heavily upon emotion rather than intellect, reason and rational persuasion. The liberal call for change arises out of emotion, is driven by emotion, and depends upon emotion for its continued survival."[35] While the discussion about liberalism and its consequences comes later in this book, it is good to know upfront what drives so much of what is labeled "Christian" religion today.

The Old Testament Example

To better appreciate the "pattern" concept and its importance, we can cite the Old Testament (OT) for a historical and biblical precedent. In Exod. 25—31, while Moses was on Mt. Sinai for forty days and nights, God spoke to him all the things that needed to be done to build a tabernacle for Him. A "tabernacle" was a glorified tent that served as a temporary temple, designed for portability from one location to another. Even so, the Mosaic tabernacle was unique, supremely special, and served as the meeting place between God and His priests, who represented the entire nation of Israel. This tabernacle would serve the people's needs as a place of worship in the wilderness until a permanent temple would be built "in a place which the LORD chooses" (see Deut. 12:1–14), which would be the city of Jerusalem several hundred years in the future.

The Mosaic tabernacle would contain certain furniture or fixtures, both within and without the tent itself, and each fixture would serve a purpose that was both practical and spiritually symbolic. Thus, God outlined the construction of the bronze altar upon which all the blood sacrifices would be offered. He gave specific instructions for the altar of incense (also known as the golden altar), the incense itself, and the ark of the covenant. He commanded the design for the table of showbread and the golden lampstand (or *menorah*) within the outer sanctuary. He detailed the frame, curtains, boards, and sockets (base supports) for the tabernacle itself, and the construction of its outer courtyard. He even gave detailed instructions for the garments of His priests, their rites of ordination, the anointing oil by which they were to be consecrated, and the food that they were to consume within the courtyard.

Not only was God specific about what He wanted, but He also made it clear to Moses that he was not to deviate from these instructions in the least. "According to all that I am going to show you," God told him, "as the pattern of the tabernacle and the pattern of all its furniture, just so you shall construct it" (Exod. 25:9). This left no room for creative interpretation, personal embellishments, ignoring details (for any reason), or justifying any departure *from* the pattern based on good intentions. God wanted a place of worship that would honor Him, the design of which was too important to let Moses or the Israelites to decide on their own. The reason for this was because the tabernacle—primitive and humanly-constructed as it was—conformed to a heavenly design and heavenly elements. God cannot be honored by something that did not come from Him; earthly versions of the "ideal" are *less-than-ideal* by comparison.

Now advance forward about 1,500 years. While Moses did construct the tabernacle "according to the pattern" dictated to him on the mountain, Christ showed Himself to *be* the Pattern—the heavenly source for all that honors God the Father. Moses was a faithful servant in God's "house," fulfilling what his limited relationship with God allowed. Yet, Christ *is* the house, so to speak (Heb. 3:1–6): He has full authority over *all* that has come into existence (Mat. 28:18, Col. 1:15–17, Heb. 1:1–3, etc.). What He provides is "more excellent" than anything Moses, Israel, the Levitical priesthood, the tabernacle, and all the animal sacrifices could have ever produced (Heb. 8:3–6). He is not merely a "copy" of the heavenly design; He is the source of it.

All this information is not to be ignored today simply because we think we have produced something better, more contemporary, or more palatable to modern expectations. God's pattern, directions, and designs serve a higher purpose than what we can even know. It is not necessary that we fully understand this purpose; it *is* necessary that we conform to what He has told us to do. Things belonging to God are important; they are not to be left to human design, wisdom, or dictation. Honoring the pattern also honors the One who gave it.

As God gave a pattern for the ancient tabernacle, so He has given us a pattern for the spiritual tabernacle: Christ's church. And, as we have a pattern for Christ's universal church, so we have a pattern for the individual churches of Christians throughout the world. We are not to guess or wonder what God wants us (individually) to do or how we (collectively) are to be organized; such details are far too important to be left to human discretion. Whatever specific direction He has given is binding, non-negotiable, and non-amendable. On the other hand, God did not provide exhaustively or comprehensively *every single* detail or implementation of His people or their churches. He has given us intelligence and discernment—all guided by the principles of godly love and godly wisdom—to fill in the blanks as needed. (This will be discussed in detail in the final section of this book.)

Just as Moses was not at liberty to alter God's detailed instructions regarding the tabernacle, so we are not at liberty to do this regarding the Christian life or Christians' churches. God has the inherent right to define whatever belongs to Him, is used in the worship of Him, and is used to represent Him. Again, this serves His best interest as well as that of all those who abide by these directions.

The Tabernacle Example Applied

In Eph. 2:19–22, quoted earlier, the apostle Paul described Christians—*all* Christians, collectively—as "a holy temple in the Lord." This holy temple, like the Mosaic tabernacle, is constructed according to a specific and heavenly-revealed pattern. This pattern begins with every individual component of the structure as well as the entire structure itself. In other words, the pattern determines the life of every individual "living stone" so that it can become part of "a spiritual house" which the Lord indwells (1 Peter 2:5).

The patterned lifestyle of the believer is necessary to contribute to the patterned design of the spiritual church. The only way for God to have fellowship with an individual Christian is to *own* him as His "possession" (Titus 2:14), thus exercising controlling influence over his life in leading him to a glorious future. The only way for God to usher the entire body of Christians (Christ's church) into glory is to have full possession of it. This spiritual "temple" must be fully, deliberately, and obediently devoted to Him in every respect to serve His heavenly purpose. Thus, whatever belongs to God—whether an individual believer or the collective of *all* believers—must live according to a godly pattern. This is not optional but necessary. To do otherwise forfeits all the promises made in the context *of* fellowship with Him.

Every single Christian is a kind of "tabernacle" or temple to God.[36] "Or do you not know that your body is a temple of the Holy Spirit who is in you, whom you have from God, and that you are not your own?" Paul asked the Corinthians rhetorically. "For you have been bought with a price: therefore glorify God in your body" (1 Cor. 6:19–20). The context here (see 6:12–20) deals with sexual purity, but the application encompasses the entirety of the believer's life. God gave detailed instructions for how the Mosaic tabernacle—a physical tent in the wilderness—was to be constructed. Much more important to Him are *living temples*, which is what Christians are (1 Peter 2:4–5). Such greater importance warrants an even greater emphasis on "building" Christians according to the pattern He has disclosed to us.

As a spiritual illustration, consider a comparison between the elements of the physical tabernacle and a Christian. The believer's heart becomes the tabernacle in which God dwells; his every act of faith is an act of worship to Him. The outer court of his tabernacle represents his sphere of influence and association with the world. His "outer sanctuary"— which corresponds to the place where the Levitical priests entered the Mosaic tabernacle—represents the more intimate and special fellowship that he has with fellow believers. Thus, the outer sanctuary is all about what Christians do *together* in collective service to God.

The innermost sanctuary of the Mosaic tabernacle was called the "Holy of Holies" (Heb. 9:3) in which the ark of the covenant was placed. The Levitical high priest alone entered this holy place once a year on the Day of Atonement to sprinkle blood on the lid of the ark of the covenant, known as the "mercy seat" (see Lev. 16). This was not a group effort but was an intensely personal and sacred work that he carried out in God's presence. This corresponds to the Christian's heart and soul—the very core of his being—where the blood of Christ cleanses his soul of its sins, and he experiences fellowship with God. Just as a copy of the Law of Moses was stored in the ark of the covenant, so God's law is treasured in the context of the believer's covenant relationship with God. To "sanctify Christ as Lord in your hearts" (1 Peter 3:15) means to revere and worship Christ in one's own Holy of Holies—that person's heart. As with the Levitical high priest, this is the believer's very sacred presentation before God in prayer, communion, and spiritual meditation. It is deeply personal between him and God; it is not an experience enjoined by others.

Outside of the Mosaic tabernacle is the bronze altar upon which the Levitical priests offered sacrifices to God and on behalf of the Israelites. These blood offerings provided atonement and consecration, cleansing the heart of sin and dedicating Israelites to God's service. In comparison, the Christian does not offer blood sacrifices since Christ has provided for all of these in the offering of His own body (Heb. 9:11–14). However, he is still required to provide gifts and sacrifices in the form of love, charity, hospitality, generosity, contributions, sharing, and "fruit of lips" (prayers, praises, and songs—Heb. 13:15).

Also outside of the original tabernacle was a bronze laver that stood between the bronze altar and the tabernacle itself (Exod. 40:7, 30). This provided for the washing of the Levitical priests before they entered the tabernacle. This corresponds to one's "washing" of regeneration (Titus 3:5), which is his baptism into Christ. No one can enter fellowship with God who has not first been cleansed in the way God has prescribed (John 3:5, Rom. 6:3–7, and Heb. 10:22). This means: a person who has not been properly cleansed cannot enter the collective work of Christians (symbolized by the outer sanctuary of the tabernacle) or the sacred communion of an individual believer (symbolized by the inner sanctuary, the "Holy of Holies").[37]

The frame, curtains, linens, and sockets of the tabernacle in the wilderness symbolize the structure and stability of the Christian's life with God. Because of this, his heart is strong, solid, and supported by nothing less than the greatest power and authority that exists. This indicates his self-discipline, self-mastery, and stewardship of his time, energy, talents, and responsibilities. Rather than God saying, in so many words, "You can just build your life however you want—I'll be pleased with whatever you choose to do," God expects the believer's life to be built according to His heavenly design.

Finally, the Levitical priests were required to clothe themselves according to the pattern God had given them, and no detail of this was to be ignored (Exod. 28:4ff). "They [all of the priestly garments—MY WORDS] shall be on Aaron and on his sons when they enter the tent of meeting, or when they approach the altar to minister in the holy place so that they do not incur guilt and die" (Exod. 28:43). The priests were also to be anointed with an oil and spice mixture that was to only be used for sacred ordinations (Lev. 8:10–12; see Exod. 30:22–33). Even the food dedicated to the priests was required to be consumed within the court of the tabernacle according to specific conditions.

Likewise, the Christian's lifestyle—his presentation to the world, his lifestyle, his conduct, and (when appropriate) even his physical attire and appearance—must reflect who he belongs to.[38] Christians are to "look" different than unbelievers; as holy "priests" of God (1 Peter 2:9), they have a sacred ministry to uphold. This must not be compromised because of peer pressure, personal preference, convenience, or laziness. Christians are to "come out" and "be separate" from the godless world in which they live (2 Cor. 6:17), not blend in so much that they cannot be distinguished from it.

Such vivid and visual patterns in the OT are not just ancient history or antiquated ideas. They are pictures of what God expects of His people (in principle) *throughout* history, regardless of which covenant they are under. He has provided a heavenly pattern by which to govern every aspect of our lives—not to burden or micromanage us but to bring us into increasing conformity with His Son (Mat. 10:24–25a, Rom. 8:29). This works to God's advantage because it creates people who are wholly devoted to His work on earth. It works to the Christian's advantage because it draws him ever closer to God, thus ensuring salvation in the life to come.

In the most basic sense, this means: the Christian's life is to follow the pattern laid out for him in the NT. His spiritual worship and service to God adhere to every aspect of the heavenly pattern, not just on Sunday services or when he is with other Christians. His heart and mind honor the holy pattern as a blueprint for how he is to think, live, and represent God to the world. His relationships with others (both believers and unbelievers) are dictated by this pattern: he knows how properly to conduct himself in any situation. His marriage—the closest earthly relationship—is built upon the heavenly pattern provided by Christ and His beautiful "bride" (the church). In this manner, he appeals to a higher order and spiritual pattern rather than simply imitating what is found in many worldly marriages. His children are brought up "in the discipline and instruction of the Lord" (Eph. 6:4) so that they will be raised, nurtured, and held accountable to expectations that correspond to his own relationship with his spiritual Father. His home will purposely provide a spiritual environment in which God is worshiped, Christ is followed, and His word is honored regularly.

Such people build their lives "according to the pattern." This not only honors the pattern-giver (God) but also gains the greatest advantages while living in a godless world. The Bible, and especially the NT, is filled with examples, models, mentors, and witnesses as to how to implement this heavenly pattern in real life. As the apostle Paul wrote, "Brethren, join in following my example, and observe those who walk according to the pattern you have in us" (Phil. 3:17). Christians are not just told *what* to do; they are also shown *how* to do it.

The "Law of the House"

This pattern of how to conduct oneself in a covenant relationship with God extends also to Christians' churches. Christ has given us a pattern for how churches are to be organized, how their assemblies are to be conducted, and how to deal with internal struggles, resistance, and even disobedient members. The fact that we have such instruction necessarily implies that this work is too important for God to leave entirely to human judgment. All congregations of God's people are to follow the same pattern. Because of this, there ought to be consistency and uniformity in the structure, work, manner of worship, and proclamation of the gospel in *all* churches that identify with Christ.

This discussion has no reference, for example, to the physical order of service, the arrangement of furniture within a church building, or the subject matter of classes and sermons offered from church to church. It has to do with a congregation's *essential* identity—whatever is critical to its identity with Christ and His gospel. Therefore, apostolic teaching—the initial instruction from Christ's apostles to the early churches—is consistent, uniform, and expected (1 Cor. 4:17). "Not only, then, was the church in the first century ordered after divine pattern, but the church throughout history is to be ordered after the same pattern to the extent of our ability to recognize and reproduce it (2 Tim. 2:2)."[39]

In another OT example, consider Ezek. 40—43, where the prophet Ezekiel watches an angelic "man" measuring a symbolic "temple" in detail. The idea was that Israel had been given instructions by Moses as to how to build the tabernacle, including the ministry of its priesthood, yet later succumbed to idolatry and cultic worship practices. This moral deviation from the Law of Moses corrupted the physical tabernacle/temple, priesthood, sacrifices, and nation itself. God openly condemned this flagrant defilement of His temple (Ezek. 43:7–8) and looked forward in time to when a new temple would be built that would not be defiled by the sins of His people (43:9). Finally, He says to Ezekiel ("son of man") (43:10–12):

> As for you, son of man, describe the temple to the house of Israel, that they may be ashamed of their iniquities; and let them measure the plan. If they are ashamed of all that they have done, make known to them the design of the house, its structure, its exits, its entrances, all its designs, all its statutes, and all its laws. And write it in their sight, so that they may observe its whole design and all its statutes and do them. This is the law of the house: its entire area on the top of the mountain all around shall be most holy. Behold, this is the law of the house.

God was not referring to a physical temple but a spiritual one. This spiritual temple is in fact Christ's church (Eph. 2:19–22). In other words, even though this temple is spiritual in nature, it still adheres to a heavenly pattern. If this is true for the spiritual church, then it is also true for the physical church: if the greater temple has a "plan," a "law," and a "design" to be "most holy" to the Lord, then the lesser temple (the individual congregation) must also have these things.

The "law of the house" is a pointed reference to how God wants things done in His churches. This "law" does not apply to unspiritual people, false religions, or earthly temples, but it most certainly does apply to God's people. Christians are to conduct themselves appropriately in their collective worship of God; they are to pay attention to the details (i.e., the "measurements" and structural components of Ezekiel's vision) that God says are important; they are not to defile God's "house" (i.e., His church) with false teaching, false religion, or false hearts.

Contemporary Views

What has just been said is such a simple, fundamental teaching of Scripture. Even so, it has been hugely ignored, dismissed, or met with open defiance in many churches today that claim to "honor Christ." What is called "worship" today is often a come-as-you-are, do-what-you-want, "God knows my heart"-experience. Reverence has been reduced to a mere attitude rather than being expressed through outward actions and appearances. (Remember the Levitical priests? They were to be reverent *through* these things, not *instead* of them.) Contemporary church "worship" has become an exercise in excessive self-fulfillment, self-gratification, and sheer entertainment. Yet, no one can truly worship Christ who refuses to abide by the pattern He has given to us. Failure to honor the pattern translates to disrespect toward the pattern-giver. When God condemned the priests Eli and his sons, He said, "Those who honor Me I will honor, and those who despise Me [through violation of His commandments—MY WORDS] will be lightly esteemed."[40]

What often passes for "Christianity" today barely resembles the NT pattern for Christians and their collective worship. Contemporary Christianity is a fractured, tormented assemblage of faiths, doctrines, practices, organizations, and social welfare programs. Little of what is done can be justified by or traced back to original apostolic teaching. (This has no reference to genuine expediencies—a subject to be addressed later—but to doctrinal teachings and their implementations.) Instead of a united body of believers that honors its head (Christ), we see a Frankenstein-like piecemeal of competing doctrines and allegiances.

Those who claim to be Christians cannot all claim to "know the truth" (John 8:31–32) yet teach doctrines that contradict the NT pattern and conflict with each other. Left to our own decisions, we can all be wrong, but we cannot all be right. It is God's revealed word that determines what (or who) is right or wrong. Paul once exclaimed, "Has Christ been divided?" (1 Cor. 1:13)—a rhetorical statement, since Christ cannot truly be divided.[41] Yet, denominationalism—and even much of "non-denominationalism"—is all about division, separation, and purposely identifying "Christians" according to one "faith" or another. This is the exact opposite of what Christ called for (John 17:20–22) and what His church is all about.[42] Paul declared that "God is not a

God of confusion but of peace, as in all the churches of the saints" (1 Cor. 14:33). Yet, God is being portrayed today as a very confused, even schizophrenic, God that endorses chaos among those who claim to be His people. It is impossible, in any context, to have peace without unity: the two states of being either rise or fall together.

It is a biblical truth—and it stands to reason—that the body of Christ must follow its head. "Christians" of numerous faiths, doctrines, and denominations cannot all be part of Christ's body if they fail to obey the head of that body. Trying to support a position otherwise begs several questions:

- If the method by which someone claims to have become a Christian does not follow the NT pattern, then is he really a Christian at all?[43] Is Christ obligated to allow people to identify with Him that refuse to honor His terms?
- If one cites the NT as the basis for his identity as a Christian, yet does not follow the NT pattern, doesn't this invalidate his genuineness and sincerity? As Christ taught, just repeating "Lord, Lord!" is not an indicator of true devotion (Mat. 7:21–23, Luke 6:46).
- What use is a pattern if it is not followed? What use is a divine pattern if it can be changed, ignored, or maligned by human authority without consequence? Since God's pattern is His revealed truth, how can we alter this "truth" and think that we will be in good standing with Him?
- If the pattern has been changed to accommodate new circumstances, social expectations, modern perspectives, etc. (as many "Christians" have claimed), then what are these changes, and how are we to know that God approves of them?
- If the NT pattern is antiquated, out-of-date, irrelevant, and unable to cope with the modern world (as many "Christians" have claimed), then what pattern *should* we follow? How do we know this for certain? Who decides this—and who has *the authority* to decide this?
- Why are some churches diligently committed to following the NT pattern while others treat it as a general suggestion and do whatever they want? Is God holding *some* churches responsible but not others? How does this reconcile with Rev. 2—3, where Jesus spoke to seven different churches and demanded that they *all* honor Him and His word or else have their fellowship with Him severed?

Summary Thoughts

Whenever God gives us laws, commandments, doctrines, or any specific instructions, He expects His people to *obey* them, not question, modify, or counteroffer them. Those who reject the Lord's *word* will themselves be rejected by Him. Jesus Himself said, "Every plant which My heavenly Father did not plant shall be uprooted" (Mat. 15:13). This means that every person, church, religion, gospel, preacher, and church leader that refuses to follow God's revealed pattern will be "uprooted."

On a positive note, God has wisely and graciously given us a pattern by which to follow. He has not left us without clear instruction and a definite direction for living in fellowship with Him. Instead, He has given us "everything pertaining to life and godliness" (2 Peter 1:3). When we do things according to God's will, we always benefit, and we are truly prepared to be the "salt" and "light" that He needs us to be to represent Him rightly (Mat. 5:13–16). Jesus said, "You are My friends if you do what I command you" (John 15:14). He could not have been clearer to His twelve disciples, or to us: He wants, needs, and expects us to honor what He has taught us and not to deviate from His instructions. This serves His best interest, but it also serves ours. It also begs the question: If we are His friends only *if* we obey Him, what are we if we *do not*?

The only way a person can be a Christian is to follow God's pattern for becoming one. The only way he can live faithfully *as* a Christian is to pattern his life after the apostolic teaching of the NT. The only way one's congregation can have fellowship with Christ and its "lampstand" be well-lit (Rev. 1:10–20) is to obey Christ's will for *all* churches that invoke His name. Since God has given all of us a pattern by which to follow, it cannot be otherwise.

Chapter Four: Why Many People Do Not Follow the Pattern

Imagine you are the head of a construction company that is building a large office complex. Your project manager has multiple blueprints for every phase of the building process—foundational, structural, electrical, plumbing, etc. Yet, instead of following these blueprints, your project manager decided to alter and customize the entire production with changes he took upon himself to make. As a result, the finished building looks nothing like it was supposed to, its internal systems do not operate correctly, and it is unsafe to use. Because of this, the ones who financed your project are extremely angry because you did not deliver on the promise you made to them in the first place: you built something far different than what they paid you to build.

The problem here is not just that the blueprints were not followed. The initial problem is *why* they were not followed by a man whom you hired to follow them. This speaks not only to improper action but also a disloyal intent. Such actions betray his commitment to you; they are offensive to your leadership of the company; he misrepresented you to anyone who would see your building debacle. In the end, people will not ridicule the project manager for a poorly-constructed building; they will ridicule the owner of the company that built it—your name is, in essence, all over it. Even though you gave the manager everything he needed to build the structure correctly and according to your expectations, he chose to override your decisions and make decisions of his own. Yet, he thinks that this is acceptable, was well within his right to do it, and expects to get paid for a job well done.

This simple illustration ought to clarify why following the pattern is so important for Christians and their churches. First, we are working not for ourselves, but for Someone higher than us (Christ). Second, we have no right to change decisions that He (in heavenly wisdom) has already made. Third, any changes we make immediately undermine our claims of respect for or loyalty to the One who gave us the blueprints in the first place. Fourth, our refusal to abide by the pattern brings reproach upon the One who oversees the entire operation: people will ridicule *Him*, not us, for creating a church that does not operate the way that it should. Fifth, we are greatly mistaken if we think that we will find favor and "get paid for a job well done" when we stand before the Owner and answer for what we did.

But aside from the failure to follow the blueprint itself, the question needs to be asked: *why* would anyone who claims to be a follower of Christ intentionally do this? If God had revealed one method, why would someone pursue a different one? How can anyone *knowingly* violate His pattern and still expect to be praised by Him for obedience, conformity, and loyalty?

A "Christianity" Foreign to the Pattern

The apostle Paul was informed by the Holy Spirit that "in later times some will fall away from the faith, paying attention to deceitful spirits and doctrines of demons" (1 Tim. 4:1–2). This "falling away" is usually referred to as an apostasy—a departure from the truth. This would not be just a personal departure (of one's private beliefs) but a doctrinal departure (that imposes upon entire congregations). The cause of this departure from the truth is cited as "deceitful spirits and doctrines of demons"—i.e., a satanic influence and temptation that leads people away from God and into rebellion (even while claiming to be "faithful" to Him). (See the chapter titled "Departures from the Pattern" for a fuller discussion of this.)

While the first-century Christians knew an apostasy was coming, they did not know all the details or the full extent of it. Now that we are on the other side of that historical prediction, we can see all kinds of departures from the pattern. Today, what passes for "Christianity" is cluttered and corrupted with all kinds of teachings, traditions, practices, and offices that many assume are biblical but, in fact, are clear departures from the NT pattern. Here's a sampling:

Clergy-laity system	The papacy	Apostolic succession
Board of directors	Titles (Reverend, Father, etc.)	Creeds (beyond the NT)
Church councils to decide or amend doctrine (beyond the NT)	Denominational system of church organization	Missionary societies (or any 3rd-party group to do church work)
Faith-healing ministries	Children's ministries	Church-sponsored holidays
Fundraisers for the church	Instrumental music	Church-sponsored concerts

Confession booths	Women ministers or elders	Calvinism (and all it implies)
Doctrine of Original Sin	Sponsors for baptism	Infant or child baptism
Salvation without baptism	Salvation by "ask Jesus into your heart to be your Savior"	Baptism for dead people[44]
Jesus is not a divine Being	Forced celibacy	Forbiddance of certain foods
Keeping the Sabbath	Purgatory	Worship of Mary

None of these beliefs or practices are biblical teachings given to Christians to teach and practice. None of these follow the NT pattern; all of them are departures from it. Even so, *all* of them are taught or practiced by groups that regard themselves as "Christian" churches. How can people claim to identify with Jesus who purposely violate the pattern He gave them to follow? In John 8:31-32, Jesus said that if we follow Him and His word, then we "will know the truth, and the truth will make you free." We cannot embrace error while claiming to be followers of Jesus and those who cling to the "truth." This is illogical, unbiblical, and unworkable.

The Heavenly Chain of Command

In John 16:13, Jesus told His disciples that the Holy Spirit would "guide you into all truth" concerning His church and its teachings. Jesus commissioned these men to communicate to the church (for all time) what the Spirit disclosed to them. You and I did not receive "all truth" individually or personally; we received it through the agency of these inspired men. This is the only way that any of us today know "truth": it was revealed to us through God having revealed it to them.

Jesus told His disciples, "All authority has been given to Me in heaven and on earth. Go therefore and make disciples of all the nations, baptizing them in the name of the Father and the Son and the Holy Spirit, teaching them to observe all that I commanded you" (Mat. 28:18–19). God the Father gave God the Son authority over *all things* (Heb. 1:2) and especially His church. Whatever decisions need to be made, whatever doctrines needed to be established, and whatever positions within the church needed to be outlined, Jesus Christ is the One who has been given "all authority" to do this (Eph. 1:18–23).

Christ's apostles understood this process. They were commissioned with the responsibility to be His spokesmen to the churches. Their apostolic authority was to be neither disregarded nor superseded. "If anyone thinks he is a prophet or spiritual, let him recognize that the things which I write to you are the Lord's commandment," Paul wrote (1 Cor. 14:37). "For you know what commandments we gave you by the authority of the Lord Jesus. ... So, he who rejects [these commandments] is not rejecting man but the God who gives His Holy Spirit to you" (1 Thess. 4:2, 8). The apostle Peter concurs: "But know this first of all, that no prophecy of Scripture is a matter of one's own interpretation [i.e., something of human origin—MY WORDS], for no prophecy was ever made by an act of human will, but men moved by the Holy Spirit spoke from God" (2 Peter 1:20–21). The apostles did not speak on their own authority, but as those who were "called as an apostle, set apart for the gospel of God" (Rom. 1:1).

This chain of command is the foundation for all authority pertaining to Christ's church—what it is, what it does, and what it teaches. The Father gave "all authority" to His Son, who sends God's Spirit to reveal to the apostles what is to be communicated and commanded to all the churches. This information was written down either by the apostles themselves or those with whom they had direct contact and oversight (i.e., Mark, Luke, the author of Hebrews, James, and Jude). This chain of command has not changed in 2,000 years because it is already perfect and complete; it remains fully functional toward the purpose for which it was intended; it does not need to be changed for any reason.

Christians are always on the receiving end of this instruction and never the source of it. The chain of command never reverses the order, allowing Christians to give *their* instructions to God the Father, as though He was obligated to accept them. We cannot honor God by pretending to be as wise as (if not wiser than) He is. We honor Him by submitting to His authority as handed down through this chain of command. The apostle Peter wrote: "I am stirring up your sincere mind by way of reminder, that you should remember the words spoken beforehand by the holy prophets and the commandment of the Lord and Savior spoken by your apostles" (2 Peter 3:1–2). The teachings of the apostles were

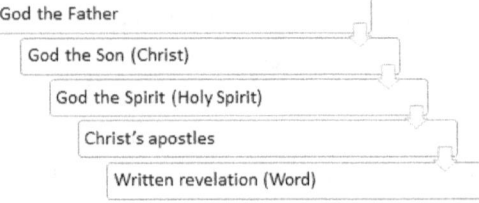

never meant to be changed, modified, or updated; they were to be "remembered." "Remembered" here does not mean merely recalled and then customized or dismissed altogether. It means to be observed, honored, practiced, and transmitted to "faithful" people (2 Tim. 2:2). The process is clear, unavoidable, and binding. It ought never to be tampered with.

Yet, as Paul pointed out (recall 1 Tim. 4:1–2), just because people desire to be identified with God and want to be recipients of His kindness, they do not always listen to Him. God always serves our best interest; people, left to themselves, will serve a lesser interest. In essence, people do not always want what is best for them, but they want to hear and do what pleases *them* rather than what pleases God. This results in a self-styled "worship" that shows little or no regard for the authority of the NT pattern, but is defined by human emotions, human "think-so's," and human appetites for power and control. Christ's church is made up of human souls, but it was never to be *led* by them. He alone is its head; Christians are His servants.

In all this turning away from the truth and turning toward something else, people confuse what *sounds* good with what *is* good. They confuse what *sounds* like "truth" with what God has declared *is* truth. They confuse their *feelings* of righteousness with the reality of it, and they forget that it is God who "credits" (or reckons) righteousness to us, never something we can credit to ourselves (Rom. 4:1–8). In doing so, they say things like, "Since I *feel* right with God, I must *be*!" These same people also confuse being "spiritual" with being *obedient*, as if experiencing one's "spirituality" was equal to being in good standing with the Lord. Yet, nowhere in the NT is anyone deemed obedient simply by feeling "spiritual." Not only this, but even pagans, witches, Satanists, and irreligious people claim to feel "spiritual" in some way or another, and yet they remain what they are.

Reasons for Failing to Follow the Pattern

Despite such clarity of the NT pattern—and such awful consequences for failing to abide by it—why do people still resist Christ's authority while claiming to be His followers? This is not merely a harmless disagreement but is something over which people lose their souls. So then, what compels them to be so bold, to go where angels fear to tread (see 2 Peter 2:10-11)? Here are some of the major reasons:

Discontentment with the NT pattern. No one may admit this, but it is necessarily implied. If someone is looking for something other than (or better than) the God-given pattern, then he is unhappy with what God provided. This is like a husband who is looking for an affair: he is obviously discontented with his wife, marriage itself, or both. Otherwise, he would remain faithful to what (and to whom) he committed in the first place.

Many today have expressed their discontent with the NT pattern in various ways. They say things like: "It is outdated." "It is unable to accommodate 'modern' life." "It does not take into account changes in society" (even though many of these "changes" are ungodly or immoral). "It is too constrictive; it is old or antiquated; it is worn out and has run its course."

Others say things like, "The NT needs clarification"—which often means, they want it to be re-interpreted or modified to fit a modern worldview. Or "We can do better; we *have* done better." Or "That was then, this is now; what worked then does not work now." All of these are human opinions, nothing more. Not only do they directly challenge what is written, but they challenge the authority of the One who wrote it: ultimately, God Himself (the head of the chain of command). So then, we have a growing discontent among people who want to belong to a "Christian" church, identify as Christ's followers, and be recipients of Christ's promises of salvation, but who are also very unhappy with *Christ Himself*. This is not going to end well for them. "Every plant which My heavenly Father did not plant shall be uprooted" (Mat. 15:13–14).

Genuine Christians are those who belong to Christ's church. It is *His* church because He died for it and rose from the dead to save it (2 Cor. 5:15, Eph. 5:25); He built it (Mat. 16:18); He is its head (Eph. 1:22–23, Col. 1:18); and He will be the One to usher it into glory in the hereafter (as His heavenly "Bride"). This is the straightforward and irrefutable teaching of the NT. Faithful Christians will accept this without turning around and challenging the gospel that carries His name and exists because of His authority.

Christians, by virtue of their own surrender to His authority, are *bound* to Christ's doctrine. We can be creative when it comes to matters of human judgments or expediencies (to be covered later in this book), but we cannot undermine the very basis for our identity: the NT pattern. In other words, we cannot say (as many have done), "We derive our identity as Christians from the NT pattern, but this pattern is outdated, antiquated, and has been superseded by a more modern understanding." This is like burning the Constitution that guarantees citizens' rights and then appealing to your constitutional rights as a citizen. It is like breaking all the rungs of a ladder and then attempting to use that ladder for any meaningful purpose. It is a self-refuting and contradictory position.

Human pride. Apart from divine influence and direction, people will believe what they want to believe and do what they want to do. This principle is as old as human history, and not even God, Christ, or the Holy Spirit can deter them from it. Human pride always seeks to exalt itself above all else, including God. It obtains self-gratification through the worship of something or someone *other* than God. While God requires that we subdue our pride and submit to His will, human pride expects God to submit to *its* will by providing us whatever we crave for attention, advancement, or profit. Following human pride always leads to misplaced worship: the creature (oneself) is exalted above the Creator (Rom. 1:25).

When people marry their personal preferences (even with the "best of intentions") with the divine pattern, the original plan is corrupted and is no longer "of God." It does not matter how seemingly small the corruption is; if it is deliberate, then it means human pride has been given preference over divine will. Just as it takes only a small percentage of sewage or contamination to corrupt a large amount of drinking water, so it takes only a small amount of human pride to corrupt the NT pattern: "A little leaven leavens the whole lump of dough" (Gal. 5:9). Human pride resents being restricted, suppressed, or denied what it wants. Pride always wants to personalize or customize God's plan to accommodate its own will. The NT pattern for collective worship, for example, seems bland and uninspiring to the proud churchgoer; he wants a service that is entertaining, self-gratifying, and emotionally rewarding.

Deception. Whether one is deceived by false religion, false teachers, the error of well-intentioned people, or even his own heart, he is still being led away from the NT pattern. Maybe someone told him, "This [practice foreign to the NT] is a good thing, a good work, or a good teaching," and the one being deceived believed it. Even a group of people—an entire congregation—may swallow what sounds good on the surface but is in fact a departure from apostolic teaching. It is not uncommon to hear someone trying to justify some behavior that is contrary to God's will with an appeal to his emotions or self-righteousness ("I know I am right—God knows my heart!"). Or someone will say, "Our church does thus-and-so, and it's a *good work*," even though this "work" is different from the work Christ has told His churches to perform.

There are many endeavors that churches do that *are* "good" by themselves, but that go beyond—or even contradict—the mission of Christ's churches. For example, donating supplies to the homeless, supporting orphanages, sponsoring women's shelters, and running soup kitchens are all good works in themselves. Even so, Christ never asked for His churches to be engaged in these. He never asked for His churches to do the same things that even ungodly or irreligious people can do. He wants His churches focused on the spiritual work of saving souls, training people according to the Scriptures (2 Tim. 3:16–17) and edifying fellow believers. *This* work is what He entrusted only to His church, never to those outside of it.

Any work, project, program, institution, third-party organization, etc. that requires modifying, re-defining, or disregarding the written word of God (the NT pattern) cannot possibly be justified as "good" for Christians and their churches. Such things may *feel* good, they may *look* good, and they may *produce* good results (as measured by worldly standards), but nothing is "good" that opposes God's instructions. This calls to mind what Jesus said to the Pharisees: "You are those who justify yourselves in the sight of men, but God knows your hearts; for that which is highly esteemed among men is detestable in the sight of God" (Luke 16:15). In another place, Jesus said, "He who is of God hears the words of God; for this reason you do not hear them, because you are not of God" (John 8:47). This is an awful condemnation, but it is one spoken by the Lord Himself. Every Christian and every person who wants to *be* a Christian ought to sit up and pay full attention to this.

The Simple (But Difficult) Solution

So then, what is the solution? It is amazingly simple—not necessarily easy to implement, but simple to understand. It can be daunting to consider all the versions of so-called "Christianity" today posing as "the real deal"—in both denominational and non-denominational groups. One might wonder how in the world all this can be rectified. But it *can* if everyone in those groups would commit to the simple plan outlined below.

First: every person who claims to be a Christian must have proper respect and regard for Christ's supreme authority over his own life *and* over all groups (congregations) of Christians.[45] Christ cannot be given merely an "honorable mention" status, and then quickly overruled by human agendas. Rather, He must be given the highest priority, the greatest honor, and full allegiance. Anything *less* than this will lead to something *less* than genuine Christians and *less* than Christ-centered churches.

The failure—really, the *refusal*—to honor Christ as "Lord" allows for an unlimited amount of personalizing and customizing ("This is what being a Christian means *to me*," or "This is how *we* think Jesus would want His church to function"). All religious error—*all of it*, no matter how seemingly harmless—stems from a rejection of Christ's authority in one form or another. But all of this can be avoided if indeed we "sanctify Christ as Lord" in our hearts and in our churches (1 Peter 3:15). One can only honor God who honors His Son, and one can only honor the Son by giving himself completely over to His headship (John 13:20).

Jesus said, "If you love Me, you will keep My commandments" (John 14:15). The two verbs here ("love" and "keep") work together: our *love* for Christ will necessitate our *obedience* to Him. This extends to whatever He has said and whatever we are called to do as His disciples. Our obedience to His will (as expressed through His teaching and commandments) will identify us with Christ; our refusal to honor His teaching will identify us as something else. Many people just want a congregation to belong to, a "church family" to socialize with, and/or a community outreach center to feel good about. Yet, Christ is looking for "good and faithful" servants (Mat. 25:21), and this is what we will be when we follow Him and His word.

Second: people need to stop listening to men's *opinions* about the Bible and start reading and studying the Bible for themselves. This does not mean that others (like me) cannot offer guidance and commentary in those studies; it means Scripture is the ultimate authority and has the final say. The lack of knowledge of God's word has always been a source of spiritual ignorance, confusion, and division (Hosea 4:6, Mat. 22:29, 1 Tim. 1:6–7, etc.). All religious error is perpetuated by preachers and other self-proclaimed religious authorities reaching false conclusions, with no one from within their congregations challenging them. Instead of an "It is written" approach (e.g., Mat. 4:4), many people will say, "My pastor said," "My priest said," "Our church teaches," "A Christian author wrote," "I read a blog," or "I saw an Internet article that said" as a final religious authority. In other words, these sources are being cited on par with or even superior to what *Christ* or *His apostles* said.

These alleged "authorities" are only human; they are not Christ; they are not smarter than Him; they have no authority to speak *instead* of Him. They have no access to divine revelations beyond what has already been revealed in the NT. The apostle Paul received the gospel "through a revelation of Jesus Christ" (Gal. 1:11–12) and verified his credentials through the visible miracles he performed (2 Cor. 12:12). No one today can say this or do this—not legitimately, anyway.[46] This fact forces us to choose: will we listen to what Christ and His apostles said, or will we listen to someone who pretends to have this same authority? (Remember what is at stake: not your church membership, but your soul's future.)

Someone says, "But I can't go against what my *pastor* says!" This person may feel very intimidated by his "pastor's" credentials; he may feel inadequate to provide a solid rebuttal. Yet, if one's "pastor" (or religious leader) is teaching something different than the NT pattern, that person *must* "go against" him since *he* is going against *Christ*. No one can honor Christ who refuses to honor His word, and we do not honor His word by letting men say things that are not true while we remain silent. Two easy and excellent questions to ask any "pastor" or teacher who promotes unbiblical teaching are: 1) Where did you get that from? and 2) Who told you that? In other words, when they make confident assertions, they should defend these from God's word rather than you having to create your own elaborate defense. If these men are honest but simply misinformed, they will correct their mistakes, like Apollos did when he was confronted with "the way of God more accurately" (see Acts 18:24–28). If they are insincere, they will continue to defy NT teaching for the sake of their position, their religious persuasion, or saving face.

Third: people need to go back to the NT pattern and read it, learn it, and follow it. While this sounds simple, it can be challenging, especially when it conflicts with modern beliefs and practices. Even so, it is what Christians have been commissioned to do, and what we *agreed* to do in our allegiance to Christ. Whatever Christ commands us, we are to do with all our might, without trying to reinterpret, redefine, add to, or subtract from it (Rev. 22:18–19, in principle). Whatever apostolic teaching was given to the early churches in the NT is meant also for *our* churches, whenever the context is the same. We are allowed to exercise expediencies when they do not change, misapply, or interfere with these instructions, but this is not a license to do whatever we want. Consider the attitude of Ezra the scribe, who "set his heart to study the law of the LORD and to practice it, and to teach His statutes and ordinances in Israel" (Ezra 7:10). This ought to be the *Christian's* disposition toward the gospel of Christ.

Summary Thoughts

God's pattern for Christians and their churches is clear, binding, and objective in nature. Whenever we allow human factors—feelings, emotions, traditions, discontent, pride, and/or deception—to interfere with His pattern, this results in confusion and division. God did not give us a pattern to confuse or divide us, but to inform, enlighten, and unite us—*all* of us who are "in Christ." If every Christian followed the same God-given pattern, then every Christian would be learning, living, and serving in the same way. Likewise, if every congregation of Christians was following the same pattern, then all these congregations would be organized the same way, teach the same gospel, and make disciples of Christ by the method described in the NT.

Sadly, as it is, many people are identifying as "Christians" today who either are *not* Christians at all or are promoting a gospel that no Christian has the right to defend. On top of this, many of these people celebrate their *separateness* as they identify, divide, and remain segregated according to whatever brand or variety of "Christianity" they have decided to endorse. No wonder so many unbelievers look upon all of this with contempt: they see it for what it really is—a mass hypocrisy.

Instead of contributing to this confusion, division, and hypocrisy, we—you, me, and every honest person—would do well to promote instead the gospel of Christ in all its simplicity and purity (2 Cor. 11:2–3). In doing so, we will proclaim the truth that leads people to Christ rather than leading them down the path of religious error. In doing so, we will be instrumental in saving souls rather than defending a religion or church system that came from men rather than from God. And in doing so, we will honor Christ, His authority, and His leadership over *His* church.

The question is: are you willing to stand in the gap and do this?

Part Two: The New Testament Pattern

Chapter Five: The Pattern for Fellowship with Christ

Imagine a random football team that wants to be identified with the National Football League (NFL). The players of this rogue team are all "good guys," and they are united among themselves as to what they want to do. However, they play by different rules than those of the NFL; they enlist players who have been *banned* from the NFL; they wear uniforms not authorized by the NFL; they organize their team differently than what the NFL allows.

The question is not, "Who *are* these guys—and what were they thinking?" Instead, the question is, "Is this team an NFL team?" Those who are *on* the team will say, "Absolutely! But *on our own terms*." The NFL, however, will say, "Absolutely *not*! That team refuses to conform to our standards or recognize our authority over the league that is under our control." Or suppose we ask, "Does this rogue team have *fellowship* with the NFL or with NFL teams?" The answer is clearly *no*, despite what this team thinks, how badly it wants this fellowship, or how it claims to identify itself.

If this is true in a secular example, can it also be true in a religious context? In other words, if a church operates by different "rules" than the NT pattern, makes "Christians" by a method unauthorized by the NT, and looks different than the churches organized by Christ's apostles, then is it a church approved by Christ? The answer is clearly *no*, despite what the members of this church think, how badly they want His fellowship, or how they claim to identify themselves.

We could also ask the question: "Does this rogue church have fellowship with Christ?" The answer remains *no*. A church that refuses to listen to Christ (by way of the NT pattern) cannot hope to have fellowship with Him. Christ will not partner with rebels, rogue churches, or wannabe Christians. He will only commune with or give endorsement to Christians that have surrendered to His leadership, and to churches that listen to Him.

How important is fellowship with Christ? It is of supreme importance for anyone who wishes to be *with* Christ in the life to come. Those who have fellowship with Him *now* are prepared for the afterlife; those who do not have fellowship with Him now remain completely unprepared for the future. Who determines what fellowship with Christ *is* and how it is *obtained*? These are questions that only Christ has the right to answer since He is the Savior of human souls and the head of the body of saved souls (His church). These questions must never be left for you, me, or anyone else to decide.

What It Means to Have Fellowship with Christ

"Fellowship," as it is used in a religious context, is a word that is nearly as misunderstood as "love," "faith," and "Christian." Those who identify as God's people may claim to have spiritual "fellowship" with people whose beliefs or lifestyle choices stand in defiant opposition to God. Regardless of the intent of either party, the result is always the same: a union that is far *different* than what Christ intended. We cannot join "the right hand of fellowship" (Gal. 2:9) with those who stand opposed to Christ's teachings. And we are not prepared to represent Christ to each other or to the world—which is one of the objectives *of* His fellowship—unless we have legitimate fellowship with Him in the first place.

Fellowship with Christ rests completely on the *doctrine* of Christ. This doctrine, which is revealed in the NT pattern, provides a solid, fixed, and unchangeable base from which stems all relations, behaviors, and acts of worship that are approved by Christ for His people. While many modern appeals to "fellowship" are based on emotions, assumptions, and good intentions, *genuine* fellowship with Christ is based upon the doctrinal evidence, truths, and teachings which the Holy Spirit has provided and preserved for us. Someone says, "What's the big deal? If Christ is being honored, there is no need to pay attention to every doctrinal detail." This begs such questions as: to which "doctrinal details" *should* we pay attention, to the neglect of all others? Who decides this? What's the point of having *any* doctrine if it can be arbitrarily or partially honored? How does one honor Christ by knowingly ignoring any of His doctrines? Can a partially honored or humanly engineered doctrine produce a fully legitimate fellowship with Christ?

Fellowship with Christ is an extremely valuable privilege. It is not something that can be entered into lightly or based upon one's own terms. Given the supremacy of Christ's position, authority, and divine nature, we are to submit to Him in every way, rather than expecting

Him to submit to us. This is right; it makes sense; it is inarguable; it is also *doctrinal*. Fellowship with Christ is based upon doctrine, never the other way around. In Eph. 4:4–6, for example, Paul lists seven doctrinal truths that *must* be accepted to have fellowship with Christ. A person cannot accept *some* of these but not others; *all* must be accepted for fellowship—and salvation itself—to exist.

Jesus had strong words for those who, like the Pharisees, fixated on *some* doctrinal teachings (of the Law of Moses) but ignored others (see Mark 7:6–8). He called this selective attention to God's law "vain" worship—i.e., worship that is empty, useless, and accomplishes nothing. If this selective approach was condemned *then*, it stands to reason that it is still condemned today. This is true regardless of how one feels about it. Feelings, emotions, traditions, assumptions, etc., are no replacement for obedience. Remember what God told Moses: "According to all that I am going to show you, as the pattern of the tabernacle and the pattern of all its furniture, just so you shall construct it" (Exod. 25:9, emphasis added). God is not pleased when we honor *some* of what He said, but only when we honor *all* of it.

Claims of "good intentions" or passionately held convictions are no replacement for divinely revealed truth. For example, Christ gave church-appointed elders (a.k.a. shepherds or overseers) the responsibility of overseeing His churches. This appointment is predicated upon specific credentials and character traits (1 Tim. 3:1–7). If Christ did not care about the character of those appointed to be elders, then He would have said so. Or He would not have been specific about what He *did* want. As it is, in having said what He *did* want, He excluded anything to the contrary. Likewise, if Christ did not care if we created a new position in His churches—e.g., that of "pastor" as it is used today—then He would have said so.[47] Or He would have not been specific about the only positions He *did* want. As it is, He appointed the different roles in His churches, and in doing so He excluded all other positions.[48]

The Importance of the Pattern

Remember, whenever Christ gives patterns or blueprints for us to follow, He expects compliance, not resistance. Compliance is never a bad thing when it serves our best interest. Since we have the pattern, now we know for certain *what* is required of us. Since it comes to us from a benevolent Savior who longs for our fellowship with Him, the pattern makes this union with Him possible and fulfilling. If we did not have a pattern, then things would be remarkably different. In view of these things, consider some conditional statements:

- If Christ were to let us do whatever we want to be pleasing to Him, then we would never have needed any NT instruction except to tell us that we can do whatever we want. (The entire gospel, in this case, would be reduced to a small paragraph.)
- If we say, "We are limited in what we can do," then we need the NT pattern to define those limits since we do not have the authority to determine them on our own.
- If we say, "We have specific objectives that Christ expects us to pursue as Christians," then the NT pattern must define those objectives and how to achieve them. We cannot know what Christ wants of us unless He reveals it to us. But, once it has been revealed, we are morally obligated to act on this information.
- If we say, "We do not need a pattern at all," then we necessarily imply that we do not need to follow Christ at all, since He is the One who provides the NT pattern. And if *this* is true, then we could claim to be "Christ-followers" (Christians) without having to follow Christ or obey His commandments—a logical and biblical impossibility.
- If the NT pattern *has not* changed, it necessarily follows that we are still expected to abide by it, regardless of any other factors or circumstances. This is because we are still in the context *of* the NT: Christ is still the Redeemer; His church is still the sanctuary of those who have *been* redeemed; His church still honors Him as its head and submits to His authority completely.
- If the NT pattern *has* changed, then we have not been told by God *how* it has been changed, *what* exactly has changed, *when* it was changed, or even *why* it was changed. If God has authorized a change, then we need to hear it from Him, not from someone less than Him (like a preacher, self-appointed prophet, modern-day "apostle," or any religious official).
- If we say that there *are* new changes, then we need proof of this new and improved "pattern" that is equal to or better than what God provided to establish the original one. The NT is the result of the inspiration of God's Holy Spirit, the earthly ministry of Christ, the direct ministry of His chosen apostles, and numerous and varied

signs and miracles to support it (Heb. 2:3–4). This is a tremendous, unprecedented, and irrefutable amount of evidence! If this is what it took to produce the original pattern, then it will take *at least* as much *if not even greater* evidence to produce one that supersedes it. Not only this, but we need a revealed explanation from God *for* this change. Conspicuously, we have neither of these things.

The NT pattern that was given to Christians and their churches in the timeframe of Christ's apostles (i.e., the first century) is still binding upon Christians today. It remains the sole authority for what we do in the name of Christ; it remains the sole authority for establishing fellowship with God *through* Christ. These facts are not meant to burden or oppress us, but to provide for us what is impossible to obtain on our own. Yet, the only way in which the NT pattern works in our favor is when we do not question it, revise it, tamper with it, or ignore it (in part or in its entirety). While it is human nature to do all these things toward whatever God has revealed to us, this fact does not legitimize these actions.

Despite the clear and unapologetic position of the NT Scriptures, contemporary preachers and churches seem to struggle with this. They will say things like:

- "Some of the NT is no longer an authority for Christ's churches." This begs the question: Which part *is* and which part *is not*? This statement puts people in the position of authority to judge God's word, rather than God being the One who provides direction for people. This is completely backward: it assumes an authority that people were never given. God's word has always been an all-or-nothing proposition: one either *accepts* all of it or *rejects* all of it. There is no middle ground here.
- "The NT is no longer relevant." Did God say this? And if He did, where is this information available? Do modern preachers, religious leaders, and/or theologians say this? If so, these men have no authority to make such statements. They certainly cannot prove them to be true. Their conclusions can only be based upon their opinions, not biblical doctrine. Christ's church has never been ruled by human opinions.
- "'Theology by nature is somewhat fluid rather than solid.'"[49] We have never heard Christ or one of His apostles say such things. In fact, they taught just the opposite of this: God's doctrine is "truth,"

and truth never changes. But if *they* never talked like this, why are *Christians* talking like this? Such doublespeak is common, popular, and readily accepted today. Preachers (and churches) like to peddle themselves as being "progressive," "mainstream," and "cutting-edge," and there is nothing more "progressive" than saying that God's doctrine is "fluid" and ever-morphing to accommodate a mass of fickle churchgoers.

In Eph. 1:18–23, Paul disclosed exactly where Christ stands in relation to His Father, His church, and all of Creation. It is a most powerful passage. It declares, in no uncertain terms, that Christ has authority over all things, except for the One who subjected all things to Him (namely, the Father—see 1 Cor. 15:27–28). It also necessarily implies that every person who is in Christ's church is to be in submission to Him. Put another way: He has controlling interest over every person who is a Christian indeed, as well as every congregation that invokes His name. Given all this, it is critical that we know His will for Christians and their churches, rather than asserting our own.

If fellowship with Christ is important to you, then His blueprint for your life must be just as important. One cannot exist without the other: since His pattern determines this fellowship, therefore fellowship must conform to His pattern. Those who faithfully pursue both are sharers in "the inheritance of the saints" (Eph. 1:18). They are "qualified" for this inheritance through having obediently "[walked] in a manner worthy of the Lord" (Col. 1:9–12). This is where you want to be, and this is where God wants you.

The Pattern for Christ's Churches

But it cannot be only yourself that you are concerned with. Your congregation must also be making every effort to follow the pattern as well. It makes no sense to choose to be associated with a church (or an entire religion) that refuses to honor the NT pattern yet preaches "fellowship" with Christ. These two positions oppose each other. One's congregation has a moral responsibility (as a group) to know the will of the Lord and to follow His blueprint for its collective work in serving Christ.

In Rev. 1:20, the apostle John saw a glorified presentation of Christ walking among seven "lampstands [or candlesticks]," which represent seven different congregations that belong to Him. This does not mean that He stands among *every* church that claims allegiance to Him, but only those that began according to the NT pattern and originally had fellowship with Him. In Rev. 2 – 3, He dictated to John letters to send to these seven churches of Asia (i.e., Asia Minor, a Roman province in modern-day western Turkey). Some of these churches were in good standing and were told to continue in their faithfulness to Him. Some were in danger of losing fellowship with Him and were told to repent and return before He came in judgment against them.[50] Once the time for repentance had passed, He would remove their "lampstand" from His presence. This is another way of saying: He will remove His fellowship from impenitent churches, and they will no longer enjoy His intercession with the Father.

The point is: Christ has specific expectations and standards for churches that claim to identify with Him. If they abide in these, they remain in fellowship with Him; if they will not abide in these, He removes His fellowship from them. (It does not matter if they *think* they have fellowship after this: He will not have a relationship with any group that resists His will.)

Based on Rev. 1 – 3, we can apply Christ's words today. Imagine a church that once began "according to the pattern," having accepted and practiced everything the apostles had taught "everywhere in every church" (1 Cor. 4:17). Yet, over time, that church lost its way; it lost its first love; it was deceived by false teaching; it allowed sin to exist in its midst; it just got sloppy, careless, or lazy in fulfilling its duties to the Lord; or it simply did not rely upon Christ's power but was self-sufficient and arrogant. These are all the problems that Christ addressed to several of the seven churches of Asia. These churches were in the process of drifting toward apostasy, and Christ did not want to lose them.

What did Christ, the head of His church, say to these wayward churches? First, it is significant what He did *not* say:

- "Well, that's not what I said to do, but at least you maintain some semblance to the original pattern. So, close enough!"
- "I did not tell you to do these wrongful things, but I'm happy that you at least still wear My name and hold to a basic concept of apostolic teaching. Well done!"
- "I'd rather that you hold to My standard rather than the one you

are presently following, but I do not want to criticize people who mean well and have good intentions. I do not want to be 'that guy' that stifles creativity and upsets people's sensitivities. So then, if you *feel* righteous and obedient, that's good enough for Me!"
- "I know you do not follow My apostles' teaching, but times are changing, and so I must learn to be more flexible with what I originally told them. I cannot fault you for simply adapting to the secular influences that are all around you!"

Of course, Christ gave no such responses. Instead, He said, "Those whom I love, I reprove and discipline; therefore be zealous and repent" (Rev. 3:19). No one needs to be *reproved* or *disciplined* for doing what meets His approval but only for violating His will. And no one needs to repent for anything except sinful action. What He teaches, then, is that any deliberate or neglectful departure from His pattern is a *sinful action*. If such a church does repent, its fellowship with Christ is preserved; if it does not, its fellowship with Him is removed.

What is true about obedience or repentance for an entire congregation is also true for the individual Christian. Christ expects the same humble obedience, allegiance, and submission from you as He does from me—and every person. He does not have multiple standards for Christians of different age groups, demographics, ethnic distinctions, cultures, or historical eras. He has *one* standard for *all* believers: one body, one calling, one faith, one baptism, and one gospel (1 Cor. 15:1–4, Eph. 4:4–6, etc.).[51] This reflects the genius of a universal gospel that serves the best interest of a global *spiritual* community. Christ is not obligated to provide any further revelatory information for you than He is for me, and vice versa. What He has said is sufficient; what the Holy Spirit has recorded as the NT is sufficient; we are not missing anything with respect to what is necessary for fellowship with God.

It is possible, however, that a few individual Christians can be justified by Christ amid a congregation that (as a whole) is teetering on the edge of losing its fellowship with Him. This is evident, for example, in the church in Sardis (Rev. 3:1–4). Christ declared that congregation to be "dead" and that it needed to "wake up" and finish what it started. Yet He also said that several "walk with Me in white, for they are worthy." It is significant that Christ never told these faithful Christians to leave (at this point, anyway); instead, He told the rest of the group, in essence, to follow their good example. On the other hand, Christ never told anyone, "Because *some* of you in a congregation walk with Me, the rest of you are 'faithful' by association." (This is apparently what many Christians believe, however: they deem *themselves* "faithful" because the congregation is faithful. Apparently, merely attending a "sound congregation" is sufficient to make a person a sound believer.) Rather, He requires *every member* of a congregation to conform, obey, love, and serve Him—and to finish what they started.

Christians must not be in the business of simply "going to church," or seeking a casual involvement with a congregation that is striving to maintain its fellowship with the Lord. Despite its popularity today, there is simply no provision made for this kind of attitude in the NT. What Christ seeks is not warm bodies sitting on pews, but active servants who are giving earnest effort toward the collective work of their congregation. If all members did this, then *every* congregation that identifies with Christ would be growing and flourishing. If every *church* followed Christ's instructions, then *all* churches would have a "lampstand" in His presence, in honor of all that He has done as our Redeemer.

Summary Thoughts

Anyone can *claim* to have fellowship with Christ—people do it all the time. But to have legitimate fellowship requires that certain criteria be met. I did not come up with these requirements, nor did you, nor did any church. Christ alone has the authority to establish fellowship with people, and He alone has the right to determine what is necessary for it to exist. These are based upon the doctrine which He has revealed, and that the Holy Spirit has recorded and preserved for us. Because of this, we can know for certain whether we *do* have fellowship with Him.

Fellowship with Christ begins with one's obedience to His gospel. The terms for becoming a Christian are all clearly laid out in the NT. Likewise, the terms for walking in a manner worthy of the Lord thereafter are also clearly laid out for us (Eph. 4:1–3). When you accept these terms and comply with them in faith, then He will do everything necessary to bring you to His heavenly home. Your *faith* is what you do for God; His *grace* is what He provides in response to your faith. Neither of these *alone* can save you, but together they create a "new creature" in Christ that is now on the path to eternal glory (2 Cor.

5:17).

On the other hand, if you just want a little bit of religion in your life or prefer to cling to a church culture that makes you feel good (regardless of what it teaches or practices), you certainly are free to do this. Or if you just want to be one of the increasingly popular "casual Christians" that "doesn't want to get involved" in church work but wants all the perks and benefits *of* a strong church, you can do that, too. Or if you want to walk away from all organized religion because you have had an all-too-common "bad experience," then that is your choice. The problem with these decisions, however, is that none of them have Christ's approval: *all* of them contradict NT teaching.

Fellowship with Christ is not something you can assume into existence. It does not happen just because you want it so badly or because you are involved in church culture. It does not happen because you have passionate convictions that you can tenaciously defend, even when they defy NT teaching. It does not happen because your preacher, "pastor," or church leadership has confirmed this for you by their own authority. (This is because they *have* no such authority.) There is a great deal of religious error in the world today, even within churches that claim to be "of Christ." It serves your best interest to avoid being swept up in all that error and its consequences.

The only correct way to escape doctrinal error is to know the truth (John 8:31–32) *and* do everything in your power to practice it. Can you do this? Of course, you *can. Will* you do this, or *are* you doing this? While I give you every benefit of doubt that you will, time will tell. You do not have need of mere religion to accomplish this. Rather, "you have need of endurance" in living by faith, "so that when you have done the will of God, you may receive what was promised" (Heb. 10:36).

Chapter Six: The Pattern for Becoming a Christian

I have a library of commentaries and biblical reference books written by denominational preachers and scholars. Most of the material in each book is excellent information. Many of the authors have made a career out of studying, researching, and writing about the Scriptures. I have benefited greatly from their accumulated efforts, wisdom, and insights.

Yet when it comes to the subject of how to become a Christian, most of these authors default to the modern evangelical formula: "Just ask Jesus into your heart to become your personal Savior." Seldom is there a call for repentance in this "asking," although one might say that it is implied. Immersion in water (baptism) is almost universally reduced to a gesture of piety *after* one's salvation, not a necessary part *of* it. Or it is simply "an outward sign of an inward grace"—a line familiar to Calvinists but nowhere found in Scripture. Baptism is, in essence, rendered expendable.

This reinvention of how one becomes a Christian is disappointing to read from men who have so much to offer otherwise. But it is also terribly disturbing. Becoming a Christian is the most important life decision anyone could ever make. To tamper with the prescription for how this is done—to purposely add to, subtract from, or outright ignore what the NT says about this—is not just poor scholarship: it is immoral. Leading someone to *think* he is a Christian when in fact he has only satisfied what some preacher or scholar has said (rather than what, say, the apostle Paul wrote) is a stumbling block of the highest order. Those who follow these scholars' poor advice ("Just ask Jesus") believe that they are saved, but they have only listened to men, not God. There is blame on both sides—the teachers and the ones being taught.

A faulty premise cannot be legitimized by what follows it; the premise itself must be right to begin with. For example, Evolutionists are fond of citing the "Big Bang" as the catalyst for how the physical universe came to be. They cannot explain how this "Big Bang" happened, much less *why* it happened, or any of the circumstances that preceded it. They say, in so many words, "Let's assume that this 'Big Bang' happened in the way that we have imagined it. After that, *everything else* seems to have naturally evolved into what it is today." The entire theory of a (godless) material universe is built upon a premise that has been fabricated to justify all the theorizing that follows. (It is not "science" when you just make stuff up.) This is like erecting a skyscraper on a single rod of rebar—or worse, a toothpick. Once the toothpick fails, so does everything that is built upon it.

Religious leaders who inform people that all they must do to be right with God is "Just ask Jesus" into their hearts are doing essentially the same thing. These teachers are using their position, credentials, and influence to persuade people to do something that the NT never taught, was never instructed by the apostles, and was never practiced among the early Christians. This flimsy, unsubstantial, and unprovable premise is then used to produce strong, stable, and responsible "Christians" who spend the rest of their lives believing that they did everything necessary to be saved.

This awful ministry of misinformation must stop. It is a violation of the NT pattern. If anyone is serious about walking with God as a faithful believer, the method for how to *become* a faithful believer must be dealt with first—and it must be dealt with correctly. The prophet Amos once asked Israel rhetorically, "Do two men walk together unless they have made an appointment [or agreement]?" (Amos 3:3). This point can be applied to the Christian faith: can anyone walk with God who has not first entered into an agreement with Him to do so? It is both dangerous and arrogant to think that we (preachers, scholars, churches, etc.) can come up with our own terms for "walking" with God and assume that all will be well thereafter.

The NT pattern is not to be followed only *after* having become a Christian; it must also be followed to *become* one. No one can be identified as a "Christian" (Christ-follower) unless or until he does what Christ has said to enter into an agreement with Him. It does not matter what I say, or what you say. It does not matter what any person thinks, feels, or believes otherwise. It only matters what the Master has said. After all, He is the head of His church, not our feelings or personal beliefs.

If you *are* a Christian, then you ought to know how you *became* one. If you cannot explain this process biblically, even in the most basic of terms, then it is quite likely you are *not* a Christian but have been misled (possibly even by yourself) to identify as one. If this is true, then you are unprepared to enter the afterlife with God, since you have not yet done what He requires of you. (Thankfully, this can all be rectified!) If you are *not* a Christian but are ready to take on the name of Christ—including all its responsibilities, sacrifices, and privileges—then God invites you to become one. But He does not offer you the popular "Just ask Jesus into your heart" formula. He tells you specifically in His word what this process involves.

Only God's Truth Will Set You Free, Not Yours

Many people come to a church looking for *acceptance* and (increasingly) *validation* rather than seeking the truth. I know this sounds pessimistic, but I have been observing people going through this experience for the last forty years, and it is only becoming more common, not less. People typically do not wish to "conform" to anything. To do so sounds constrictive, even oppressive, and interferes with their desire to live life on their own terms. All they want, really, is to get rid of that nagging "guilt" thing and identify with a bunch of people with whom they can have a personally gratifying "worship" experience every now and then. Often, people do not really want their life to *change*, they just want their beliefs, convictions, and spirituality to be approved by an authority greater than themselves—i.e., a preacher, "pastor," scholar, or priest.

Our modern feel-good philosophy has conditioned people to think this way. People claim to want "the truth" about God, but what they really want is *their* "truth" to be validated and then lived out on their own terms. This is not a fact-based perspective, but a subjective, emotional, and often gullible means of regarding Christianity. Such people will believe *anything* if it fulfills an emotional longing. Some of these might say (in so many words), "I want a church that will give approval to my personal beliefs and embrace my worldview." Or they might say, "I want a religion that will gratify my longing for spiritual awareness" (whatever that means). Others might say, "I don't want to be bound to a 'church system'; I just want to commune with God and experience this joy with other 'seekers' like myself."

Those who say such things are also clear about what they *don't* want. In so many words, they express, "I do not want to learn about 'authority' and 'doctrines' and 'prescriptions'; I just want to embrace God's love, forgiveness, and fellowship." This emotionally based perspective fails to recognize that the object of His love, the reality of His forgiveness, and the joy of His fellowship are all based upon His authority, His doctrine, and His prescriptions for the believer. In fact, forgiveness and fellowship cannot exist *apart from* obedience to His authority and doctrine. God never establishes a relationship with *anyone* based upon emotions or feelings.

Others will say, in so many words, "I do not want anyone questioning my beliefs as a Christian. What I believe is *my* choice; it is not something that should come under the scrutiny of another!" This position fails to recognize that *all* Christians believe in the same gospel, the same doctrine, the same divinely revealed truths, and the same Savior. These are foundational beliefs; they are solid, unchangeable, and consistent among *all* Christians. If someone claims to be a Christian based upon something other than these, then he has falsely identified with Christ. We cannot have spiritual fellowship with people who falsely identify with the Lord; we can only have such fellowship with those who genuinely follow Him. The apostle Paul challenged *any* "Christian" that believed in something other than what Christ revealed to him (2 Cor. 13:5, Gal. 1:8, and 1 Tim. 6:3–4a). Christ Himself challenged *all* those who claimed to follow God but did so in serious error (Luke 16:15 and John 8:46–51). Nothing has changed: we still hold every Christian's professed faith up to the standard of God's word. That word either justifies his faith or exposes it as a fraud. (Better to find this out now than in the life to come.)

Someone else will say, "This is what the gospel means to *me*"— and then goes on to relate a gospel of his own making. This treats Bible study like participation in a book club ("This is how *I* saw the character"; "This how *I* felt about the plot"; etc.). This person allows his personal convictions to color how he reads God's communication with His creation—the exact opposite of what should be happening. It really does not matter what the gospel means to this person (or to you, me, or anyone); what matters is what God *says* and what His gospel means to *Him*. Only when we accept the gospel of Christ for what it is are we in the right frame of mind to respond to it properly.

Another will say, "The church needs to accept me as I am." Exactly! You (meaning: *every person*) are a sinner in need of God's saving grace. You are incapable of doing anything good (for God) apart from Christ's help (John 15:5). You need to humble your heart and submit to God to be saved from His condemnation of your sins. You need to come to Him broken and shattered, not all duct-taped together according to your own homemade repair job. You are in the same boat as every other person who has come to Christ: "you" are no different; your spiritual circumstances are not unique; we *all* have the same problem.

But what if this person meant was, "I do not expect to change," or "I'll change when I good and well please," or "It is not *I* who must change to do the work of God's church, but His church must change to fulfill *my* expectations"? Such attitudes are completely foreign to the NT pattern. They are resistant, defiant, and disobedient. No one can come into Christ's church with a list of demands, expectations, and a personal wish list of things Christians must do for him.

There is only one Lord for Christ's church; the rest of us are *all* servants to Him and servants *equally* to one another. Yet, some people come into Christ's church with a chip on their shoulder, or conditioned to getting what they want, or having been "burned" before by religion. Now, they sit as skeptics, critics, and complainers ("How are they going to treat me?"; "How will I be regarded?"; "How *dare* they question me!"; etc.). I want to say that Christians will treat a new Christian well, but even if they do not, this is irrelevant to that person's situation. We must never base our faithfulness to *Christ* upon how well or badly we are treated by His *people*. Christ is worthy of our faithful service to Him no matter what.

Finally, someone says, "This is how *I* want to become a Christian"— and then lays out his preferred method of conversion. Yet, it is irrelevant what any person wants; it is essential to follow what Christ has instructed. We simply cannot go any further in the discussion with someone who will not submit to His word, even if he claims to want to be a Christian. It is each person's decision to follow Christ; it is *Christ's* decision as to how this is to be done.

What Is Required to Become a Christian

We are pleasing to God only "if we keep His commandments" (see 1 John 2:3–6). This is true in the case of *becoming* a Christian as well as the lifestyle that *follows* this. No one can truly "know" God who deliberately refuses to obey Him. On the other hand, those who *do* obey Him *will* "know" Him, and He will accept them as His holy children, and He will be a Father to them, and "'they shall be sons and daughters to Me,' says the Lord Almighty" (2 Cor. 6:18). Christ said plainly, "If you love Me, you will keep My commandments" (John 14:15). It does not matter which of His "commandments" are under discussion; one who claims to love Him must "keep" them all. Love and obedience are not two separate objectives; we are not given permission to separate them.

The commandments regarding salvation must be followed if one wishes to *be* saved. Yet, no single verse or passage provides the full explanation of what must be done to be saved. A sincere Bible student will not pick only verses that agree with what he wants to believe while ignoring others.[52] The study of "conversion" or "salvation" *as a subject* requires that we consider all verses that apply to that subject.

Becoming a Christian is both a *process* and an *event*. It is process-oriented because there are several things that must be done to meet this objective. It is also an event because it does culminate in a final decision—one that requires an historical, irrevocable, and life-changing point of division between the "old self" and "newness of life" (Rom. 6:3–7). (Likewise, Christ's earthly ministry was a process but culminated in a crowning event—His sacrificial death on the cross.) To turn salvation into *only* a process is to blur the point in time when one does identify with God and when he doesn't. It allows the "believer" to decide when he has become a Christian, not God.

So then, what does the NT pattern show us concerning how to become a Christian? The information is clear and defensible:

- **You must *read the message*.** No one can decide to become a Christian who has not first learned *why* this is needed, *what* being a "Christ-follower" means, and *when* and *how* this is to be accomplished. The "word of Christ" is the foundation for one's faith in God (Rom. 10:17). Yet, this "word" means nothing to the person who has never read it. The reason to believe in Christ is based upon the written record of who He was and what He did for us (John 20:31). Every single conversion account in the book of Acts begins with the *preaching* of the message and (when properly received) *obedience* to what it instructs one to do (e.g., Acts 8:26–38).
- **You must *believe* the message.** To "believe," in the context of becoming a Christian, means to put one's faith in something and

then to obey it (compare John 3:16 and 3:36). "Believe" does not mean merely to accept the facts of Christ and His gospel; it requires one to act upon it (Mat. 7:24–27). "Faith" is the necessary reason for why everything else from this point forward is done. Many have been taught (as I once was, too), "You need to have faith, and then move on to the next step." Instead, *each step* and *every act of obedience* is also an act of faith.

- You must *deny yourself, take up your cross,* and *follow Christ* (Mat. 16:24). To "deny" yourself has to do with a change of allegiance: you no longer live according to your own will but allow Christ's will to direct your life. To "take up your cross" refers to the sacrifice that is required in this decision. Historically, a person only literally carried his cross when he was going to his death. Thus, the cost of discipleship to Christ must be accepted "daily" (Luke 9:23) to identify with Him. Finally, to "follow" Christ means far more than just calling oneself a Christian or attending a church service. It means that whatever Christ asks of you, wherever He takes you, and even whatever He *denies* you, you will respond with humble submission rather than resistance or defiance.
- You must *confess* Christ. To "confess" in this context means to say the same thing that God says—about His Son, the world, sin, and you. It also means to admit or proclaim what you believe (about Christ) to others. For example, if God says that you are a sinner in need of salvation, then you must agree to this. If He says that, after your conversion, you are forgiven of all your sins, you must agree with Him. Also, the believer must "confess" that Jesus is a Divine Person who came from (was sent by) the Father (Rom. 10:9–10). He must also publicly identify as a Christ-follower rather than one who still belongs to a lost and dying world (Mat. 10:32–33).
- You must *repent* of your sins. No one can become a Christian who willfully and deliberately clings to the very sins that caused his spiritual death in the first place. The "word of the cross" cannot help one who continues to indulge in the pleasures of sin (1 Cor. 1:18). Repentance requires first a change of *heart*—a commitment to no longer follow sin but to follow Christ instead. It also requires a change of *action*: whatever had caused that person to sin (or "stumble") must be cut out of his life and cast from him, so to speak (Mat. 5:29–30). At the same time, the penitent person must seek to replace his sinful behavior with *holy* behavior instead (1 Peter 1:13–16). The entire gospel message is predicated

upon these changes being made (Luke 24:46–47, Acts 2:38, 3:19, and 2 Cor. 7:10, for example). Hardly anyone has a problem understanding this requirement, yet many struggle to *comply* with it.

- **You must be *born again*.** Immersion in water (baptism) is the visible and historical event that signifies one's change of allegiance to sin to his loyalty to Christ, his new Master (Rom. 6:3–7). Being "born of water" (John 3:5) has no other meaning in the context of salvation than baptism (see Heb. 10:22, where "our bodies washed with pure water" has the same necessary implication). Peter said that "baptism now saves you" (1 Peter 3:15)—not the *act* of baptism itself but what is accomplished *through* it. In it, the death, burial, and resurrection of Christ is replicated (symbolically) in one's burial in water and being raised to "newness of life." It is through baptism that one becomes "clothed" with Christ (Gal. 3:27). One writer says, "One of the most difficult challenges of 'in Christ' fellowship is embracing the fact that the bright line between Christians and non-Christians is both *inclusive* and *exclusive*. It's a line of demarcation: no unbaptized believer is a Christian; no biblically-baptized believer is *not* a Christian."[53]

> Many have concluded, "Since baptism is only a symbolic rite, it is not required." The word "only" in this statement is forced into the NT pattern, not a natural conclusion of it. There is no question that baptism is rich with symbolism, but just because an act of faith is symbolic does not render it optional or expendable. The ancient Passover was brimming with symbolism, but it was also required of every Israelite *by law* (Exod. 12:1–13). Likewise, Jesus' cross was immensely symbolic, but it was also *necessary* as a means of providing atonement for our sins.

Water baptism has become a magnet of controversy and resistance. Many people believe that they have been made Christians prior to or even in the absence of it. Yet, their method is foreign to the NT pattern. If we assume that some are made Christians at their baptism, while others are made Christians without baptism, now we have two different methods based upon two different standards of authority. One standard is that of modern "Christian" religion; the other is what the NT Scriptures teach.[54] We cannot be united with Christ (or in Him) if we have two different ways to come *into* Him. As one author put it, "There were not two plans revealed [in the NT pattern—MY WORDS]—one with baptism and one without."⁵⁵ If we can justify two different methods, why stop there? Why not recognize *anyone* as a Christian by *any means* that he chose to become one?

Instruction and Implementation

Between His resurrection and ascension, Jesus gave specific instructions to His disciples about how to make new disciples in His name. "All authority has been given to Me in heaven and on earth," He declared. "Go therefore and make disciples of all the nations, baptizing them in the name of the Father and the Son and the Holy Spirit, teaching them to observe all that I commanded you" (Mat. 28:18–20). Thus, how disciples are made includes teaching, baptism, and further teaching. The first teaching *leads* to baptism; the second teaching *follows* it and continues throughout the rest of the new disciple's entire life. If anyone is wondering what evangelism ought to look like today, it is this same strategy.

The book of Acts provides the historical implementation of Jesus' instructions to His disciples-turned-apostles. Once the Holy Spirit made it abundantly clear that the time was right (Acts 2:1–12), Peter took his stand with the other eleven apostles and preached the first message of the gospel of Christ. He concluded his basic message with a call to obey the Lord Jesus Christ and become His disciple. Some of those who heard Peter's preaching believed in the message he spoke and responded obediently to it. Thus, they repented of their sins and were baptized into Christ (Acts 2:37–38).⁵⁶ Having carried out these acts of faith (and whatever else was required of them), three thousand people became Christians on that day (Acts 2:41).

This pattern of making disciples (a.k.a. Christians—see Acts 11:26) is repeated throughout the entire book of Acts. Christ's instructions are implemented in the form of preaching His gospel and convicting human hearts. Those who were sincere responded with obedience, and this obedience culminated in their baptism into Christ. This is the NT pattern for how Christians are made. This pattern was given by Christ, communicated to His apostles, and recorded and preserved by the Holy Spirit. It now serves as *our* pattern for making disciples/Christians. We have no other authority or teaching by which Christians *are* made—

certainly nothing that has come to us from Christ. The pattern is repeated in each individual conversion account in the book of Acts:

- **Acts 8:12:** the gospel is preached in Samaria, and people respond with obedience, as expressed through their baptism. (Confession, repentance, etc., are all necessarily implied; baptism, however, is specifically stated.)
- **Acts 8:35–38:** Philip "preached Jesus" to the Ethiopian official, and this man responded with obedience, as expressed through his baptism into Christ. There is no way he could have known to request this unless "preaching Jesus" necessarily involves this instruction.
- **Acts 10:** Cornelius and company hear Peter preach the gospel of Christ, and these people respond with obedience to Peter's command to be baptized. The Holy Spirit's work gave *approval* for these Gentiles to be included in Christ's church, but they still had to be baptized in water to gain *entrance* into it, just as the Jews did in Acts 2:38–41. Cornelius could not demonstrate faith in Christ if he had refused this command.
- **Acts 16:14–15:** Lydia heard Paul and Silas preach the gospel of Christ and she responded by demonstrating obedience to it, culminating in her baptism.
- **Acts 16:30–33:** the Philippian jailer was told up front to "believe in the Lord Jesus, and you will be saved," but he could not believe in what he had not yet been told. After he heard Paul and Silas preach the gospel to him, he responded with obedience, resulting in his baptism.
- **Acts 18:8:** Crispus, the leader of the Jewish synagogue in Corinth, heard the gospel preached by Paul and obeyed it when he was baptized into Christ (as did many other Corinthians).
- **Acts 22:16:** even though Jesus met him on the road to Damascus (Acts 9:1–16), Saul (a.k.a. Paul) still had to become a Christian in the same way as everyone else. Thus, he was instructed by Ananias to be baptized into Christ. This passage also informs us that baptism is how the believer "calls upon" the name of Christ for salvation (see Acts 2:21, Rom. 10:13).

Is anyone *anywhere* in the NT told to "Just ask Jesus...to be your personal Savior"? Is anyone taught that they were *already* saved by grace but could not discover this until they heard the gospel preached (i.e., the basic premise of modern Calvinism)? Is anyone taught that baptism in water is something that happens *after* one becomes a Christian rather than being instrumental in *becoming* one? Is anyone taught that being baptized with the Holy Spirit—a phrase that is nearly always misapplied to salvation or taken out of context—is a *replacement* for acts of obedience, including water baptism?

The answer to all these questions is a resounding *no*. Despite this, the popular, mainstream, "progressive," and so-called "evangelical" methods for becoming a Christian use one or all these negative scenarios as *positive proof* of one's conversion to God. This is the proclamation of a *new* gospel. Yet, such a gospel is being proclaimed without authority, stands opposed to the teaching of Christ and His apostles, and defies the example of every believer-turned-Christian in the book of Acts (and elsewhere in the NT). It is an impostor gospel (Gal. 1:6–8).

How did *you* become a Christian, if indeed you identify as one? Did *you* listen to this "new" gospel? Or did you follow the instructions of Christ, as communicated to His apostles and endorsed by God's Holy Spirit? If you were "saved" by "just asking Jesus into your heart," are you willing to trust your soul's future to this plucked-out-of-thin-air instruction? If you were baptized as an infant or young child—another teaching missing from the NT pattern—are you willing to enter eternity based upon this man-made instruction? Or is there more that you must do—acts of faith that you must carry out—to satisfy what Christ requires of you?

I want to clarify: If you once listened to mere men telling you how to become a Christian, this does not mean that you intentionally chose to disregard the NT pattern. It does not mean that you have a wicked heart, are foolish and irresponsible, or have no love for God. But it *does* mean that you allowed someone with far less authority than Christ to tell you how to be saved, and this error must be corrected. You may be a God-fearing person, and you may intellectually agree with who Christ is and what He has done for you, but you have not yet demonstrated faith in Him *in the way He has required*. Now you are at a crossroads. The NT pattern will not change to accommodate you; you must conform to it. Something must be done, and now you know far too much to claim ignorance of *what* must be done.

Summary Thoughts

What is strikingly and conspicuously absent from the NT pattern are the following:

- Anyone becoming a Christian and *then* (after the fact) being baptized into Christ.
- Anyone being recognized as a Christian *before* he is baptized into Christ.
- Anyone being told to pray a scripted "sinner's prayer" as a means of becoming a Christian and instead of being baptized into Christ.[57]
- Anyone being told, "Just accept Jesus as your personal Savior" (or any form of this), despite its immense popularity and convenience in contemporary "Christian" preaching.
- Any infants or children being baptized; anyone being identified as a "sponsor" for infant baptism; any young children becoming Christians (or having their own children's ministry); or the confirmation ritual of a teenager who had been baptized when an infant. All these things are completely foreign to the NT pattern, yet extremely popular in many contemporary churches.

Someone says, "I've been baptized in water, so therefore I'm a Christian!" This is like saying, "I've spent time in a garage, so therefore I'm a car!" The one does not, by itself, produce the other. Baptism is necessary for salvation, but it is not *equal* to or a *replacement* for salvation. Baptism must be for the right reason, based upon the right teaching, and carried out by the right heart. Practice follows teaching, not the other way around. There is only "one baptism" (Eph. 4:5) that God seeks from the believer: the one that demonstrates full surrender to His will and His Son's gospel. All others are for show, are empty attempts at appeasing one's conscience, or are for the purpose of joining a congregation rather than becoming a Christian (another practice foreign to the NT).

The only reason I have been emphasizing baptism here is because the NT pattern speaks of it often, both in teaching and practice. Yet, despite such abundant teaching and example, most "Christian" churches today reject it as essential for salvation. Baptism is not more important than belief or repentance, but it is often the sticking point in any discussion about conversion. This is largely because people have been far more conditioned by denominational teaching than

NT teaching. Water does not save anyone, but it does provide access to what *does* save us—the blood of Christ (the essential teaching of 1 Peter 3:21–22). The only way to be "united with Christ in the likeness of His death" is through baptism (Rom. 6:3–7). How in the *world* anyone can read the NT and come to a conclusion that *omits* or even *rejects* baptism as part of one's conversion to Christ is inexplicable and inexcusable.

Any church that claims to be a "Christian" church but deviates from the pattern of teaching people how to become Christians is a church that you should *avoid*. Any preacher who does this is someone whom you should *avoid*. Human-made teachings do not produce Christ-followers; they only mislead, misdirect, and outright misinform people to conform to something other than God's pattern. We have no authority to redefine or reinvent the gospel for any reason. A person cannot redefine Christ's gospel and still be obedient to it. This makes no sense, yet it is extremely popular today.

The NT pattern for becoming a Christian is the important one. If one is not born of God, then it does not matter what else he does in God's name: he is still not "in Christ." Those who are not made Christians according to the NT pattern are not Christians at all. If you disagree with this, your disagreement is not with me but with Christ who gave the pattern. I have no authority of my own to determine your fellowship with God, but Christ does. His authority is what we ought to respect above every other authority, including our own.

On the other hand, if you do exactly what God asks of you, then you can know for certain that you are "in Christ" and where you stand with God. You can also have full confidence that you abide in Him, and He abides in you, so that you have no need to fear the future or the Judgment to come. You are already prepared for your presentation before Christ (2 Cor. 5:10). This is exactly where God wants you; this serves your very best interest.

Chapter Seven: The Pattern for Church Organization

Near my home is a major food and household goods store that is part of a much larger chain of stores that bear the same name. Each store is headed by a store manager, then an assistant manager, then department managers, and so forth. The store manager does not act alone, however, but complies with the decisions made by a governing body of people that oversees *all* the stores in this chain. This governing body determines the layout (floor plan) of every store, as well as the schematics (product placements) of all the merchandise on the shelves. All the stores look pretty much the same regarding layout and schematics, with only slight variations due to building configurations, local clientele, and seasonal departments. These variations, however, do not affect the overall "look" and function of all the stores in this chain.

This illustration lends itself to understanding the *organization* of churches. Each congregation of God's people is overseen at the local level by its own eldership (parallel to store managers, in a sense). Under them are other workers and servants (preachers, deacons, teachers, etc.). But every congregation answers *not* to a governing board of people that dictates the form and function of every church under them. Instead, every congregation answers directly and submissively to Christ and His word. He, and He alone, is the overseer of all churches that operate according to His pattern.

All groups of people—regardless of size—need organization and leadership if they hope to reach any meaningful objective.[58] Churches are no different from marriages, families, companies, sports teams, states, and nations in this respect. People do not function well (or at all) if they do not know what to do, how to do it, or even when to do it. Christ, in His wisdom, did not expect Christians to assemble randomly, chaotically, or without purpose. Paul's instructions to the Corinthian church, for example, speak to keeping their assemblies stabilized, organized, and well-run (1 Cor. 11 – 14).

Unfortunately, many churches do not *have* a stated objective (beyond mere survival) or a known purpose for existence (beyond meeting every Sunday). Not surprisingly, churches that do not know why they exist or where they are going are "tossed here and there by waves and carried about by every wind of doctrine" (Eph. 4:14). Or they just lose members through attrition, having no real plan for replacing an aging membership. Or they just stagnate, decline, and disappear over time. Church organization is not just for managing the status quo of a group but also for providing the leadership, teaching, and reinforcement necessary to carry that group into the next generation.

The Need for Organization

"Church organization" has no direct reference to the physical layout of a church *building*. (However, it is true that some aspects of church organization will affect this layout to provide an effective and efficient means of conducting a worship assembly.) It has to do with the mission of each congregation, the entire body of people that comprise that congregation, its leadership, and its workers—especially those workers that are dedicated to a specific work in that group (such as deacons).

The modern idea of church *buildings* being called "churches" comes to us from denominationalism, and especially ancient Catholicism, but is irrelevant to the organization, mission, and work of a given congregation. Churches are comprised of people, not structures, fixtures, or furniture. God's gospel is all about saving people, not preserving a tradition, heritage, or church building culture. A church that meets in a rented hall or gymnasium is no less of a body of God's people than one that meets in a building of its own. The meeting place does not define a church, but Christ does.

Even the spiritual body of Christ (taken as a whole) is not without organization.[59] Consider a few passages that speak to this:

- "And He [God] put all things in subjection under His [Christ's] feet, and gave Him as head over all things to the church, which is His body, the fullness of Him who fills all in all." (Eph. 1:22–23)
- "And God has appointed in the church, first apostles, second prophets, third teachers, then miracles, then gifts of healings, helps, administrations, various kinds of tongues." (1 Cor. 12:28)[60]
- "And He [Christ] gave some as apostles, and some as prophets, and some as evangelists, and some as pastors and teachers, for the equipping of the saints for the work of service, to the building up of the body of Christ; until we all attain to the unity of the faith, and of the knowledge of the Son of God, to a mature man, to the measure of the stature which belongs to the fullness of Christ." (Eph. 4:11–13)

When Christ's church was first established, it had no written record or instruction by which to guide it. This guidance was instead provided through two primary means: 1) apostolic teaching, whether in person (by the apostles themselves) or by an extension (through men sent *by* the apostles, like Titus, Timothy, Epaphroditus, etc.); and 2) miraculous gifts that served to confirm what was being said, taught, or required was truly from God (Mark 16:20). Today, we no longer have apostles, but we do have all their instructions that the Holy Spirit saw fit to record and preserve for us. Also, we no longer are given the ability to perform miracles (despite modern claims), but we do have the record of all the miracles that the Holy Spirit *once* performed, which serve as a witness to the facts (Heb. 2:3–4).[61]

Even so, apostles and miracles were instrumental in providing for the original organization of Christ's church. Other "gifts" that Christ has given to us (preachers, pastors [shepherds], teachers, etc.) are always needed; their roles and functions will never be done away with.[62] Christ, being the head of His church, oversaw the initial development of the body of believers, and knew which functions would be temporary and which would be permanent. His oversight did not end with the spiritual church but extends to each physical congregation as well. Just as His spiritual church required organization, so does every physical church.

The Only Church We Can Organize

To get a clearer and better understanding of church organization, it might be good to back up a bit and lay the groundwork before proceeding any further.

Once a person becomes a Christian, he is added to a group of all other saved people. He did not add himself to this group, since he has no authority or ability to do so. The spiritual body of Christ did not add him to itself since it also has no authority or ability to do so. It is God who adds this person to this group since He *does* have the authority and ability to do so (Acts 2:41, 47). Once added to this *body* of believers, the *individual* believer now has a responsibility to this group as a demonstration of his responsibility to Christ. These two moral responsibilities—to Christ (or God) and his fellow believers—are inseparable: one cannot be done without the other. For example, one cannot claim to be a part of Christ who refuses (for any reason) to demonstrate love to anyone else who belongs to Him (1 John 4:20–21, 5:1).[63]

While all Christians (living and dead) are a part of the spiritual body of Christ, and all *living* Christians are part of the worldwide brotherhood of believers, only *some* Christians are a part of any given congregation. This has to do with being a specific member of a known and identifiable group of believers. For example, as a Christian, I am a member of the spiritual body of Christ *and* the worldwide brotherhood of believers. But I am only a member of one specific congregation at a time—not two or more at once, and certainly not all of them.

Thus, while "the body" is expressed in a spiritual context in the NT, it is also carried over into a physical or literal context. Sometimes it has a dual meaning. For example, in Rom. 12:5, Paul says that "we who are many, are one body in Christ, and individually members one of another." His statement here is true *spiritually* as well as it is *physically*. Christians who are members of the church(es) in Rome are "individually members of one another"—i.e., they do not live for themselves, act alone, or serve Christ apart from their fellow believers. They are part of a *physical* body of believers as well as a far larger *spiritual* body of believers. "Members" whom they *can* see, touch, speak to, and serve are as much "in Christ" as those whom they have never met, or even those who have died. However, being "members of one another" applies to those in this immediate physical membership—their own congregation.

The word "church," then, has more than one meaning in the NT.[64] It is context, and not the word itself, that determines this meaning. In some cases, there are dual meanings where two related but different contexts can be meant at the same time. For example, consider 1 Cor. 12:12: "even as the body is one and yet has many members, and all the members of the body, though they are many, are one body, so also is Christ." Paul is speaking of the physical church in Corinth, yet he alludes to the spiritual church of Christ that comprises *all* believers. Both meanings are valid, even though one is (here) being emphasized rather than the other.

What has been said so far: there are three meanings for "church" in the NT with reference to Christ's people. First, there is the spiritual body of Christ, which is often referred to (by Christians) as the universal church. This is "His body" as stated in Col. 1:18. Second, there is the body of Christians everywhere in the physical world, the collective of all living believers. This is meant in Acts 8:1, 9:31, 12:1, 1 Cor. 10:32, etc. It is also meant in the revelation given to the apostle John, symbolically referred to as the "one hundred and forty-four thousand" who stand with "the Lamb" (Christ) on "Mount Zion" (Rev. 14:1–3).

Third, there is a specific group of believers in a particular city or congregation, such as Rome, Corinth, Ephesus, Philippi, or Colossae (cities of the ancient world). These Christians are intimately related to the first two groups but are identified separately from them as well. When Paul wrote to "the church of God which is at Corinth" (1 Cor. 1:2), for example, he wrote to a specific congregation, not to all Christians everywhere. (While what he *instructed* them may apply to Christians everywhere, his initial reading audience was only these Christians.) When Jesus wrote to "the seven churches" of Asia Minor, He did the same thing: He sent seven different messages to seven different congregations in seven different cities.

This understanding is very important because "church organization" refers to our responsibility for only *one* of these contexts, not all of them. We do not have the authority—much less the ability—to organize the spiritual body of Christ. Christ is already the head of it; to put us on par with or even above Him is to usurp His authority. Not only this, but it is impossible for us, in our limited and fallible human wisdom, to organize and govern a spiritual church. Christ is the builder of His church (Mat. 16:18), not us. From His heavenly perspective (not our earthly one), there are *no distinctions* among believers according to age, gender, status, nationality, number of talents, kinds of responsibilities, etc. We are "all one in Christ Jesus" (Gal. 3:28). (This does not mean, however, that all our earthly distinctions, relationships, and responsibilities are irrelevant.)

We also have no business—no right, authority, or ability—to organize the entire brotherhood of believers on earth. This, too, is exclusively Christ's work, and we are not to assume or interfere with it.[65] For this reason, the entire brotherhood of believers on earth has no central headquarters, no board of directors, and no legislative body of officials to which all satellite churches must answer. The body of believers is also not broken down into different regions, districts, dioceses, wards, or other collectives of churches. All such decisions to do this came *after* and *apart from* the NT pattern, not because of it. The NT provides for no greater organization of Christians on earth than the individual, standalone, and autonomous congregation.

Therefore, the only group we *do* have the right, authority, and ability to organize is the individual congregation of God's people. This group is often defined simply as "the church" in each city or locale, such as the church in Corinth, Ephesus, Philippi, or the seven churches of Asia. Christ did not establish these churches; men did. Christ recognizes and oversees these churches, but only when they conform to His will. (Recall my opening illustration of the retail chain store: it may be managed independently in each location, but no store has the right to do whatever it chooses.) We cannot control what happens with the spiritual church, nor the entire brotherhood of believers, but we *can* and *must* control what happens in our own congregations.[66]

However, principles that apply to the spiritual church *and* the worldwide brotherhood may also extend to each individual congregation. For example, the local church does not have the right to define "fellowship" with Christ or make final decisions concerning this. However, Christ does have the right to do these things. Just as the spiritual church and the brotherhood are not to be divided, so each congregation is to "all agree and that there be no divisions among you, but that you be made complete in the same mind and in the same judgment" (1 Cor. 1:10). And, just as the spiritual body and the brotherhood must abide by the NT pattern, so must each individual congregation. No church that refuses to honor this pattern has the right to invoke Jesus Christ in its name, organization, or teaching.

According to the pattern, each congregation is autonomous [lit., self-governed] in nature.[67] This means that it is not dependent upon another church, but it does not rule over another church, either. As far as its identity and operations are concerned, it is not connected to any other church at all. (The *members* of this church are also members of Christ's body and the brotherhood, yet the congregation has its own unique identification and specific membership.) The best example of this is found in Christ's letters to the seven churches in Rev. 2—3. Each church was addressed independent of any other church; the members of the church in Smyrna were not members of the church in Thyatira. Even so, the members of all seven churches belonged to the earthly brotherhood of believers *and* to the body of Christ.

All legitimate churches will recognize Christ as the head of the body (*His* church). Yet, the body of Christ is not comprised of churches, but individual members (people). Christ does not save congregations, but only individual members of His body. He does not save couples, families, nations, causes, movements, denominations, or religions. He only saves genuine *Christians* who have entered a covenant relationship with God *through* Christ in the manner described by the NT. At the same time, He does expect *all* believers to cooperate and work together toward a common objective: the proclamation of His message to believers and non-believers alike. The only context in which Christians can work together as an identifiable body of believers is the local congregation. The NT allows for no other organizational grouping of people.

The Organization of a Congregation

The independent, standalone, and autonomous congregation has a distinct membership *and* distinct leadership. It is the membership that appoints its own leaders; no one outside of the membership has any say in this process. Church-appointed elders are responsible for the spiritual oversight and well-being of the membership that appointed them and no one else.[68] These men—always men, never women; and always plural, never singular—provide spiritual teaching, leadership, and protection for the congregation that appointed them. They are men who are husbands of honorable marriages, are heads of well-established families, and have a proven track record of maturity, wisdom, and life experiences to draw upon (1 Tim. 3:1–7). They are also active teachers who positively and proactively promote God's word as well as defend against any teaching that rivals it (Titus 1:9).

Church elders are also identified as "overseers [or, bishops]" (Acts 20:28, Phil. 1:1, 1 Tim. 3:1, Titus 1:7) and "shepherds" (1 Peter 5:1-3). "Elders" identifies them by age and experience; "overseers" identifies them as managers and supervisors; "shepherds" identifies them as caretakers, feeders, and protectors. Elders are not to choose which of these functions they wish to exercise; they are to be *all* of them at once. All these functions contribute to their *leadership*.[69] Elders are also to be living examples of what it means to be faithful to Christ (1 Cor. 11:1, Phil. 3:17, 1 Peter 5:3). They are not to be mere figureheads, administrators, sheriffs with a gun and a badge (so to speak), or "lording it over those allotted to your charge" (1 Peter 5:3).

Each church appoints its own elders because each church is its own family and requires its own unique leadership. Nowhere in the NT are elders appointed over multiple churches, and nowhere is one church involved in the appointment of another church's elders. Just as each group is singularly identified, so its spiritual leadership is singularly identified. Elders cannot oversee members whom they do not know, with whom they have zero contact, or with whom they have zero influence. Likewise, members of congregations cannot be led, taught, taken care of, or even disciplined (if needed) by elders whom they do not know, whom they have never seen, and who have no idea of the members' needs or situations.[70]

People (and "Christian" religions) tend to draw upon church history to justify a different arrangement, in which one or more men oversee multiple congregations. However, what men decided to do long after the apostolic instruction was given in the NT is always an inferior standard to the NT itself. One writer says it well:

> Since … we are committed finally and ultimately to biblical authority, we all recognize that whatever conclusions can be drawn from the practice of the church in its earliest centuries, while instructive and important, can only rightly be viewed as secondary and under both the critique and correction of Scripture itself. … Appeals to early church theology and/or practice on any given issue are no guarantee that one is directed rightly in accord with the teaching of Scripture.[71]

It is neither necessary nor always prudent to cite what earlier churches or church leaders have done to know what God expects us to do. If such men are wrong, then we simply copy their error by following them. If they are right, then it will only be because they had followed the NT pattern—something we can do with or without them.

Church leadership requires church followship: if there is no one to lead, then there is no point in being a leader. A known and identifiable congregation necessitates a specific church membership that follows that group's leadership. Christians are expected to be *members* of a particular congregation because it is in this context that they both serve that congregation *and* submit to its leadership (Heb. 13:17). Drawing on my own situation, it is my Christian obligation to a certain group (or spiritual family) to know its members and for them to know me. It is also necessary for the appointed elders of that group to know those whom they are to oversee. Shepherds cannot manage a "flock" that is undefined, changes without their knowledge, or ignores their oversight.

Every Christian has limited obligations to the entire brotherhood, but he has considerable obligations to the members of his own congregation. Nearly all the "one another" appeals in the NT (love one another, serve one another, encourage one another, etc.) have reference to the fellow members of one's own church. I cannot show love to, serve, or encourage Christians whom I have never met, but I am expected to do these things to the members of my own spiritual "family."[72]

While membership in Christ's church is determined by Christ, membership in each congregation is determined by that group's shepherds. Shepherds/elders serve as the gatekeepers (for lack of a better word) of who does or does not belong to the congregation that appointed them. Those within the group are under their watch; they (shepherds) will "give an account" for how they tended to them (Heb. 13:17). Those outside their group are also outside of their oversight; they have no obligation to shepherd them. Thus, while Christ determines who will be members of His spiritual church, elders/shepherds determine (ultimately) who will be members of their congregation. This is necessary for the work, integrity, and security of each group to be maintained and enforced.

It is necessary that one be a Christian to be a member of a congregation. However, just because a person identifies as a Christian does not mean that he will be an asset to a church. Some Christians simply bounce from one group to the next, often because they are troublemakers, resistant to the elders' oversight, and/or are generally unyielding and uncooperative. It stands to reason that a church should exercise some degree of vetting, investigation, and checking the references of any candidate for membership. There is nothing in the NT that says that Christians can demand that they be made members of a congregation. It is well within the right of an eldership to deny membership to a candidate whom they view as a liability rather than an asset. In the same way, the eldership has the right to *revoke* membership from those who endanger the group's well-being, integrity, or sound teaching.

On the other hand, the candidate for membership is also entitled to certain information to make some decisions of his own. He needs to know what membership will require of him; he needs to commit to the work of the congregation. In all this, he must agree to submit to the congregation's elders. If the elders are godly men leading in a godly manner, then there is no good reason to withhold his submission to them. Members who refuse to submit to their church's spiritual leadership are not being faithful to Christ.[73] Elders are to be honored and respected, not defied or ignored (1 Thess. 5:12–13, Heb. 13:17). If a candidate for membership will not honor the elders' role, then he is not prepared to accept the spiritual responsibilities of what is expected of all members.[74]

At the same time, it is the elders' job to inform the candidate of what *is* expected of him. Many memberships have been decided upon a casual conversation and a handshake, but with nothing in the way of clear communication of what is expected of all parties involved. While this seems to work for the moment, it becomes very difficult later when the elders try to enforce membership responsibilities upon members who never knew about or never agreed to these things.[75] Likewise, it becomes difficult for members to communicate with elders who themselves are not given to open communication but simply "lead" according to a traditional yet often unbiblical course of action.

A final point here: church membership—i.e., one's acknowledged identification with a particular congregation—must never be used to determine one's faithfulness to Christ. Just because someone is regular in attendance or is listed in a congregation's directory does not guarantee whatsoever that he is righteous.[76] Faithful membership (or attendance) and faithfulness to Christ are not necessarily the same thing. While faithful Christians will always seek to be active members of a congregation, it is not true God has ever used church membership as the defining factor of faithful obedience.

Likewise, if shepherds do remove a person from their church's membership, this does not mean that that person is indeed unfaithful to Christ. Members can make mistakes in assessing shepherds; shepherds can make mistakes in assessing members. There is an example in the NT of a big-headed man named Diotrephes who was apparently single-handedly kicking members out of his congregation, even though the apostle John upheld these members' faithfulness (3 John 1:9–10). No doubt there have been many Diotrephes' since then.

Workers in the Congregation

Aside from the apostles themselves, there is no other office in the brotherhood (or in any given congregation) than that of elders.[77] Members in each congregation will have different responsibilities, but these responsibilities are never referred to as "offices." Deacons (1 Tim. 3:8–13) are servants who are specifically recognized and appointed by their own congregation (as in Acts 6:1–6), but they do not hold an office. They are workers and servants, to be sure, but not officers.[78]

Preachers (or ministers; evangelists) might be regarded as specialized deacons. While they may serve a particular congregation, they have no specific appointment process in the NT. On the other hand, both 1 Timothy and Titus describe in detail the kind of men that are to be recognized for this role. Preachers are not above elders in church organization, but they do provide a kind of checks and balances for both the elders and their congregations. The elders' ministries are primarily to the people themselves: as shepherds, they oversee the "flock" (1 Peter 5:1–3). The preacher's ministry is primarily to the revealed word of God: he is to preach it without reservation and safeguard its usage (2 Tim. 2:15, 3:16—4:2). Elders oversee the spiritual well-being of the group; preachers make sure that whatever is done by the elders and within the group agrees with the NT pattern. Preachers are to use their biblical knowledge and expertise to teach, train, correct, and (if necessary) rebuke the congregation for which they work. They are also instrumental in the appointment of elders (Titus 1:5).

Beyond these specific roles, there are non-specific roles within the church, such as teachers, workers, and those with various (non-miraculous) gifts. Teachers are those who teach, train, and develop Christians within the congregation so that all the members have opportunity to grow in knowledge and exercise their own personal ministries. This training is perpetual (Mat. 28:19, Col. 2:6–7, 2 Tim. 2:2, etc.), so that the congregation is always filled with people of varying levels of spiritual knowledge and experience. The NT pattern dictates that women are not allowed to teach the entire congregation (1 Cor. 14:34–35, 1 Tim. 2:9–15). However, women can and should be teachers in private settings (Acts 18:26), and especially among Christian women younger than themselves (Titus 2:3–4).

Paul speaks of those with various ministries in the church such as prophesying, service, teaching, etc. (Rom. 12:4–8). While miraculous ministries are no longer exercised or necessary, non-miraculous ministries are always needed. Just because God is not empowering His people to perform miraculous gifts does not mean He has not gifted them in some other manner. Some Christians are particularly skilled at evangelism; others, at carrying out missions of mercy; others, at providing hospitality; still others, at leading or writing songs; and so on. All these work under the leadership of their elders *and* toward the collective mission of the church, which is all about discipleship to Christ.

This is all that the NT talks about: elders, deacons, preachers, teachers, workers, and servants of varying degrees of spiritual maturity and ability. There is no authority for any other offices, "official" positions, or levels of administration.[79] Conspicuously, there are no popes, archbishops, cardinals, or priests (as a position rather than a description). There are no special names, creeds, catechisms, or manuals for different groups. There is no money from satellite congregations being funneled to a "mother church," or one congregation dictating the operations of another congregation. There are no third-party missionary societies, no youth ministries, no praise teams, no church-sponsored social events that have nothing to do with the work of the church, no social services, and no "directors" to oversee any of these things.

Instead, the NT provides the picture of congregations of believers who study the Bible, do their best to follow its teachings, submit to their elders, are exhorted by their ministers, and are helped by various teachers and servants. We see all members entrusted with the God-given responsibility to "proclaim the excellencies of God" (1 Peter 2:9) and striving to carry out "the will of the Lord" (Eph. 5:15–17). The idea of only *some* Christians working and *everyone else* doing little or nothing, which is common in many churches today, is foreign to the NT pattern. Every Christian has been given one or more "talents" (Mat. 25:14–30, in principle), and is expected to serve Christ and His church to the degree that he has been equipped to do so.

Summary Thoughts

The NT pattern—through specific commands, apostolic teachings, and godly principles—provides a heavenly blueprint of what Christ expects of Christians everywhere. This blueprint provides everything we need to know about why we need fellowship with Christ; how to become a Christian; how to live like a Christian; how to define and teach "sound doctrine"; and how to organize congregations of His people.

The fact that these things are spelled out for us means that they are important to Christ and therefore must be treated with importance by His people. We honor Christ when we honor His instructions. There is a wealth of information about Christians, congregations, elders, preachers, and doctrinal teachings in the NT. It is our responsibility to study these things out and teach them accurately and in their proper context.

There will always be people who are "looking for a church" by visiting various groups of Christians. While this is a worthwhile pursuit, the *first* thing anyone should seek is *the truth*. Instead of looking for a church that fits one's own belief system, traditional views, or personality, a person should first know for certain whether he is a Christian. Once this is positively established, he should look for a *congregation* of other Christians that is teaching God's truth and is organized according to His pattern. Upon finding one, he should identify with that group (by agreeing to submit to its leadership) and throw himself into the work that God has prepared for him. The NT pattern is the basis for determining all these things.

Chapter Eight: The Pattern for Collective Worship

"Worship" is all about giving God what He deserves because He *is* God. He is worthy of being honored, which has to do with the origin of our English word for it ("worthship").[80] Often, its usage in the NT has to do with physically bending the knee or prostrating (bowing down) before someone (Mat. 8:2, 15:25, Acts 10:25, Eph. 3:14, Rev. 5:14, 7:11, etc.). Even when the physical act is not carried out, one who worships God is to bow his heart, so to speak, in reverence and full submission to Him.

Worship can be private, as what one does personally and apart from all others, or it can be done collectively. The NT pattern does not speak to private or personal worship very often, because the entirety of the Christian life is to be a "spiritual service of worship" (Rom. 12:1–2). Our attention presently is not to address this kind of worship, except to say that each individual Christian has his own responsibility in the matter. Instead, we will focus on collective worship, as what is carried out by a congregation in having assembled for this very purpose. What we do in worship together (collectively) may be different than what an individual believer does alone (privately), as in his own home. The two contexts may share some common ground but are not interchangeable.

Just as the NT pattern provides instruction for how congregations are to be organized, so it does for how collective worship is to be carried out. The function of Christ's churches is too important to be left up to human wisdom or human decisions. Likewise, the worship of the Creator of the world is far too important to be left to human dictation or imagination. We are not worshiping an idol or an idea, or even another human being—an equal. Since we are worshiping the Almighty God, we are in no position to tell Him how He (and His Son) ought to be worshiped. Some people worship what they do not know (John 4:22); some worship in ignorance (Acts 17:23); others, with irreverence (Isa. 1:10–17, in principle). Our worship—especially, what we do together—is to be done "in spirit and truth" (John 4:24). God is the One who defines what this means.

Why We Come Together

As they are depicted in the NT, churches are much more than just groups of friends coming together, even in the context of religion. They are not social clubs, casual meetups, or family get-togethers; they are not defined by potlucks, devotionals, or singings. A church-supported *function* (such as a Bible study in someone's home on a Thursday evening) must not be confused with or even become its purpose. Congregations will most certainly have Bible studies, yet home Bible studies are not why we have congregations.

A congregation that just wants everyone to be friends with each other does not understand its mission or the reason for its existence. The assembly is not about maintaining friendship with one another, but an exercise of our discipleship to Christ. While friendship may be (and often is) included in this, it is not the primary objective or even necessary. We are commanded to *love* one another with godly love; nowhere in the NT does it say that we must *like* everyone we love. Sometimes, personalities, temperaments, and differing interests get in the way of Christians "liking" each other. However, *nothing* should get in the way of us loving one another with Christ-like love (John 13:34–35, 1 John 5:1–2).

A congregation that seeks friendship over discipleship to Christ will not be interested in carrying out what this discipleship requires of them. For example, its members will not be interested in speaking the truth, because their primary interest will be to keep everyone happy and content, not obedience to Christ. "The truth" often gets in the way of human perceptions of contentment. They will not admonish one another to remain true to their commitment to Christ, because their objective is to provide a friendly, non-confrontational environment in which everyone is welcomed, and no one is criticized. This often masquerades as "love," but this is not how godly love is described in the NT. When Jesus called Peter "Satan" and rebuked him for putting human interests ahead of God's, He did this out of love (Mat. 16:21–23). When Paul rebuked Peter for his hypocrisy, he did this out of love for Peter *and* the many Christians who were following his poor example (Gal. 2:11–21). Seldom, if ever, will you see this kind of straightforward talk among a friend-seeking group.

A congregation seeking friendship above discipleship will talk about friendly, non-threatening subjects like love, fellowship, faith, and unity, but these will be based upon the consensus of the group rather than the divinely revealed truth of God. They will seek emotional gratification in their friendships, not spiritual completion in their submission to Christ

(Col. 1:28). Congregations that cater to the desires of their members must do so at Christ's expense since they cannot serve themselves and Him equally (Mat. 6:24).

This point gets to the heart of *why* Christians come together in the first place. There are two main reasons for this. First, it is to worship God in whatever way He has prescribed. If we believe that He is our Creator, then it stands to reason that He knows best how we (the ones He created) are to honor Him. Second, it is to support one another—fellow Christians and members of one's congregation. This is not about self-gratification or catering to the desires of the group; it is about seeking the best personal and spiritual interest of the group. All the Holy Spirit's involvement with groups of Christians—whether it had to do with miraculous gifts in the early church or assemblies in general—is "for the common good" of the group (1 Cor. 12:7). It is Christ who decides what is "good" for His people since He is the head of His church, and thus the head of all churches that identify with Him.

The assembly is a time of great influence and mutual edification. (To "edify" means "to build up," as in the erection of a literal structure. "Edification" is the process of building up one another.[81]) Paul instructed the church at Corinth, "Let all things [in the assemblies—MY WORDS] be done for edification" (1 Cor. 14:26b), which provides the basic, all-encompassing principle for all church assemblies. These gatherings are to have a positive effect on all those involved—adult members, their young children, guests who are seeking the truth, and even those who might be attending for lesser motives (i.e., out of guilt, peer pressure, against their own will, etc.). Specifically, the assembly is a time to:

- **Reinforce our commitment to God.** This is the emphasis of Heb. 10:23–25: "Let us hold fast the confession of our hope without wavering, for He who promised is faithful; and let us consider how to stimulate one another to love and good deeds, not forsaking our own assembling together, as is the habit of some, but encouraging one another...." Our "hope" can be obscured by the darkness of the sinful world all around us; we need to have it regularly rejuvenated. To "stimulate" means to prod, provoke, or incite; here, it is used in a good way, as positive peer pressure. We all need the encouragement (even prodding) of others to overcome this world and remain faithful to God.

- **Enjoy our collective fellowship with God through prayers, songs, studies, and mutual edification.** In this context, we are all seeking "the grace of the Lord Jesus Christ, and the love of God, and the fellowship of the Holy Spirit" (2 Cor. 13:14). To do this, it is necessary that we follow the pattern God has given us for this very purpose. The true seekers of God are those who submit to His word.
- **Promote godliness, Christian love, peace, and unity within the congregation.** Christians who assemble to worship God are to do so with "the same mind, maintaining the same love, united in spirit, intent on one purpose" (Phil. 2:2; see 1 Cor. 1:10). We do not come together to seek a consensus of viewpoints or opinions; this contradicts our purpose. Rather, we seek to teach and uphold the basis for our fellowship in Christ. We are to be of the same mind, love, spirit, and purpose in whatever binds us together "in Christ." The assembly provides an excellent time to admonish the unruly, encourage the fainthearted, help those who are weak in faith, and be patient with everyone. We are to "seek after that which is good for one another" (1 Thess. 5:14–15); "each of us is to please his neighbor [i.e., fellow believer—MY WORDS] for his good, to his edification" (Rom. 15:1).
- **Open the door to guests and open our hearts to one another.** "Therefore, accept one another, just as Christ also accepted us to the glory of God" (Rom. 15:7). Our assemblies, especially on Sundays, are one of the few times during the week when we are face-to-face with the entire membership as well as potential candidates for conversion to Christ. This opportune time allows us to put into practice what the word of God has taught us, whether by command or in principle.
- **Prepare ourselves for sharing and defending the faith by way of engaging in a deeper study of God's word.** The assembly is a kind of training center for what we need to do or will be confronted with during the rest of the week. "All Scripture" is "profitable" for those who study and learn from it, particularly for "reproof, for correction, [and] for training in righteousness" in order that we might be "equipped for every good work" (2 Tim. 3:16–17). While certainly some of this studying and training can be done on one's own, the assembly is when we pursue and reinforce this together.
- **Sing songs to God and to one another, as another form of teaching, training, and edification.** Most denominational (and even non-

denominational) religion marries this with instrumental music, even to the point where the instruments overwhelm or replace human voices. Yet, Christians in their assemblies are to be "speaking to one another in psalms and hymns and spiritual songs, singing and making melody" with their hearts to God (Eph. 5:19, Col. 3:16).[82] The only instruments God wants to hear in the context of collective worship are the shared voices of His people. (What Christians do outside of this context is a different matter.) Singing together is the only form of collective worship in which *all* members vocally participate at the same time. It is meant to be a special and meaningful experience.

These are the positive, biblical, and God-given reasons for why we come together. Sadly, the modern, "contemporary," "mainstream," and "progressive" churches today often seek a different path. They claim, "It's all about Jesus!" but their actions say otherwise. This is what is often seen:

- Ministers or "pastors" elevated to celebrity status: people come to hear *them* more than they do the word of God. Many of these "pastors" have become quite wealthy from their ministries, some of them worth several millions of dollars.
- Easy-to-swallow messages, often saturated with emotional anecdotes, colorful illustrations, inspirational quotes from famous people, and selected passages of Scripture that are certain not to offend anyone. These allegedly "life-changing messages" expect little in the way of self-denial, cross-bearing, and following Jesus as He asked us to do.
- Often, a conspicuous avoidance of unpopular and uncomfortable subjects. Such difficult-to-hear messages are replaced with lessons on God's love, mercy, grace, and forgiveness. While these latter subjects are certainly worthy of our study (and I have written entire books on them for this reason), modern churches often have a lack of *balance* in their teaching content. Seldom will you hear lessons on the conditions of forgiveness, God's wrath, God's condemnation of unholy lifestyles, or hell—all things that Jesus Himself talked about.
- Services formatted to be exciting and dramatic, with stimulating video presentations, live musical performances with state-of-the-art sound systems, light shows, choirs, and celebrity singers.

Some "worship services" are nothing more than thinly veiled rock concerts to attract young people and keep them enthralled and entertained.
- Coffee kiosks in the lobby, because no one should have to go for an entire *church service* without a cookies-and-cream Frappuccino and a blueberry scone. The objective is to make people feel comfortable so that they will return, not call them to true discipleship.
- Staffed daycares and children's ministries, because contemporary Christianity puts a tremendous emphasis on children, often treating them as mini adults. Churches want to keep the parents coming by providing an entertaining diversion for their children. If they can win the children's hearts, then they will keep the parents' membership—and the revenue that comes with this.
- Church-sponsored support groups for divorced people, single parents, widows, those with young children, singles groups, senior citizens, war vets, book clubs, bikers, etc. In other words, it is not a church of blood-bought disciples working together toward a transcendent objective, but a thinly disguised social outreach program that caters to various demographics and secular interests.
- Rescheduling or canceling a Sunday service so that everyone can watch the Superbowl on the church's big-screen TV—then *advertising this*, being oblivious to the irony.

Regardless of the claims, this is not "all about Jesus." It is about keeping people feeling good, socially connected, and entertained. Entertainment distracts people from reality, but it cannot feed the soul or please God. It is a travesty to call this "Christianity" or "worship of God," because it shows little concern for the NT pattern that Christ provided for all His people. Instead, Christ is relegated to a mere sideshow rather than being exalted as the head over the His church, the body of those redeemed by His blood.

What We Do When We Come Together

When Christians come together in the manner that the early churches did, we are to follow the same pattern that they were given. What they practiced in their assemblies is what we are to practice in ours; as the apostles directed them, so the apostles' teaching continues to direct us. The early churches did not design a worship format of their own volition or pluck acts of worship out of thin air. Instead, they strove to honor the pattern as it was revealed to them. These specific actions include:

Assembling on the first day of the week (Sunday). This is because the "first day" is the day of the week in which Christ rose from the dead and established His church on the day of Pentecost (in Acts 2).[83] The "first day" of the week is also the *eighth* day of the previous seven-day cycle. The number eight is significant in Scripture since it nearly always signifies a new beginning, new identity, new strength, new power, or new dynasty. It was for this reason that the Israelite males were circumcised on the eighth day (Lev. 12:3). For seven days, the male child belonged exclusively to his parents; on the eighth day, his circumcision identified him as a member of the covenantal community established between God and Israel. It is no wonder, then, that Christians come together to celebrate a *new* covenant in Christ's blood (Luke 22:20), and that their spiritual "circumcision" is performed by Christ upon their hearts in their baptism (Col. 2:10–12).[84]

Assembling on the first day of the week does not forbid assemblies on other days, but the first day must be the primary assembly to partake of the Lord's Supper (see below). What *time* on Sunday, or where, or how are decisions God has left for us to decide; likely, such decisions will be different for every church, according to what is expedient for each one. Yet, meeting *together* is expected, so that the church, at least once a week, has a face-to-face encounter with all its members. The idea of a "virtual" assembly (as through video conferencing) is completely foreign to the NT. The problem with this has nothing to do with the technology itself; it has to do with what Christians are called to do *together*. It is impossible to carry out the mission of the congregation remotely.[85]

Observing the Lord's Supper. The central point of reference in the first day-of-the-week assembly is the memorial of Christ's life and death. Jesus told us to "do this in remembrance of Me" (Luke 22:19). Paul reiterated this command—it is a *command*, not a suggestion or option—in 1 Cor. 11:23–26. This is something for which Christians are to leave their homes and come together to observe (1 Cor. 11:22, 33-34).[86] This is also something Christ has called us to do in honor of Him. Take this memorial out of the picture, and we are no longer assembling for Him, but only for ourselves. This memorial is not a time to talk about our life experiences, our loved ones, someone else's death, or someone else's heroic accomplishments. These all pale in comparison to Christ; others' accomplishments, no matter how monumental they may seem to us, cannot hold a candle to what Christ did for *all* people. No one else died for you and resurrected *from* the dead for you; no one else's death can save your soul from spiritual ruin.

The Lord's Supper—Paul's designation, not ours (1 Cor. 11:20)—has been criticized by some when it is observed in the morning rather than in the evening (at suppertime). But the "supper" part alludes to when Jesus instituted it with His disciples in the upper room, not when we partake of it in our assemblies. It has also been criticized because its bite of bread and sip of juice hardly constitutes a "supper" or meal, but this is not its function. Paul's entire discourse on this subject (1 Cor. 11:17-31) is to deliberately *separate* it from any common meal. The elements of the Lord's Supper are unleavened bread and "fruit of the vine" (i.e., grape juice), since these are what Jesus used with His disciples to identify with His body and blood (Mat. 26:26-29).

The Lord's Supper is often referred to as "communion," since in it we commune with Christ as well as with believers all around the world. It is as if we are *all* partaking of "one bread" as "one body" of people (1 Cor. 10:16-18). This makes the Lord's Supper the only ritual observance which is shared on the same day by the entire brotherhood of believers. In Acts 20:7, we see this carried out as a common practice on the first day of the week.[87] Christians are commanded to "come together" *not* to segregate into party factions or to exalt some believers over others (which is what Corinth was doing, requiring Paul's strong rebuke). Rather, it is to "eat the Lord's Supper" in a reverent, respectful, and communal manner.

Exhortation and edification of fellow members. The weekly assembly of Christians is an ideal opportunity for the spiritual encouragement of one another. All members of the congregation are important, and no one is to exalt himself above his fellow believers. Instead, Christians are told to lay aside our "own personal interests" and seek "the interests of others" (Phil. 2:3-4). This illustrates our humility toward Christ and our mutual subjection to "one another" out of reverence for Him (Eph. 5:21). We are to conduct ourselves "so that there may be no division" in the body (1 Cor. 12:25); "Let all things be done [in the assembly—MY WORDS] for edification" (14:26b). This is done through:

- **Prayers to God.** Prayer is the Christian's lifeline to God. It is a necessary function of every believer as well as of every congregation. It manifests our dependence upon God and His grace rather than our trust in human strength and our accomplishments. In prayer, Christians petition God for divine intervention; thank Him for blessings and help; praise Him for who He is and all that He has offered us through His Son. We are to be "devoted to prayer" (Rom. 12:12, Col. 4:2), which means we are to be prayerful people. Prayer ought not to be reduced to a ritual feature of a church service, but an active and ongoing appeal to God for divine help, intercession, and forgiveness of sins.
  - Prayers in the assembly ought to be for the benefit of all members, and for the general welfare of the entire group. However, they can (and should) be offered for specific members or situations as well, as the need arises. Paul asked the Colossian Christians, for example, to "[pray] for us as well" as for one another in their own congregation (Col. 4:3). We may pray on behalf of those who are seeking God or whose faith is struggling.
  - If anyone "lacks wisdom," he is to pray to God for this (James 1:5), and others can pray for him as well. If anyone is sick, suffering, seeking forgiveness, struggling with temptation, or even cheerful, fellow members are expected to pray for him. "The effective prayer of a righteous man can accomplish much" (James 5:16).
- **Teaching and preaching God's word.** This is evident throughout the book of Acts. Paul also wrote letters (epistles) for churches and insisted that these letters be read in other churches as well (as in Col. 4:16). His purpose for this was so that *all* Christians could "read and understand" what had been revealed to him by God *for* the churches (Eph. 3:4-7). God's word is "profitable" for spiritual growth, nurturing of the Christian faith, and providing instruction for how to operate churches and solve problems that they will face (2 Tim. 3:16-17, 2 Peter 1:5-7, etc.). Christians are to "give attention" to the reading of Scripture, and "to exhortation and teaching" (1 Tim. 4:13). "Exhortation" is the process of offering encouragement, consolation, and help (as obtained through a deeper understanding of God's word). Preachers and teachers are those who have devoted themselves and/or been trained over time to provide and expedite all such teaching.

- **Singing as a special form of teaching, encouraging, and admonishing.** This aspect of collective worship has largely been lost on contemporary "Christianity." Modern churches do not always engage in congregational singing, but often provide a soloist, choir, and/or band to provide music for them. Music has become a form of church entertainment, not a shared practice of teaching and admonition (Eph. 5:19, Col. 3:16). The purpose of singing is to "speak to one another" spiritual content, values, and even warnings in a musical context. (To "admonish" is to offer encouragement *and* a warning: an encouragement to do what is right, alongside a warning *not* to stray from this.) As mentioned earlier, instrumental music redirects the purpose of the singing or ignores it altogether.

The collection of money for the work of the church and (as a specific work) benevolence. While this "giving" (as it is often called) is based upon the Levitical system of tithing (Deut. 14:22, etc.), it is no longer called a "tithe" [lit., tenth] nor is it something a church can demand of its members. Money is to be given voluntarily, "as [each believer] has purposed in his heart, not grudgingly or under compulsion" (2 Cor. 9:7).[88] While the offering is not commanded (2 Cor. 8:8), it is most certainly *expected* by those who have benefited from God's grace and the work of His church. Such donations are to be collected on the first day of the week. This not only makes sense (because it is when Christians come together) but is further supported by Paul's instructions to the Corinthians (1 Cor. 16:1–2, in principle).[89]

- The NT pattern allows for only one method of revenue for churches: the voluntary donations of its own members or donations from Christians in other churches. Likewise, the money collected by a congregation is never used for anyone or anything outside of the immediate needs of or expenses for its own members. This rules out church bake sales, rummage sales, firework stands, car washes, raffle tickets, and a variety of other revenue-generating gimmicks commonly employed by churches. The idea of asking *unbelievers* (i.e., the general public) to donate money to a work that only *believers* directly benefit from is both unethical and unbiblical.
- Similarly, the NT church is never told to give money that has been collected by God's saints as a form of benevolence to anyone who is not a Christian. This rules out church-sponsored food kitchens, homeless shelters, orphanages, political campaigns, social causes,

etc. The church is not to duplicate work that *unbelievers* do; its mission is to address spiritual work that *believers alone* are qualified to do. To give God's work to unbelievers, or to give money collected in God's name to unbelievers, is a complete mishandling of our stewardship to Christ.[90]

While Paul did also give instructions for the use of "spiritual gifts" (miraculous works) within an assembly, this *kind* of gift is no longer given by the Holy Spirit as it was at first.[91] Christians have many other non-miraculous gifts, however, and these are to be exercised properly and generously (Rom. 12:4–8, Eph. 4:16, 1 Peter 4:11, etc.). *These* gifts may be practiced both in the assembly and outside of the assembly, as the need for them arises. On the other hand, no assembly should be turned into a stage performance of one person's "gift" at the expense of (or being imposed upon) everyone else. Our assemblies are to carry out collective worship, not to become a talent show. Likewise, no assembly should be a free-for-all in which everyone does as he pleases (1 Cor. 14:33, 40).

If we believe that God is in our midst and Christ is our head, then our congregations must conduct themselves with reverence and appropriate behavior. "If anyone thinks he is a prophet or spiritual, let him recognize that the things which I write to you are the Lord's commandment," Paul wrote. "But if anyone does not recognize this, he is not recognized" (1 Cor. 14:37). This is no less true today than it was 2,000 years ago.

Summary Thoughts

If we all follow the same script, so to speak, the collective worship of God's people will look fundamentally the same in every church that belongs to Christ. This is how it was meant to be from the beginning, and there is no reason to change it. Christ is the head of His people today just as He was in the first century. We honor Him when we submit to His instructions; whenever He is honored, those who do the honoring always benefit (John 13:17).

On the other hand, doing something other than what Christ has authorized is neither submission nor obedience, but open rebellion. Before Israel left the wilderness and entered the Promised Land, Moses warned them: "You shall not do at all [in that land] what we are doing here today, every man doing whatever is right in his own eyes"

(Deut. 12:8). Later, after Israel *had* entered the Promised Land, they did not listen to what Moses had said. "In those days [of the judges] there was no king in Israel; every man did what was right in his own eyes" (Judges 17:6, 21:25). This was completely unnecessary and inappropriate, as God had told Israel how to live and how to worship Him. This also directly contributed to Israel's downfall.

This principle is timeless and universal: the things *of* God are determined *by* God, not His people. We have a King who rules over the universal kingdom of God. We have a head, Husband, and Shepherd who rules over the body of believers.[92] There is no reason why any church ought to be doing whatever seems "right in [its] own eyes" when we have clear instruction otherwise. The chain of command always begins at the top and trickles down; it never comes from below, as if to tell God how *we* have decided to worship *Him*. This is true for individual believers as it is for groups of believers.

For many people today, a "church" is basically a community outreach center, a social welfare system, and/or a Sunday filled with tradition, family history, and ceremonial importance. Yet, to Christ, it is the assembly of His people who reverently observe His life, death, and resurrection in their worship of Him. It is a time of prayers in His name, the study of His word, and songs that communicate His teachings. It is also a time for fellowship and edification among its members. The assembly of God's people is a time to honor Christ—the Savior of the world—through communal worship and selfless service toward one another. The NT pattern provides clear instruction for all of this because these things are important to God.

Are they important to *you*?

Part Three: Policies, Expedients, and Departures
Chapter Nine: Human Policies within a Church

A church that follows the NT pattern will "look" like all other churches that are also following this same pattern. This makes sense: if a house builder builds twenty houses from the same blueprint, then all these houses will look virtually the same. I say "virtually," because the blueprints usually have to do with the essential layout, structure, and utilities of each house. However, suppose the builder decides to decorate each house a bit differently regarding paint scheme, flooring, molding, light fixtures, and exterior colors. Structurally and functionally speaking, all twenty houses will be the same, yet they may manifest cosmetic differences due to the artistic license of the builder (or the buyers).

Similarly, all churches that follow the same pattern will: have the same reason for their existence; pursue the same spiritual mission; preach the same gospel; make Christians by the same method; engage in the same acts of worship in their assemblies; and act like the same kind of people. Christ, and not each church, determines all these things through a universal pattern. However, each church may look slightly different regarding how some of these things are done, as long as these decisions do not impose upon, conflict with, or altogether ignore the original pattern. In other words, each congregation has the freedom to exercise its own decisions or policies in the realm of human judgment.

Doctrine comes from God, but doctrine does not address or give instruction for every single decision that must be made within a believer's life or within a church of believers. Doctrine is required of *all* Christians: no one can become a Christian apart from it. Doctrine, like truth, is timeless, changeless, universally applied, impartial, and reaches only one conclusion. Human policies, however, are not on par with divinely revealed doctrine and so they do not share its attributes. The human policy of one congregation may be very different from another: twenty different churches may exercise twenty different policies. If this is done correctly, then, despite their *policy* differences, they will all follow the same NT pattern. Doctrine affects fellowship with God, the impartation of His grace and forgiveness, and His salvation. Human policies are limited to one congregation's way of "doing business" that does not interfere with these things.

Human judgment, human wisdom, and human policies among Christians are not free-for-all decisions. They are exercised in lieu of specific commands and apostolic examples within the early churches. In some cases, they cover what must be done by necessity; in other cases, they cover what is determined to be best for one group's own membership (which may be very different than what seems best for another group). This principle works upon individual Christian lives as well. All Christians ought to "look" the same regarding essential beliefs, Christian conduct, and the content of the gospel that we share with others. However, each Christian has the freedom to exercise a certain amount of individuality regarding lesser things, as long as these decisions do not come into conflict with how Christ has told us how to live.

Human Judgments in the Form of Church Traditions

The realm of human judgments has been one of the most misunderstood, abused, or outright ignored subjects among Christians and their churches. Many people think that since "God knows my heart," He automatically endorses whatever one's "heart" decides regarding his relationship with God. This same free-flowing, doctrine-ignoring, and customizing attitude spills over into churches. Essentially, churches operate by a "We can do pretty much whatever we want, as long as we call Jesus 'Lord' and carry out the basic functions of a Christian church"-kind of logic. But Jesus said, "Why do you call Me, 'Lord, Lord,' and *do not do what I say?*" (Luke 6:46, emphasis added). Then He went on to talk about "wise" and "foolish" people. Wise people are those who listen to Jesus and do what He says. Fools may claim to listen to Jesus, but then do whatever seems best or right to themselves. This simple, fundamental point is so often and so easily violated today.

Some think, "Laws were meant to be broken"—but these are the words of immature, unwise, and often ungrateful people. Yet, laws were meant to be kept, not broken. Contempt for law produces contempt for the lawgiver(s), which leads to the breakdown of society. Without law and order, people slide into anarchy, and anarchy (the absence of law and order) is always catastrophic. Breaking God's laws also shows contempt for God Himself (the Lawgiver), and while someone may not experience an immediate consequence for this, it is most certainly coming. God is honored only when we keep His laws, never when we

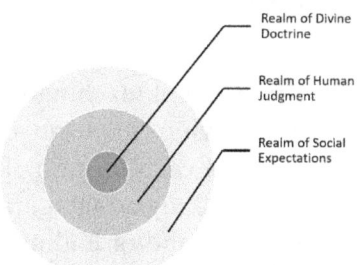

break them, modify them, or ignore them altogether.

But not everything in life is specifically defined by law. Jesus did not tell us *everything* that needs to be done or how to do it. He allows for a limited amount of creative expression to work alongside divinely revealed truth. The critical difference is that while this creative expression may accompany divine truth, it is never equal to it and must never supersede it. While doctrine remains at the core of the Christians' beliefs and is much smaller than the realm of human judgments, it is nonetheless more important than this other realm.

Even so, human judgments are still necessary, and God gives Christians and their churches the right to exercise them. People, families, churches, and even societies all have their set ways of doing things, and there is nothing inherently wrong with this. In the postmodern world, social "traditions" are seen as part of the old establishment, so to speak, and are no longer valued. (We are not talking, for example, about the "tradition" of marriage in this case, because marriage is a teaching of Scripture, not a mere human tradition that has been handed down through generations.[93]) Many newer generations today have no respect for the homesteaders, civil engineers, noble statesmen, military heroes, and other men and women who built roads, communities, and cities from which people presently benefit. Many of these earlier people established or perpetuated traditions that helped to identify society and keep it knitted together. While someone might disagree over the benefit of one tradition or another, the concept of *having* them is appropriate, healthy, and approved by God.

Traditions, conventions, customs, routines, etc., are all a part of human life. I have my traditions, you have yours: these are chosen, established, and often cherished ways in which we like to live our lives. Even so, these traditions are flexible and even changeable, if necessary. For example, I *used* to have a tradition of having a cup of coffee and a bagel with cream cheese every morning at a local café. Since that got expensive (and a bit unhealthy), I modified my tradition to simply having a black coffee every morning. I have the right to make this tradition, and I have the right to modify it, or even get rid of it altogether.

Churches most certainly have human traditions amid teaching the word of God. For example, many churches known to me have a tradition of offering an "invitation" at the end of each sermon. This is not a biblically binding action but is one that many congregations have adopted. Other traditions include beginning and/or ending each assembly with a song (or prayer); having a brief message before the Lord's Supper; devoting an evening service only to songs and prayers; holding special meetings twice a year with guest speakers. None of these are required by Scripture, but none of them violate it, either. The only time when this goes wrong is when a church tradition is elevated to the status of divine law. For example, suppose members of a congregation accuse a preacher of being in *sin* for not offering an invitation at the end of his lesson. They have crossed a serious line in doing so. The preacher may have violated their tradition (or expectation), but not Scripture. To charge someone with "sin" over an action that *God* has not defined as sin is, itself, sinful (James 4:11–12, for example).

Human Judgments in the Form of Policies

A specific form of human judgment is that of a policy. "Policy" is from an old French word meaning "government," "civil administration," or the management of something.[94] It is the "wisdom in the management of affairs"; "a definite course or method of action selected from alternatives and considering existing conditions to guide and determine present and future decisions."[95] This is very formal language, but it is also accurate and descriptive. Policy is related to our modern word "police," but this does not mean the policy is a police action, as in the case of civil authorities whose job it is to protect civil law. To "police" something, however, means to manage, organize, straighten up, or limit the extent of something. In this sense, a "policy" *does* become a "policing" action. When you rake a leaf-covered lawn into piles of leaves, technically speaking you have "policed" that lawn. When you clean up a messy kitchen and wash and put away all the dishes, you have "policed" the kitchen. You would never say it this way, of course, but this shows how common the action is in everyday life.

Still, raking leaves and cleaning kitchens do not necessarily require a definable "policy," unless this is what you wish to call it. If you said, "It is my policy to rake leaves into piles" or "to clean the kitchen every night," then this does become a definable policy: this is what you do as a matter of governing something within your realm of responsibility. This offers a *general response* to an expected set of circumstances. In the case of exceptional circumstances, however, this general response may be superseded. For example, if you suddenly take ill right after dinner and need to go to bed, the policy for cleaning the kitchen can wait, and no laws have been broken by putting it off.

A policy is a guiding principle or course of action. Policies that govern groups of people (including congregations) are often preceded with "should" or "ought": "We should do this"; "We ought to do that." In the absence of specific legal or biblical direction, a person saying this is recommending a policy, outlining a general rule, or offering a strategy for normal expected conditions. For example, a member of a church might say, "If it's raining outside, we should help our elderly members into the church building by escorting them with an umbrella." This may be the accepted policy of that church from then on because it seems good and benefits those involved. On the other hand, it is not a law, and it can be broken without punitive consequences. After all, elderly people have been walking into buildings unescorted, even in the rain, for most of human history.

Such policies can be collective or individual. A collective policy serves a group of people and is most often made by those who preside over those people. The elders (shepherds) of a congregation, for example, are often the ones who ultimately make policies for their own "flock." These policies pertain only to *that* congregation and no other; likewise, that congregation is not bound by a different congregation's policies. An individual policy serves only the perceived needs of the one who made it. For example, it might be one's individual policy to pay cash instead of credit, buy Chevrolet instead of Ford, never access his phone during dinner, or only cite from one Bible version over all others. These are *his* (or *her*) policies; they are not laws, and they cannot be imposed upon anyone else.

Policies are like traditions, and sometimes even confused with them, but serve a higher purpose. A tradition says, "This is what we've always done," or, "This is what we have come to accept as 'the norm.'" A policy says, "This is what seems good and appropriate (for us)." One is a matter of habit, custom, or common practice; the other seeks to provide benefit or advantage to those involved, whether it be one person or a group of people. Traditions are repeated customary practices that often come into existence unconsciously or over time; policies are deliberately chosen practices that fulfill a certain purpose. For example, pews and pulpits in church buildings are based on long-standing tradition; how to handle someone who wants to be a member of a congregation is often a matter of policy.

Policies are also like expediencies but are not interchangeable with them. An expedient facilitates a necessary action, as in helping to carry out a specific command. A policy is an acceptance of expedient as a guiding course of action thereafter. Both can be changed if a better or more efficient course of action is discovered. Church leaders create policies to regulate conduct that is not specifically addressed in Scripture. For example, it would not be unusual for a standard policy of expected conduct to be posted in a classroom of a church building. It may be expedient to *have* such a class; the policy simply governs the behavior *of* the class. Yet, neither the class nor the posted policy are required by Scripture.

Up front, there are two major limitations to policies. First, they cannot be imposed upon anyone outside of the person or group of people for which they serve to govern. Regardless of how wise, rational, or sound they might seem to the policymakers, they are not laws, and certainly not doctrine. They cannot extend beyond their intended purpose; they cannot be expected of the entire brotherhood of believers. What is policy for one congregation has no bearing on what another congregation does. Second, they cannot be absolute, inflexible, or unalterable. God's doctrine cannot be changed or broken without serious consequence; human policies, however, *can* be changed or broken, if there is good reason to do so. Doctrine is God's business; human policies are our business. While God provides the basic structure and overarching principles that govern human judgment, He leaves this judgment up to us to decide.

Policies are never a replacement for the NT pattern; they do not carry the same authority as Scripture. However, policies that govern the general function of a given congregation are often based on Scripture.

Likewise, personal policies that govern one's own practice of Scripture are themselves based (ideally) on Scripture. For example, Paul wrote that we are to be "contributing to the needs of the saints, practicing hospitality" (Rom. 12:13). This is a command, not a policy; this is something all Christians are to do, not just a select few. However, not all Christians will contribute to the needs of the saints in the same way. It might be one Christian's policy to make meals for those going through difficult times; it might be another Christian's policy to fix members' cars as a gesture of his kindness toward them. Both policies are self-chosen, both are legitimate, and yet neither one violates or ignores the command itself.

God does not have "policies" about obedience. Instead, He has commands that define this. God does not have a "policy" regarding salvation, but laws, commandments, and binding terms that one either agrees to or rejects. Doctrine is necessary for defining, establishing, and maintaining fellowship with God; policies are not. We should never confuse doctrine (and its commandments) with policies of human judgment.

God's doctrine does not have exceptions but serves as binding governing authority for all Christians and their churches. Human policies, on the other hand, can and often do have exceptions. Policies can also be changed, modified, or ended. The same human authority by which the policy was made also can be used to discontinue it. Yet just because a policy can or does have exceptions does not mean it is weak, ineffective, or has no value. For example, on my congregation's visitor cards, it reads, "Every visitor is an honored guest." This is our policy; for all I know, it is every congregation's policy. Yet, there are limits to this, at least for us. If a visitor chooses to heckle the preacher, steal some of our songbooks, brandish a weapon, or act very inappropriately with women or children, we will no longer treat him as an honored guest. Instead, we will discreetly usher him out of our assembly.

In another example, it might be a congregation's policy to have a final prayer at the end of its worship assemblies. This is a good practice and serves a particular need. However, suppose the song leader decided (with the shepherds' permission) to end the service with a song instead of a prayer. No harm is done in this; the policy has been temporarily suspended but not invalidated or permanently ended. Policies are made by men for limited, earthly conditions; they are finite in nature; they are not cast in stone, so to speak. No one is saved or lost if the closing prayer is not offered according to standard policy. But if one rejects God's doctrine, he cannot be saved by any other method, no matter how well-intentioned that method might seem.

Practical Applications

From a practical point of view, policies are good things to have for individual Christians as well as their churches. Policies contribute to the structure, stability, and uniformity of one's life, or for the general conduct of a congregation. Church policies provide a known course of action under normal circumstances. Everyone knows what is expected, and the group can operate more effectively and efficiently because of this.

Policies also serve as boundaries and protections: they keep us from doing too much, going too far, or allowing too much leniency. They provide pre-determined safeguards against temptations, abuses, and avoidable trouble. For example, it is a good policy for a man not to meet (say, for the purpose of counseling) a woman who is not his wife or family member. While there might be exceptions to this (say, choosing to meet in a public place and with his wife's full knowledge), the policy itself is meant to protect all parties involved.

Personal policies do not have to conform to group policies or expectations. You are allowed to have private policies that may be very different from what the group expects of you. For example, it may be a church's policy for its song leaders to use a pitch pipe to begin each song; however, it may be your personal policy *not* to do this. If it does not create conflict with the church leadership, your personal decision is entirely appropriate.

I have my own personal policies. For example, it is my policy to wear a shirt and tie to Sunday assemblies. I have my reasons for this which may differ from someone else's reasons for doing the same thing. However, I do not look down upon those who disagree with this: it is my policy, not everyone else's. There also may be exceptions to my policy (e.g., extreme weather conditions, I spilled coffee on my tie, etc.), yet this remains my standard and expected course of action. In another example, I (as the preacher) refuse to baptize anyone less than thirteen years of age. I do not impose my policy on others, and yet this is a matter of principle for me (based on my understanding of Scripture).

There may be exceptions to this policy, but this remains my standard course of action, regardless of what others think about it.

In another (but less significant) example, if my wife and I are hosting a potluck in our home, I always announce that the adults and youngest children are to dish up first, and the older children (and especially teenagers) are to wait until last. There may be exceptions to this, of course, but this is the general expectation. As the host and homeowner, I have the right to dictate the policy for those who are invited. But my home policy is only for occasions at *my* home. I do not go to someone else's potluck event and insist that they abide by my policy.

In other words, I have personal policies that I have deliberately put in place for (what I believe are) good reasons. Often, these policies are for the protection of my reputation, setting an example for others to follow, and consistency with my personal beliefs and conscience. These policies are limited to me and those within my household; they are not extended to those beyond my household or to my congregation. They are privately held and personally implemented. They are not universally applied, and I have no right to use them as a test of one's fellowship with or faithfulness to God.

Jesus Himself operated according to personal policies. These policies indicated His standard and expected course of action under typical circumstances. Yet, because they were policies and not law (or doctrine), exceptions could and did exist. For example, in Mat. 8:1–13, a Gentile centurion made (from afar) an appeal to Jesus to heal his servant. Jesus agreed to help but allowed the centurion to dictate the terms of *how* He was to heal the servant: the centurion asked that Jesus would not come into his home, but "just say the word" and the servant would be healed. It was normally Jesus' policy to dictate the means of healing, but He obviously allowed for exceptions to this.

In another (and related) example, it was not Jesus' policy to heal those who were not Israelites. Yet, in Mat. 15:24, He made an exception for a Canaanite woman (a Gentile) because of her insistent and reasonable request for this. Jesus' exception did not nullify His policy, but special circumstances allowed Him to set aside His normal and expected routine to fulfill a need that He deemed more important than adhering to policy. Likewise, it was Jesus' policy to have His disciples go only to the cities of Israel to preach the gospel of the kingdom (Mat. 10:5).

Yet, He made an exception to this for Himself when He preached to the Samaritans in their own cities (John 4:39–42). As He saw it, it was more important *under the circumstances* to temporarily suspend the policy for a need that was greater than the policy itself.[96]

The Pharisees gave Jesus much grief over His alleged "violations" of the Sabbath (particularly, because of His healings performed on that day). Yet, Jesus never violated God's law concerning the Sabbath, only the Pharisees' policies concerning it. The problem was that they had illegally elevated their policies to the level of divinely revealed law. Jesus exposed their inconsistency by pointing out that if one of their animals fell into a well on the Sabbath, they would violate their own policy to rescue it (Luke 14:1–6). (In a sense, this is what Jesus was doing: rescuing *people* who had fallen into a spiritual well, so to speak.) God never said that it was unlawful to do necessary (or good) work, only *unnecessary* work that could have waited until another day (Exod. 20:8–11). God revealed His doctrine concerning the Sabbath; the Pharisees wrongly assumed that their policies were on par with His doctrine. On the other hand, the Pharisees would make exceptions to God's revealed doctrine (Mark 7:9)—something Jesus never did.

The apostle Paul also had some policies for which he made exceptions when he deemed it appropriate to do so. For example, it was his policy *not* to perform baptisms while preaching the gospel of Christ to a given group of people. However, he did make exceptions, as he himself admits (1 Cor. 1:14–17). Obviously, to "not baptize" was a personal policy of his; this cannot be misconstrued as a doctrine against baptism, or a doctrine to invalidate the *need* for baptism in salvation (since Paul himself was baptized into Christ—Acts 22:16). Those today who cite this passage (1 Cor. 1:14–17) as a doctrine fail to see that it is a policy. Policies can and do have exceptions; doctrine does not. In another example, it was Paul's policy *not* to circumcise men who became Christians (Gal. 2:1–5), yet he made an exception for Timothy (Acts 16:3) because of special or overriding circumstances. As Paul saw it, removing the stumbling block of Timothy's non-circumcision (while preaching to Jews) was more important than upholding his personal policy.

Christians never have God's permission to violate His doctrine. At the same time, there is no need for Christians to get upset if a mere policy is broken or suspended, especially when the reason for this serves a higher purpose than the policy was meant to govern. The Pharisees erred not because they had policies and expectations, but because they allowed these to blind them to the higher calling to which God had called them. They put their policies above human compassion, human suffering, and the spiritually lost and oppressed (Mat. 12:1–7). To them, policies and policy-keeping were more important than people.

Jesus' rebuke of the Pharisees is an important warning to us. No policy (or tradition or expediency, for that matter) is to be held on par with or above God's laws. No policy is worthwhile that already violates these. For example, one's "policy" to lie when questioned about a certain subject or to defend a certain person is a moral error that needs to be rejected immediately. No policy ought to interfere with our compassion for and the practice of "good deeds" toward our fellow man, and especially fellow believers (Gal. 6:9–10). And no policy is worthwhile that puts a stumbling block in one's own path or someone else's path. If a head of household had a family policy that purposely forsakes the assembly whenever the family wants to have a "play day," this creates a deterrent for serving and sacrificing for God. This is not just a bad policy; it is a stumbling block to him and his family.

Summary Thoughts

If handled rightly, policies have a healthy place in the lives of Christians and their churches. It is our human nature to function more effectively and efficiently when there are known, established, and meaningful expectations for us to follow. It is good to have wise courses of action to govern our behavior and our work. This is true individually as well as collectively. Just as Jesus and Paul had policies that they followed whenever it was appropriate to do so, we can have these in our own lives.

Policies serve to support and protect our beliefs. They reinforce what we know to be true, or what we know to be the right thing to do. They prescribe a certain kind of response or behavior based on typical scenarios. In special or extreme circumstances, a different course of action may be taken, but never one that violates God's commandments or is at the expense of someone else's well-being. If policies are handled wrongly (through misuse or misapplication), then what was meant for good becomes harmful and even sinful. At the same time, just because bad policies do exist does not make policy-making a bad thing.

Similarly, there are a lot of abusive or dysfunctional marriages out there, but this does not mean marriage itself is to be discontinued or held in contempt.

I am not in a position to tell you what your policies ought to be. That is for you to decide. In the case of one's congregation, that is for the group to decide. On the other hand, I am saying that it is a good thing to have policies, so long as everyone involved understands what they are, what they are *not*, and the limitations of their usage. There is no book-chapter-verse commandment for policymaking. All the biblical information we have on this subject comes to us deductively (or is necessarily implied), not prescriptively. All policies are matters of human judgment, not divine decrees. We all would do well to acknowledge this simple fact and keep our policies where they rightly belong. God's doctrine, on the other hand, *is* a matter of divine decree, and therefore must be honored and obeyed, even to our own hurt.

Chapter Ten: What Expediency Is and Is Not

In an earlier chapter, we examined why so many self-professed Christians and Christian churches do not follow the NT pattern. This departure has to do with the method of becoming a Christian, church organization, collective worship, and/or specific acts of worship. Such people will likely respond, "Our church doesn't 'depart' from the pattern, but we practice *expediency* regarding it." This begs the question: what *is* "expediency"? Or what is the difference between an expedient and a violation?

Appeals to "expediency" serve as justification for all sorts of innovations, practices, and activities that have little or nothing to do with spiritual fellowship or the biblical work of the church. Instead, they are often the personal preferences of individual Christians and church leadership. In this usage, expediencies are purposely relegated to an undefinable and uncontestable gray area that seems to override or even defy any written NT instruction. The realm of expediency is treated as almost unlimited permission to do whatever seems best for a given situation.

Yet, what *seems* best falls into the realm of human policies, whereas what is *always* and *universally* best falls into the category of divinely revealed doctrine. These are two realms that must not be made equal or interchangeable. God never allows for an equally authoritative "blend" of His doctrine and human opinion. One remains superior to the other; one is always subordinate to the other; one is always required, and the other is always expendable.

On the other hand, the NT does allow for expediencies (or expedient actions), if we keep to the rules about what an "expediency" is in the first place. This is not something for us to define and then apply to the Scriptures, but quite the opposite: God defines this and then we apply it to a given situation. This keeps God's word where it belongs: always in the driver's seat, rather than taking a back seat to our opinions and human perceptions.

While we do have permission to use expediencies, expediency itself never becomes an authority of its own. We have *no* permission to allow expediency to create new or revised teachings for Christians, congregations, or the entire brotherhood. Expedients never become law, and expressed laws never become expedient: these are two separate things. Any so-called "expediency" that changes, usurps, or simply ignores the NT pattern cannot *be* expedient but is an unauthorized action.

The NT pattern cannot be modified *and* obeyed all at once. Likewise, we cannot be in submission to God *and* act in defiance all at once. Genuine Christians will not be those who are always looking for loopholes, escape clauses, and a means by which to exceed the boundaries of what is written while still claiming to compliant. Instead, they will learn what the pattern teaches and do their very best to honor it.

Definition of "Expediency"

Expediency, whether religious or otherwise, is often loosely defined as "whatever it takes to get the job done." If you are asked to paint someone's house, then a paint sprayer, ladder, and scaffolding are all expedient to accomplish this. These are used to get "the job" done. They do not interfere with the job, however, for then they would cease to be expedient. They do not *become* the job, either: painting the house is the mission, not lining up the equipment to do so. Depending on the size of the house, one may be able to paint without any of these expediencies.

The word "expedient" comes from a Latin word (*expedire*) which literally means "to free the foot." In its classical usage, it referred to freeing the foot of a soldier so that he would be able to march or fight without encumbrance. The more contemporary idea of taking off our jacket or rolling up our sleeves to do work mirrors this ancient usage. In a general sense, something is expedient when it facilitates carrying out a certain purpose or addressing a particular circumstance. For example, a car's navigation system is expedient when driving to a new destination, an umbrella is expedient for walking in the rain, and a minister's lectern is expedient for holding his Bible and sermon notes.

The word "facilitate" helps us in understanding the correct implementation of an expedient. "Facilitate" comes from a Latin word (*facilis*) which means "easy to do." By extension, something is facilitative when it simplifies, eases the difficulty of, or assists in carrying out a particular action. All expedients are facilitative in nature or intention. If something must get done, an expedient makes getting the thing done *easier* than without it. An expedient is advantageous: it not only makes the job easier but does so through greater effectiveness or efficiency. This means, when used properly, expedients are very profitable.

Back to my "paint the house" illustration: in doing so, you can use a paintbrush, a roller, or a sprayer. Any of these are expedient. None of them change the objective (paint the house), but each of them provides a different level of effectiveness or efficiency in meeting that objective. You could, of course, just throw cans of paint against the house and smooth it out with your hands, but this might be the most *in*effective and *in*efficient manner possible. The idea is not to make the work harder (or to keep it hard) but to make it easier. This is the role of expediencies.

On the other hand, suppose you hired me to paint your house and left it up to me to decide how to get it done. But, instead of painting, I decided (on my own authority) to tear off all the wood siding and install aluminum siding instead. I then defended this by telling you, "I think it looks better than painted wood." Whether it looks better or not, my decision violated what I was told to do. I arbitrarily imposed my will over your own. After all, it is your house, so you have the right to decide what to do with it. This is exactly what is happening when Christ gives direction for His church, but members of His church decide to do something completely different, while citing "it looks better" or "we like it this way."

The biblical definition of an expedient is more tightly defined than just "whatever gets the job done." In 1 Cor. 10, Paul warned the Corinthians against succumbing to the temptation of idolatry by eating meat sacrificed to an idol or dining in an idol's temple. While these things were not morally wrong in themselves, some Corinthians thought that they could participate in them without any harm to their conscience or in misleading others. On the heels of this, Paul wrote, "All things are lawful, but not all things are profitable. All things are lawful, but not all things edify. Let no one seek his own good, but that of his neighbor" (1 Cor. 10:23–24). The phrase "all things are lawful" may have been an argument used by the Corinthians to defend their Christian liberty. They might have said, "I have the liberty to eat whatever I want!"—a conclusion to which Paul agreed, but with conditions. These *are* the conditions:

- **First, one's "liberty" cannot violate or corrupt his own personal relationship with God.** While the basic premise of whatever is being done might be legal, any violation of conscience or injury to one's own faith renders this "not profitable." Violating one's conscience to justify Christian liberty is a no-win situation; it is never "lawful" to sin against one's conscience. Any violation of one's conscience—regardless of what others do—is no longer expedient to that person because whatever is "not profitable" is also *not expedient*. Any violation of doctrine *or* one's conscience is "not from faith; and whatever is not from faith is sin" (Rom. 14:23).
- **Second, one's liberty cannot purposely or carelessly lead *someone else* to violate or corrupt *his* conscience, causing *him* to sin against God.** This describes a case in which a Christian imposes his "liberty" at the expense of a weaker brother or sister in Christ, causing that person to go against what he believes to be right. If what a Christian does is required by God (for all believers), then it does not matter if someone else is offended by it: that other person's issue is with God, not him. However, if what a Christian chooses to do tramples on the weaker conscience of a fellow believer, then the one causing the stumbling is at fault.[97] It is never edifying *or* profitable to be the cause of someone else's sin (by misleading, poor influence, intimidation, etc.). This does not mean that another's tender conscience cannot be re-trained or better taught, but as it stands, "we who are strong ought to bear the weaknesses of those without strength [i.e., whose consciences and/or faith are lacking in knowledge or experience—MY WORDS] and not just please ourselves" (Rom. 15:1).

Paul wrote something similar in 1 Cor. 6:12: "All things are lawful for me, but not all things are profitable. All things are lawful for me, but I will not be mastered by anything." To paraphrase: "Just because an action is technically not sinful in itself, it can *become* sinful to me or someone else if I put my 'liberty' ahead of what is best for myself or a fellow believer." Even more simply: just because something is doable does not make it automatically profitable or edifying. In the verses prior to this statement, Paul spoke of the self-defeating action of one believer taking another believer (presumably, of the same congregation) to court (6:1–8). In another publication, I commented on this passage:

> Going to court is not wrong in itself; taking your *brother* [to court] out of greed, distrust, spite, vengeance, etc. *is* wrong.

Likewise, sex is not wrong in itself; illicit sexual relations (fornications) *is* wrong. ... Whatever God says is good is also "profitable" (2 Tim. 3:16–17); whatever is born of jealousy, self-ambition, and satanic desires is not good and therefore is not profitable.[98]

"I will not be mastered by anything" (1 Cor. 6:12) means that Paul will not allow what *can* be done to dictate what he *will* do. Indulging in the temporary things (or liberties) of this world at the expense of spiritual profitability is never wise or advantageous.

What all this means is: an action cannot be "expedient" according to the NT pattern if it is not profitable or does not edify. "Profitable" (1 Cor. 10:23) means that it advances the teaching or cause of Christ; something is *not* profitable that interferes with or corrupts this. "Edify" means to build up through encouragement, exhortation, and/or positive influence. Nothing is edifying that purposely, spitefully, or carelessly puts a stumbling block in anyone's path. Thus, Paul established a measurement by which we can know if something is truly expedient or whether it poses as expedient but is harmful:

- If a given action is lawful <u>and</u> profitable <u>and</u> edifying, it is acceptable to God and is expedient by biblical definition.
- If a given action is lawful but <u>not</u> profitable <u>or</u> edifying, it is not acceptable to God and is *not* expedient, no matter how one tries to justify it otherwise.
- If a given action is <u>not</u> lawful, it is never expedient, regardless of any other reasons, justifications, or circumstances.
- If one's Christian liberty is knowingly not in the best interest of one's "neighbor," it is not expedient to practice it in that person's presence.
- Every action must be done in godly love and godly wisdom [implied]. These two things drive all Christian actions outside of the specific commandments of God.[99]

These modifying conditions ("acceptable to God," "best interest," "godly love," and "godly wisdom") must be defined or qualified by God's word, never by our own estimation. For example, it is not within my ability, left to myself, to know what God deems acceptable or what serves anyone's best spiritual interest. But God knows these things perfectly and absolutely, so I defer to Him on this. Likewise, godly love and godly wisdom are *of God* and not of human origin. In other words, we cannot arbitrarily *choose* what is loving or wise, if indeed we have already been *told* what is loving or wise by a higher authority than ourselves.

The Alleged "Authority of Silence"

Many people appeal to a so-called "authority of silence" as a form of expediency to justify things not specifically forbidden by Scripture. This translates to a "The Bible didn't say I *can't*, so that must mean I *can*" mentality. This becomes absurd in a hurry. God didn't say we *couldn't* sacrifice chickens to Him in the church assembly; He didn't say we *couldn't* play bingo during the church assembly; He didn't say we *couldn't* ... well, you can fill in the rest with whatever ridiculous scenario you come up with. Someone will respond, "Of course, we cannot do *those* things because they violate what He *has* told us to do!"—and this is correct. But it also makes my point: **silence does not give us permission to do whatever we want when we have already been told what to do instead.**

The authority of silence is a concept that is foreign to Scripture. Nowhere in the NT is it taught, implied, or practiced. Yet, in the modern context, it is almost invariably used to justify what *people want to do* rather than honestly striving to fulfill the mission and purpose of Christ's church. As discussed previously, the mission of Christ's church is not to pursue whatever Jesus did not expressly forbid. Rather, it is all about discipleship to Him. His church is commissioned with making disciples, promoting discipleship, and teaching His disciples how to make more disciples. We are not created anew in Him to choose our own good works, but to carry out the good works He has "prepared beforehand so that we would walk in them" (Eph. 2:10). In other words, it is not left up to us to decide how discipleship is to be done; Christ has already decided this in His gospel message.

Silence is not an authority to do anything. Appealing to something that is *not there* as "authorization" for a certain action is not only illogical but unbiblical. With such reasoning, we can sanction virtually *anything* and call it "the Lord's work" if He did not expressly forbid it. This is not a demonstration of godly love or godly wisdom. Just because the Holy Spirit is silent on a given subject does not mean He endorses *or* prohibits it. It means: His silence is *insufficient by itself* to determine a right(eous) course of action.

This does not mean we are flying blindly but that we must look elsewhere in God's word for direction. Godly principles, for example, may not say "yes" or "no" to a specific subject, but they do provide overarching guidance for several subjects or actions to be considered. Returning to my earlier ridiculous examples—sacrificing chickens or playing bingo in the assembly because "God didn't say we *couldn't!*"—we can cite godly principles rather than a "Thus-sayeth-the-Lord" dictation. We are not to give attention to *any* sacrifice (as a means of worship) rather than Christ's sacrifice for our sins (1 Cor. 2:1–2, 15:3–4, etc.). And we are not to marry worldly recreation or entertainment with our solemn worship of God and His Son (1 Cor. 14:40, 2 Cor. 6:14–18, etc.). The passages I cited do not specifically say "yes" or "no" to my hypothetical actions, but they do speak to the *overarching purpose* of what we do with our churches.

Where direct instructions or definitions are absent, we have governing principles to guide us in the direction God wants us to go. For example:

- We are to "treat people the same way you want them to treat you" (Mat. 7:12), but Jesus did not detail every instance or way this is to be done. This guiding principle affects *everything we do* but it does not spell out everything that *will be done.*
- Christians are to "love one another" in the way Jesus has loved us (John 13:34–35). This passage does not provide an exhaustive list of *how* to do this but does modify *all* actions that we are to do. Whatever is not of godly love, no matter how noble or significant it appears otherwise, is empty and useless (1 Cor. 13:1–3).
- Christians are to "do good to all people, and especially of those who are of the household of the faith" (Gal. 6:10). Again, "doing good" is not something left fully to our own imagination but is governed by what *God* defines in His word. Anything that "seems" good but contradicts or disregards this is not good in His sight.
- Christians are to "examine everything carefully; hold fast to that which is good; abstain from every form of evil" (1 Thess. 5:21–22). This is obviously a very general instruction but also a binding one. In other words, it is not left to us to decide what is "good" *or* "evil," nor which of these we should "hold fast to" or "abstain

from." The direction here may not be specific but it is most important, and it touches on *everything* we do as God's people.

The combination of **godly love** and **godly wisdom** provides an overall guiding principle to all other biblical principles. Godly love provides the right spiritual attitude and frame of mind for all that we do in Christ's name. Godly wisdom always leads us to the right action in which God wants His people to engage. For example, Paul instructed Christians to demonstrate godly love *and* godly wisdom in dealing with one another (1 Cor. 10:24, 32–33, Col. 3:12–15, etc.), as befits God's people. It's not all about me or you, so we must look outside of ourselves to live in agreement with the one (Christ) to whom we belong. We are not to be "children in [our] thinking; yet in evil be infants, but in [our] thinking be mature" (1 Cor. 14:20). This does not mean that we choose between love and maturity, but that we pursue *both* at the same time.

In other cases, the method or means is not given in Scripture as a direct command but as a precedent established by Christ's apostles. Such examples are not offered in a one-time instance for a very specific situation but are regular, typical, and repeated examples that are practiced "in every church" (1 Cor. 4:17). For example, the gospel was spread not through a third-party missionary society or evangelism campaign, as we often see today, but through individual Christians carrying the message of salvation personally to whomever needed it.[100] It is not a church's job to evangelize; this responsibility falls to individual Christians. A church can *support* evangelism, however (as seen in Acts 8:14–15, 11:19–24, 13:1–3, etc.). But nowhere in the NT pattern do we see both Christians *and* the churches hand off the responsibility of evangelism to an agency outside of themselves—not only to represent them but to *do their work*.

Someone says, "But missionary societies [or, whatever one chooses to call this third-party agency] are expedient to preaching the gospel!" This would be true if we did not have instructions otherwise. Since we *do*, these societies are no longer expedient but are alterations of what we have been told to do. For a thing to be genuinely expedient, it will not and cannot change what is commanded (even through examples) but must only aid in getting such commands done. Whatever alters the NT pattern cannot be expedient; biblical expedients cannot alter *anything*. When God gives us patterns and precedents to follow, He is telling us how He wants things done. If we did not have such a pattern, then we could do whatever we want. But if we ignore the pattern which He has given us, we are disobeying rather than honoring Him. This is also true regarding:

- Church-run or -sponsored bands, musical concerts, and celebrity singers which are allegedly for the purpose of attracting people to the gospel or edifying Christians. This all sounds good to the human appetite but defies the NT pattern. Neither Christ nor His apostles ever resorted to entertainment as a means of spreading the gospel. Using entertainment to appeal to the masses may *seem* good but it is not expedient.
- Partaking of the Lord's Supper once a quarter, twice a year (at Christmas and Easter—two traditional but unbiblical holidays), or at random times throughout the year. It is not expedient to decide arbitrarily when (and even how) to carry out this memorial of Christ's death when biblical precedent says otherwise. All indications in the NT show that the apostles partook of this memorial with the early church regularly in every first day-of-the-week assembly and not at random times throughout the year (Acts 2:42, 20:7, and 1 Cor. 11:17–33 [implied]). Someone will say, "Since it doesn't say exactly 'when,' we can do it whenever we choose." But the weight of evidence all says "every first day"; any other view has zero support, having been plucked out of thin air.
- Church-run food banks (and related services). A food bank is certainly a noble effort toward helping people in need. Sadly, it may also become an enabler to people who refuse to work—something to which the NT speaks directly (2 Thess. 3:10). Assuming the better of these two things, this remains a work that any secular group can do; there is no NT authority for churches to be involved such efforts.[101] If a group of Christians, acting on their own, wish to run a food bank, there is no problem with this. But the collective work of Christ's churches is to support the preaching of the gospel in a manner consistent (or at least not in conflict) with the apostolic examples of the NT.

Returning to what Paul said about expediencies (1 Cor. 10:23–24): just because something is not specifically prohibited in Scripture does not make it profitable or edifying. On the other hand, this does not make it inherently evil, either. It simply means that we must look elsewhere in God's word for justification for it—if indeed it should be practiced at all. Everything we do as a church that identifies with Christ is defined by law (specific commandments) or precedent (apostolic-approved examples).[102] This is the NT pattern. We are allowed to exercise expediencies in carrying out these actions if we adhere to God's definition of what an "expedient" is and not our own. Again, an "authority of silence" is contrived, not legitimate.

The Congregational Application

An expedient is not a means to bypass godly authority and do whatever we want. We also cannot use expediencies to *create* an authority for this same reason—again, to do whatever we want. An expedient has no authority of its own; it is merely something that carries out what *is* authorized without violating or usurping it.

An expedient is always optional and expendable: it does not *have* to be done, and if it is done, then it can be undone without consequence or condemnation. This means that an expedient action cannot be turned into a test of one's faithfulness to Christ or a test of whether we can have fellowship with a person. One Christian cannot charge another Christian with sin just because he "violated" the first person's expectation. A violation of an optional action (or of a group's expectations) may annoy those who implemented it, but it is not a moral error. God defines what sin is, not Christians or congregations. We do not have the authority to create a new definition of sin, nor do we have the power to enforce this.

Simply put, we cannot make laws—which, if broken, lead to sin—concerning things that are optional in the first place. For example, many Christians in the more conservative churches have claimed that no one is allowed to eat (as in, have a meal) in their church buildings because these buildings are dedicated to one purpose: the assembly of the saints and class teaching.[103] This prohibition goes well beyond the time of the assemblies and extends to anytime during the week. Thus, Christians cannot come into the church building on, say, a Thursday and share a pizza as they engage in a Bible study. To state it more plainly, these Christians are said to be *in sin* to do so, since it is allegedly *unlawful* for them to eat in the building.

This kind of reasoning, while perhaps well-intentioned (see below), is completely unjustifiable. The same Christians who legislate the "laws" of the church building will also concede that such buildings are expedient in the first place. So then, they have made laws—and charges of sin—in a realm in which God has not made laws or charged sin. They have turned their optional, expendable, and human-determined expedient (the building) into a case in which someone could lose his soul if he did not properly comply. James sums up the problem well: "There is only one Lawgiver and Judge, the One who is able to save and to destroy; but who are you to judge your neighbor?" (James 4:12).

At the same time, just because it is not unlawful to eat in a church building does not mean that *all* eating there is immediately advantageous, or that *anything goes* within the building. (It is these latter actions that those who forbid *any* eating in the building are trying to avoid.) Biblical principles of godly love and godly wisdom may lead us away from doing certain things, and most certainly will cause us to avoid other actions altogether. But every human interpretation of love and wisdom cannot be held to the same level as divine law. It may be *my* congregation's decision (as a group policy) not to eat pizza on Thursdays in our building, but not because it is a sinful action. Rather, it may be because we do not want to confuse weaker members into reducing a Bible study into a pizza party, or we do not want to set a precedent for what happens in our building on occasions in which no studying is done at all. These are personal decisions of the church leadership for their group only; they are not on par with doctrine, and they cannot be extended to all other churches. In fact, another church's leadership may have no problem with the Thursday night pizza-and-Bible-study-in-the-building scenario.

Expediencies cannot make laws (and laws cannot be made from expedient actions) because they have no authority of their own. The so-called "authority of expediency" is a phrase cited by Christians who do not understand what expedients are, how they are implemented, or their limitations. In effect, this phrase is an oxymoron—a self-refuting or self-contradicting statement. (Those who cite this phrase are often the same ones who cite an "authority of silence" discussed earlier.) If an expedient is cited *as* an authority to do anything, then it is cited illegitimately: it is neither authorized by God nor can it be defended biblically.

The principle of expediency is itself violated whenever an expedient is re-defined as law and enforced as law. It is also violated when an expedient ignores, exceeds, or modifies any written authority of the NT pattern (Christ's revealed instruction to His churches). For example:

- Some churches believe that the only way the offering can be collected from their members is to pass a tray around and have those in the assembly put some form of money into it. While this is an expedient way to get the job done, it is not the only way. The congregation could just as easily—and legitimately—install a box in the building foyer for the members to put their money into as they come into or leave the building.[104] Or, given modern means of financial transactions, members could electronically transfer funds to the church's account on the first day of the week. Or a few other methods could be used. But to charge a congregation with not being "scriptural" because it does not pass a plate around is to turn expediency into law, and then to judge Christians by that self-made "law."
- Nowhere in the NT is the role, position, or authority of a congregational song leader mentioned or defined. Yet, this has not stopped many churches from virtually legislating what a song leader can or cannot do. Some churches have an entire list of "responsibilities" of the song leader—which is not a bad thing in itself, except when this list is regarded as a binding legal document, and sin is charged if it is violated. It is amazing to me that more may be expected from song leaders than a group's own appointed deacons. Yet, song leaders (and even song leading) are expedient: we do not *have* to have them, and we have no business legislating their function.
- Many churches have a tradition of an opening or closing prayer—which, again, is a good idea. The assembly of God's people *should* (as a matter of propriety, not law) entreat God to be present with the group as it engages in the worship of Him and do *something* to close out the assembly. But policies and traditions are not on par with divine law. It is expedient to offer an opening prayer; it is just as expedient to have an opening song *instead* or *in place* of that prayer; it is also expedient to have a Scripture read for the same reason. Often, church traditions are based upon good ideas, and may well be retained for this same reason. Yet, traditions are not laws, and whatever is not law cannot be violated in the same way (or with the same consequence) as law.

The latest example of an expediency-turned-into-law is the idea that congregations must use video conferencing as a means of including their members who are not physically present. The reasons *why* these people are not present vary considerably; sometimes the reasons are legitimate, and sometimes people just want the freedom and convenience of "worshiping" while lounging on their living room sofa. Prior to video conferencing, if someone could not attend (let's assume for a good reason), then he would simply stay home and wait until a time when his circumstances allowed otherwise. But with modern technology, churches now feel morally obligated to offer "virtual" or "remote" assemblies, leading to remote membership, and thus, remote fellowship.

Whether a church offers video conferencing is up to each congregation. (Whether it is *wise* to offer this is another discussion.[105]) Yet this offering must be recognized as an expediency and not a binding legal requirement. Just because a congregation has access to technological services does not mean it is morally obligated to use them. This equally applies to sound systems, smart boards, PowerPoint slideshows, HVAC equipment, etc. When we allow technology to redefine how we function as one of Christ's churches, we give godlike power to a human invention rather than following the God-given prescription of the NT pattern. If video conferencing is chosen, then it must only be used as an expedient; and if it is expedient, then it is optional, changeable, and expendable without consequence.[106]

On the other hand, if video conferencing (or any other action deemed expedient) disrupts or interferes with Christian assemblies, then it is no longer expedient. Anything of human origin that divides the congregation must be rejected simply because it *is* divisive, whether it is people (Rom. 16:17), teachings (2 Tim. 4:3–4), or innovations of any kind. Even things that are not wrong in themselves can be disruptive and divisive and therefore no longer expedient. Other examples of this include:

- **Instrumental music in the assembly.** Certainly, instrumental music is not evil, even if it is combined with religious songs in a private setting. But it has no place in the assembly because it violates how and why the NT pattern teaches churches to use music in this context (Eph. 5:19, Col. 3:16–17). Instruments are not expedient when they add something to our worship of God that He never called for in the first place. When instrumental music was first introduced into the assemblies (particularly in the 19th century), it was controversial and divided numerous churches. If preachers today would teach what the Bible teaches about singing, instrumental music would be just as controversial and divisive as it was then. The almost universal acceptance of this practice today does not make NT teaching irrelevant or expendable.

- **Placing the human desire for food (and meals) over worship of God.** There is nothing wrong with having a desire for food. But food, while harmless by itself, can interfere with the priority treatment that God deserves when we assemble in His name.[107] When Christians refuse to put aside their food and drink to give sole attention to prayer, teaching, singing, and praise for God, then this food and drink is no longer expedient but a disruption.[108] Similarly, having a kitchen in a church building (or meeting place) to prepare food is not sinful. However, if members are forsaking the Christian assembly to spend time in the kitchen fixing meals, it is no longer expedient but is a cause for stumbling. Or if the aromas of coffee and lasagna fill the place of worship as a distraction from the purpose *of* the assembly, it is no longer being used expediently but has become a disruption and interference.

- **Treating the assembly as if it were one's home.** For example, imagine if members were all invited to bring their pets into the church assembly: dogs, cats, birds, hamsters, llamas, etc. It is not wrong to have a pet, but it is not expedient to allow them to interfere with the solemn worship of God and the memorial to Jesus Christ (the Lord's Supper). Imagine all the noise, smells, food dishes, water dishes, and other paraphernalia—not to mention the visual distraction—as the group struggles to maintain its focus on why it came together in the first place. God should not have to compete with pets (or iPhones, iPads, video games, social media, excessive creature comforts, etc.) for our attention. Whatever unnecessarily robs Him of that attention is anything but expedient.

- **Anything that looks bad even if it isn't.** Christians are to "abstain from every form [lit., look; appearance] of evil" (1 Thess. 5:22). This means that we are not only to abstain from literal evil but also things that *appear* evil to the casual observer. For example, imagine several of the men of a congregation tipping back non-alcoholic beers in the foyer—or the front porch—of the church building after services. While there may be nothing sinful about non-alcoholic beer, in this case (if not in other cases as well) it provides a poor example, negative influence, and a cause for stumbling among weaker and possibly younger members. This is not an act of godly love or godly wisdom, but instead manifests an irresponsible conduct that cannot be defended as expedient. (Thankfully, this is a fictitious example meant to prove the point and not one based on a real-life experience.)

Anything that necessarily imposes upon *all* the members of a congregation yet unnecessarily offends the consciences of some (or most) is no longer expedient. This is not profitable or edifying; instead, it sows seeds of confusion, discord, and division. Christians must never choose such actions, as they are in clear defiance of the NT pattern.

The Personal Application

This discussion must be kept in the context of our fellowship with God. It has nothing to do with the realm of personal preferences. In other words, we cannot extend what has been said to "offending" someone over the color of the carpet in a building, using folding chairs instead of pews, the chronological order of our assemblies, or the choice of songs selected from our hymnals. Such things have nothing to do with our fellowship with God, our mutual fellowship with each other (Eph. 3:6), or the reason why we have assembled in the first place. "Offended" does not mean "I don't like it" or even "This annoys me." The biblical usage is, "This causes me to sin, either by violating God's law or my own conscience."[109] This applies to personal situations as well. Suppose you do not like the kind of truck I drive, the kind of house I live in, or the way I prepare my coffee. These things have no bearing on God's law (unless there is something sinful in any of this) or your conscience. It may "offend" you that I drive a Nissan rather than a Ford, but that is simply one opinion over another. I have not caused you to sin, and you have no reason to charge me with causing you to stumble.

On the other hand, just because one engages in an activity on his own, apart from the physical assembly of the church, does not mean all such activities legal, profitable, or edifying. Again, even good things can be misused and abused to render them detrimental to our own spiritual well-being. Whatever endangers one's soul or is at the expense of your fellowship with God cannot be considered harmless, justifiable, or expedient. One's so-called Christian liberty does not give him the license or permission to do whatever he wants in the privacy of his own home simply on the grounds that "it's not imposing on anyone else." If it is imposing on God, your relationship with Jesus Christ, and the leadership of the Holy Spirit, then this is sinful and not expedient.

For example, a Christian cannot be getting drunk on the weekends, watching X-rated movies, or shooting up heroin in his own home and claim that these are "expedient" because they do not affect anyone but himself (which is not even true). Engaging in sin in the privacy of one's home does not make the "sin" designation suddenly disappear.

In another example, the internet can be a very good resource for information or getting things done. Sadly, it also is the source of all kinds of unholy and satanic activity. One cannot make a blanket statement that "the internet is merely an expedient" when in fact many Christians are losing their souls over what they have chosen to do with it. Even the *time* spent on the internet can corrupt one's marriage, family, and Christian lifestyle. While the internet is "lawful," it can be used in such a way that is not profitable or edifying, and therefore not expedient. Thus, to some, the internet *is* expedient; to others, it is a stumbling block.

The same can be said about television, gaming, network marketing, and a host of other activities that are permissible yet often abused. A new car is expedient, if indeed it is affordable and serves the needs of the one buying it. On the other hand, if paying for a new car forces a Christian to get a second job, and this becomes the reason why he cannot assemble with fellow believers or engage in nearly any church work, then the permissible purchase is no longer expedient. It is instead a serious interference to his walk with God. Christians are not merely to exercise their "liberties" as much as they possibly can; more importantly, they are to exercise godly love, godly wisdom, godly virtues, and good stewardship of the gifts God has given them. Otherwise, the abuse of that which was meant as a gift may become a curse and lead a person away from God rather than drawing near to Him (James 4:8).

Summary Thoughts

For a thing to be biblically expedient, it must be lawful, profitable, and edifying (1 Cor. 10:23). Nothing is lawful that contradicts the teaching of the NT; all things are profitable that agree with biblical teaching. Nothing is profitable that compromises one's fellowship with God; all things are profitable that concur with the instructions revealed to us in God's word (2 Tim. 3:16–17). Nothing is edifying that tramples our own conscience or that of a fellow believer; all things are edifying that are done according to godly love and godly wisdom. While none of this is rocket science, these teachings are extremely important and need to be understood by all who are "in Christ."

Expediency is never an *authority* to do anything. You have the authority to use expedients, but you cannot use expedients to create new laws (or revise God's existing laws) for yourself, your congregation, or the entire brotherhood. Expediency never becomes law and expressed laws never must be treated as expedient. An expedient is optional, and therefore expendable; laws are never optional and therefore are never expendable. Laws and expediencies must never be used interchangeably since they belong to very different realms.

Just because something *sounds* good to you or me does not automatically mean it is loving or wise to pursue it. This is especially true in the case of a congregation, where many people of varying degrees of faith must be considered, not just one's own conscience or faith. Christ has already determined what is best for His churches; it is not your place or mine to disregard this and choose a different course of action, and then justify it as "expedient." Nothing is expedient that defies the instruction of the head of *the* church (Col. 1:18) and of *every* congregation.

God has given us laws, boundaries, and moral responsibilities to respect and exercise in honor of Him. Whatever human decisions we make, whether we call it a tradition, policy, or expediency, must be kept within those boundaries. You cannot redefine the boundary of your property just because you want to build on the other side of the fence. Likewise, we cannot redefine the NT pattern just because we want to do something on the other side of the fence, so to speak. Many "expediencies" today have nothing to do with honoring God's word, but are the self-willed preferences of church leaders, individual members, and entire congregations.

Paul summed everything up succinctly: "For he who in this way serves Christ [i.e., walking according to love] is acceptable to God and approved by men. So then let us pursue the things which make for peace and the building up [or, edification] of one another" (Rom. 14:18–19, bracketed words are mine). This should be our overall pursuit in every realm of our lives: to be acceptable to God and approved by His people. This must be the overarching endeavor of every individual Christian, as well as the collective pursuit of every congregation of Christians. If you are "in Christ," hopefully it is yours as well.

Chapter Eleven: The Danger of Unwarranted Interpretations

Christ's pattern for His people and their churches seems straightforward enough. After all, we are not dealing with higher math, quantum physics, or electrical engineering (all of which are well over my head). The overall divine plan is, thankfully, far simpler than most of our modern sciences. Anyone with reasonable intelligence can understand it.

Yet, some people see this simplicity as the problem. If God's heavenly plan is so wise and profound, then maybe He should have made it more difficult, so that only a limited number of people *could* understand it. Then, they reason, we could maintain greater *control* over His word, so people with lesser education or understanding could not misconstrue or misrepresent what it is saying. This assumes, of course, that those with greater intelligence will always have the right understanding, which is not always true. Historically, we have seen those who have greater control over the people often abuse that control for their own advantage. No wonder Jesus prayed, "I praise You, Father, Lord of heaven and earth, that You have hidden these things from the wise and intelligent and have revealed them to infants. Yes, Father, for this way was well-pleasing in Your sight" (Mat. 11:25–26).

Even so, the Pharisees of Jesus' day had the mindset that they—and they *supremely*—had the correct understanding of God's Law. No one could know God's will better than they did; no one could *teach* God's word better than they did. Yet, it was such pompous thinking that blinded them to Jesus' identity as the Son of God (John 7:48–49, 8:12–18, and 9:24–34). No wonder they were so incensed when Jesus, a man not educated in their rabbinic schools, ran circles around them, and dared to challenge their conclusions (John 7:14–15).

If God did not make His word so difficult, then, some have reasoned, maybe *teachers* should make it more difficult to justify the need for them. Again, the control issue underlies this mentality. This also seems to be the logic behind seminaries and theological schools that turn the simplest of God's instructions into complex dissertations. The fact is that we *do* need scholars and theologians—those who have spent a great deal of time mining and explaining those far deeper concepts in Scripture that challenge most everyone else.[110] Yet, there is no need to *make* God's word more difficult, since it already contains spiritual truths that no one will be able to master fully. But we do not need such men (or women) to control the usage of God's word; we only need them to help us see it more clearly and accurately.

So then, we have a paradox: a heavenly message that the "average Joe" can understand, yet complex enough to keep scholars and theologians busy for their entire careers. And no matter how basic, simplistic, or understandable God's word is, there will *always* be a need for teachers of it. This is not because people are generally stupid: it is because enlightenment of this kind requires a deliberate mental shift to transition from physical-based, mundane, and humanistic thinking to heaven-sent, spiritual, and godly thinking. This paradigm shift is not only needed in understanding certain passages but also in making practical applications. Even very educated people will struggle with making these shifts and can be greatly helped by those who have already made them.

"That's Just Your Interpretation"

There is another aspect to consider in all of this. I have spent some time already in this book (and will do so again) citing careless departures from God's pattern and, in some cases, some people's blatant refusal to follow it. A common response to all this is, "What you are seeing is not a *refusal* to follow the pattern, but simply different *interpretations* of it." In other words, the problem does not lie with those who are doing something different than what the pattern calls for. Rather, the problem is *my* failure to accept their "interpretation" of it, as though any person's understanding of God's word is immediately legitimized simply by designating it *as* an "interpretation."

People often invoke the "interpretation" defense when they want to justify what they are doing rather than admit the obvious. This is very common when it comes to religion but is seldom used otherwise. For example, you do not want your bank "interpreting" your account balance; you want your balance to be exactly what your bank statement says it is. You do not want someone "interpreting" the title to your car, your college diploma, the deed to your house, or your marriage license; you want these things to be honored *exactly* as they are written. You do not want someone "interpreting" your truthful statements; you want those statements to be taken at face value.

God's word is incalculably more important than your bank account, car title, college diploma, house deed, marriage license, or your words. If it is wrong for someone to interpret these lesser things arbitrarily or preferentially, then it stands to reason that it is wrong to use this same approach toward more important things, and especially God's word. We are not dealing with the mundane things of the world here but with our standing before God in the hereafter. This is something that you, me, and every person ought to treat with the utmost care.

The "interpretation" rebuttal to this is, in effect: "God is not so 'legalistic' to require a rigid obedience to His word. It is enough that the *spirit* of His word be carried out, and we are permitted to convey that spirit in diverse ways without violating the essence of what He said." Clever sidestepping will invoke words like "spirit" and "essence" in place of "conformity" and "obedience." It is the language of those who are dissatisfied with the given instructions and want to read them differently. This different reading purposely allows for creative human expressions of Christian teaching rather than simply communicating exactly what Christ and His apostles taught "in every church" (1 Cor. 4:17).[111]

The charge of "legalistic" is meant to paint anyone who takes God's word at face value as a Puritanical, pickle-faced, word-mincing prude that lacks spiritual understanding, creativity, or compassion. Those who read God's word literally are deemed "legalists" because they are (allegedly) only concerned with making sure that laws are followed, nothing more. This is not to say that some Christians are not legalists, for some most certainly are. But just because someone quotes God's *laws* for His people, and then insists that no one has the right to *violate* such laws, does not make him a legalist. (Such a definition would make Jesus Himself a legalist.) Having respect for, showing reverence toward, and expressing appreciation for *divine law* is a good thing, not something to be held in contempt (Rom. 7:12). Respect for God as Lawgiver and Judge is necessary for law and order to be maintained (James 4:11–12).

"Legalism," on the other hand (as with all "-isms"), originates from human will, not divine law. Legalism wants to impose one's own expectations, convictions, or conclusions about Scripture upon others *as though these were equal to* God's revealed truth. Rather than allowing God's actual teaching to instruct and guide people, legalists want to make sure everyone is doing things according to their *own* hypercritical standards. The Pharisees did this often, and Jesus called them on it. They put their traditions on par with the Law of Moses; they assumed that sinning against their traditions was equal to sinning against God's Law. Jesus condemned this kind of logic then (Mat. 15:1–9) and there is no reason to believe that He would approve of it today.

Even so, those today who make accusations of legalism will quote, for example, Jesus' own words He spoke to the legalistic Pharisees: "But if you had known what this means, 'I desire compassion, and not a sacrifice,' you would not have condemned the innocent" (Mat. 12:7). The point they want to reach is: "Following God's law is good, but showing love and compassion *trumps* all laws of God." Yet, this is not at all what Jesus said, meant, or taught. In fact, it was Jesus who also said that not a single letter or stroke of the Law of Moses was to be violated—and that He Himself would not do this (Mat. 5:17–18). Taking words, phrases, and quotes out of biblical context is one of the easiest and most misleading ways to twist Scripture into saying something different than what it says *in its context*.[112]

Using Jesus' words as a springboard (but misinterpreting what He said), many people today are putting *their versions* of love, faith, and compassion for others ahead of God's instructions. They are doing so with no point of reference other than their own "take" on a given situation. This is the mentality behind involving churches in social causes, social reform, sexual identification, political issues, video "assembling," virtual membership, etc. Under the subjectively defined banner of "compassion," Christians (and those who think they are Christians) have elected to set aside the NT pattern to promote a humanistic brand of Christianity that makes them feel good but is conspicuously foreign to apostolic teachings.

The Scientific Approach to Studying Scripture

Sincere Bible interpretation is not a free-for-all approach, as if we can make a qualified rendering of its text without any guidelines. Rather, there is an actual science to biblical interpretation called hermeneutics.[113] Hermeneutics involves a critical-thinking and common-sense approach to studying the Scriptures. It involves, among other things:[114]

- **Deep respect for God as the sovereign, final, and unchallengeable authority.** The God of the Bible has absolute say over all things. Whatever He has revealed in His word is *the truth*—the foundational premise from which all spiritual teaching is derived (Rom. 11:36, 1 Cor. 8:6, Eph. 4:6, etc.). God alone defines truth, righteousness, morality, and justice; any deviation from what He has declared is a departure from *the truth*. Biblical scholar Carl Henry says: "All creaturely authority and power is derived from that of God. As the sovereign Creator of all, the God of the Bible wills and has the right to be obeyed."[115] No interpretation process that fails to honor God's supreme authority should ever be seriously considered.
- **Deep respect for the Bible as sacred writing.** The Bible is not a novel that can be edited or revised; a collection of random teachings that can be altered or manipulated; an allegorical story version of human history; or the product of human wisdom, ideas, or creativity. The teaching of Scripture is to be regarded as God's breathed-out revelation (2 Tim. 3:16–17, 2 Peter 1:20–21). Whatever God wants us to know about Himself, His Son, His Spirit, His "eternal purpose" (Eph. 3:11–12), and His dealings with people through the ages, He has had recorded and preserved for us to read (Rom. 15:4). Henry continues: "The inspired Scriptures, revealing God's transcendent will in objective written form, are the rule of faith and conduct through which Christ exercises His divine authority in the lives of Christians."[116] All genuine Christianity rests entirely upon an accurate understanding and implementation of this record (cf. 1 Cor. 15:1–2). One who loses sight of the *sacredness* of Scripture will have no problem *reinventing* it to accommodate his personal version of Christianity, and then promote this version as though it were the "the gospel truth."
- **Apostolic authority.** In the NT, all recorded teaching was either written by or had to be consistent with the teaching of Christ's apostles, since they were appointed as His spokesmen of the gospel (Rom. 1:1–6, Gal. 1:11–12, Eph. 2:19–20, 2 Pet. 3:1–2, etc.). Any gospel teaching that was inconsistent with apostolic teaching was regarded as a counterfeit and thus soundly condemned (Gal. 1:8). One notable characteristic of liberal biblical interpretations is the failure to honor the role, authority, and significance of Christ's chosen apostles.[117]

- **Word definitions.** These are based on both original meaning *and* textual usage, not one or the other. Some word meanings will be modified by how the ancient writers used them. For example, the Greek word *pneuma* can mean spirit, ghost, breath, or wind, depending on the context. Also, whether this word is capitalized (referring to God's Holy Spirit) or lowercase (referring to something else) also depends on context. Other word meanings can be used either positively or negatively, depending upon how the writer applied them. In Acts 15:39, Paul and Barnabas had a "sharp disagreement" over whether to bring Mark along with them; in Heb. 10:24, Christians are to "stimulate one another to love and good deeds." The same Greek word [*paroxusmos*] is used in both places—in one, negatively; in the other, positively.[118] It is both the word definition *and* its usage that gives us a clear meaning of these passages.
- **Context, context, context.** This refers to the natural environment in which we find words, phrases, and teachings. All of Jesus' teachings, for example, must be viewed in the context of His position (as Son of God), His generation and its outlook, the Jews and their Law, God's covenant with Israel, and the Jews' anticipation for the coming kingdom of God. When we read Jesus' teachings through the lens of a person in the 21st century without considering the original context of His words, we come up with something different than what He meant.[119] In doing so, we can justify all kinds of things that He never justified—and would never justify today.

  Contextual study involves the who, what, when, where, and why questions that form the basis for any objective investigation. This includes both the immediate context (say, the verse, chapter, or book in which a passage is being considered) as well as the larger context (as in *all* similar books, *all* verses dealing with the subject at hand, or the entire Bible). When passages are pulled out of context, they are no longer connected with their original environment. Once this happens, they can be made to say whatever a person *wants* them to say, since their original meaning has been compromised.[120]
- **Critical thinking.** This involves using factual evidence and sound reasoning in pursuit of (if possible) an inescapable conclusion. This method is based on objectivity rather than subjectivity; facts and evidence rather than speculations and suppositions; and letting the Scripture speak for (and defend) itself rather than injecting

personal opinions or traditions into the text.[121] In many cases where modern religious teaching violates Scripture, people have reached a desired conclusion *first*, then go throughout the Bible looking for passages that appear to support their conclusion.[122] Modern denominationalists, liberal teachers, and end-of-the-world enthusiasts are famous for this. This kind of "interpretation" is completely backward and shows great disrespect for the *purpose* of Scripture in the first place.[123]

Suffice it to say: biblical interpretation should never be reduced to, "This is how *I* take Jesus' words," or, "This is what *I* think God is teaching." Jesus' words and God's doctrinal teachings are never to be evaluated or communicated with "I think," "I feel," or "I heard" statements. If you ever find yourself defending what you believe to be *doctrinal truth* with "I think/feel/heard," you are only stating your opinions (or someone else's), not citing divine law. No one can be saved by adhering to your (or my) opinions about God and His word. On the other hand, *everyone* will be saved who obeys "the truth" which He has revealed (1 Tim. 2:4). God's laws should be viewed with a "Thus says the Lord"-kind of respect and reverence. Jesus often said "It is written" in response to His opponents, including Satan himself (Mat. 4:1–10). The written word of God always trumps our feelings or opinions. People who think that their emotional "take" on any given Scripture equates to obedience to God are deeply mistaken.

Today, it is not hard to find disparity between what has been written in Scripture and what is dubbed "Christianity." This happens whenever the *world's* version of "truth" is accepted over *God's* truth. This violates, among other things, one of the basic rules of biblical interpretation: "An interpretation must not be influenced by a preconceived notion."[124] Otherwise, "Men can find what they look for, but what they do not want to see, it is difficult to make them understand. Hence if there be not a good and honest heart, there will be but little fruit from the sowing."[125] Abandoning the rules of interpretation never produces a sincere student of the Bible and should never be regarded as genuine Bible "study." Staring at a box of carpenter's tools does not make you a carpenter, much less a very skilled one. So it is with Bible study: a person can stare at the tools of interpretation all he wants, but until he applies them properly, he really does not know what he is doing (cf. 1 Tim. 1:6–7).

God's word must be revered as commandment teachings, never as mere good advice. When God gave Moses a pattern to follow for the construction of the tabernacle, He was not merely "suggesting" what Moses *could* do: He was telling him what *must* be done. So it is with us: we have not been given a bunch of divine suggestions to consider, but divine commandments to follow. **Commandments do not need to be interpreted but obeyed.** If a general gives a command to his troops when confronting an enemy, the troops do not respond with, "Sir, we've all been talking, and while we see where you're coming from, we have a plan that is just as good *if not better* than what you have said." This is nothing short of insubordination and is cause for a court-martial.

Peter said that the instruction given by the apostles to the churches were not the apostles' private interpretations (2 Peter 1:20–21). Jesus' commandments, whether spoken by Him personally or by His hand-picked apostles, originated from His Father (John 5:30, 8:28, 12:49, etc.). He said, "If you continue in My word, then you are truly disciples of Mine; and you will know the truth, and the truth will make you free" (John 8:31–32). He did *not* say, "you will know your interpretation of the truth, and this interpretation will make you free." Truth does not need to be interpreted, evaluated, dissected, second-guessed, or suppressed. It only needs to be *heard* and then *acted upon* (Mat. 7:24–27). It is not "a matter of interpretation" when a person or church acts in direct violation of the NT pattern. Instead, this is rebellion and open defiance, and "rebellion is as the sin of divination, and insubordination is as iniquity and idolatry" (1 Sam. 15:23).

Seeking a Different Objective

Given all this, one can see the stark contrast between the "casual churchgoer"—at one time, a disgraceful thing to be, but now fully acceptable in contemporary religion—and those who have accepted God's great invitation into His fellowship. How are we to reconcile all of what the Bible teaches about being a Christian and what passes for "Christianity" today? The fact is, we are unable to do so. Even so, many will cite the interpretation factor to clear up all contradictions between the two. Conspicuously, it is always the ones who disagree with the straightforward and contextual understanding of Scripture that want to "reinterpret" it into something else. Then these people insist that *their* "interpretation" is correct, while any interpretation that does not allow for their creative interpretation is deemed legalistic, bigoted, or unloving. "They are *dogmatic* in their insistence that no one should be dogmatic."[126]

Yet, this claim begs several questions. First, who decides that subjective interpretations are permissible? If this premise is never established, then nothing that follows matters. Second, whose interpretations are we to follow—especially when they boldly contradict what has been written—and who has the authority to lead the rest of us? Third, when Christ says, "Believe this!" or His apostles say, "Teach this!" or "Do this!", who today is qualified to modify such commandments through his own interpretation of them? Fourth, who also decides when one command is to be obeyed at face value (*literally*) and another command is to be interpreted in a different way? When the straightforward truth of God is subjected to human interpretations, then what exactly is the *worth* of such truth? If God's truth can always be reconfigured to become someone *else's* truth, then why do we need God to tell us anything at all? Once we make private interpretations on par with or even more important than revealed truth, we have lost sight of what it means to be *walking* in truth (2 John 1:4).

The "That's your interpretation" accusation is always used very selectively, not consistently. When Christ or His apostles say whatever supports one's views, brand of faith, or religion of choice, everyone is content with what is written. When the two things disagree, however, then "interpretation" is invoked to (allegedly) harmonize two contradictory positions: theirs and Christ's. Anyone who dares to challenge *their* unfounded interpretation is disparaged as a legalist or false teacher. They *need* their interpretation to prevail for their belief system to work. Instead of allowing the NT pattern to define their belief system, they (consciously or not) redefine the NT pattern.

For example, when Paul says that you must "believe" and "confess" for salvation, most people see no need to interpret this (Rom. 10:9–10). Believing and confessing are standard and acceptable terms across denominational lines. But when Peter says you must "repent" and "be baptized" for salvation (Acts 2:38), suddenly it's not clear what he meant about baptism (and it is *always* baptism that is debated here, never repentance), and we need to have denominational theologians and word experts wade in with their scholarly "interpretation" of the passage. The clear, natural, and contextual meaning of this passage becomes so dissected and overanalyzed, it can mean whatever they want it to mean rather than what it says. (Not surprisingly, their "interpretation" will always conform to their denominational persuasion—an entirely backward and thus insincere approach.)

Consider some other examples of this:

- In several cases, people have interpreted Jesus' words to the Jews as being doctrinal teachings for His church. This ignores the context of His teaching and misapplies it in ways that He never meant. For example, Christians say things like, "Jesus' teaching *superseded* the Law of Moses," which is untrue and violates what He had said (Mat. 5:17–19).[127] It *is* true that moral teachings are consistent with *all* covenants with God, and Jesus did teach a great deal about morality. In all other cases, however, Jesus was not speaking to the church but to the Jews (concerning their Law and their covenant relationship with God). Thus, His words must not be automatically assumed to be "church law," because His church was not even in existence until He ascended to the right hand of God following His resurrection (Acts 2:33).[128]
- When Jesus told His people not to elevate some men over others with special statuses, titles, and distinguished positions (Mat. 23:6–12), no one seems to have a problem with this. (Clearly, this passage has dual application: first, to the Jews themselves; second, to His church, in anticipation of it.) Yet, many "Christian" churches commonly elevate some men (and women) over other church members with these very things. Titles like "Pastor," "Reverend," "Father," "Cardinal," "Pope," etc. succumb to the very thing about which the Master warned us. Some men are deemed closer to God than others, based especially on the created position they hold in their church. Only through clever interpretations (and other imaginative explanations) can anyone skirt around Christ's prohibition for this.
- When Jesus prayed for unity for His disciples (and those who would become His disciples), no one seems to have a problem with this (John 17:17–23). Yet, the religious world is fractured with numerous groups, each with its own doctrine, faith, identity, practice, and organizational structure, yet *all* of them claim to be "united" with Christ.[129] Through clever and diverse interpretations of Scripture—all of them being unfaithful to the NT pattern— people have made a mockery of Christ's call for unity. No one can

be united with Him *and at the same time* separated from anyone else who is united with Him. Yet, amazingly, most of what is dubbed "Christendom" is filled with segregation and division.

- When Christ is identified as the head of His church (Eph. 1:22–23), no one seems to have a problem with this. But when a church that invokes His name and claims to preach His gospel is faced with social pressure to conform to politically correct social issues, suddenly it is permissible to *vote* on moral teachings or lifestyle choices that defy what *Christ's hand-chosen apostles* preached as "the doctrine conforming to godliness" (1 Tim. 6:3–4a).[130] No longer is Christ recognized as the head of His church since those who do the voting apparently can overrule Him.
- When John wrote, "God is love" (1 John 4:8), no one seems to have a problem with this. But instead of letting God *define* love with His own divine nature, people feel very comfortable interpreting "love" in a way that is self-gratifying, embraces unholy lifestyles, or *defies* all that God said is holy. Thus, godly love—and, by implication, God's holy nature—is subject to human interpretation, which has led to many diverse and conflicting beliefs and practices among those claiming to be Christians. Ironically, those who disagree with the progressive *version* of "love" are the ones deemed "unloving" rather than the progressives who redefine God's love.
- When Paul says that fornicators, idolators, adulterers, thieves, and drunkards "will not inherit the kingdom of God" (1 Cor. 6:9–10), no one seems to have a problem with this. But when, in the exact same passage, Paul says that the "effeminate"[131] and "homosexuals"[132] *also* will not inherit the kingdom of God, then suddenly Paul is accused of being a homophobe and we should not trust what he says; "homosexual" doesn't really mean, well, *homosexual*; and since God loves all people, therefore He will welcome all forms of love *between* people, including homosexual love and its accompanying lifestyle. Such people, if they *love* each other, must be allowed to be in Christ's churches in good standing. Anyone who disagrees with this interpretation is painted as a legalist, a bigot, and unloving.
- When we are instructed (by apostolic example) to appoint elders in every church (Acts 14:23), no one seems to have a problem with this. But when we are told that those elders need to be married *men* and heads of households (1 Tim. 3:1–5), suddenly we must interpret such passages to allow *women* to be elders and *marriage* to be

between two people of the same gender. And, of course, anyone who says otherwise is labeled a legalist and a bigot.[133]
- When a believer is told to believe, confess, and repent to become a Christian, no one seems to have a problem with this. But when Paul says that he must also be baptized in order identify with Christ's death and "walk in newness of life" (Rom. 6:3–7), denominational theologians are quick to interpret baptism as a mere *symbol* of salvation rather than a necessary *component* of it. (Belief and repentance are never reduced to mere symbols, only baptism.) Baptism is often interpreted to be merely "an outward sign of an inward grace"—a teaching of Calvinism (an "-ism"), not Scripture—and therefore is deemed optional or expendable. All this defies what Paul said in this passage, as well as other corresponding passages.

It is amazing what people can and will come up with in their quest to "interpret" Scripture to conform to what they already believe, *want* to believe, or *need* to believe to walk in step with modern socio-political-religious issues. Instead of respecting the authority of Scripture as the divinely revealed word of God, they are "daring, self-willed," and go where angels fear to tread—something characteristic of false teachers, never faithful Christ-followers (2 Peter 2:10–11).

Instead of letting Scripture draw its own conclusions and then each person accepting those conclusions as "the truth"—however they impact his own life or belief system—many people are ignorant of Scripture, are not trained to study Scripture, or simply do not really care what Scripture says. In the end, some people just want to do what they want to do, regardless of what God or anyone else says about it. Yet, they expect the full approval of Christ's church. They also want (and think that they will receive) God's approval.

The people I just described can hardly be called Christians, since no genuine Christ-follower would adopt such an attitude toward or show such disregard for his Lord. Yet, modern interpretations of Scripture—what some have dubbed "the new hermeneutic"—have taken deep root among so-called Christian churches. Once people are indoctrinated with the casual, opinionated, and feel-good approach to "interpreting" the NT pattern, then it is very difficult for them to see it any other way. It is hard to get people to follow the "narrow" way once they have developed an insatiable appetite for the wide path of least resistance (Mat. 7:13–14).

Creative interpretations of preachers and theologians have no place in genuine Bible study. Even worse is the subjective, often plucked-out-of-thin-air interpretations of people who think they are qualified to "know" what the Scriptures teach simply because they are reading them. This happens in many so-called Bible studies (where "study" is not really what is happening at all): suddenly everyone is an expert on Scripture only because they read a verse and felt immediately qualified to explain or expound upon it. To be truly qualified requires a great deal of time and reading, as well as many years of genuine biblical education. Even so, I have sat through many such occasions in which a "study" was nothing more than each person offering their personal reflection on a given passage, rather than honoring either the specific or general context in which it was found.

Honest, open-minded, and discerning interpretation is one thing. I deeply respect all those who have made a great investment into an objective study of the Bible. Such people have done their homework; even if I disagree with them, I still admire what they bring to the table. But offering a cold reading of a passage and then declaring "This is what it means *to me*" requires no meaningful effort. This allows one's personal emotions to impose upon and often redefine what God said is *true*. Truth is something to discover, learn, and live by; it is never something that we are allowed to interpret according to our own "take" on it. If one is being honest in his pursuit of God's truth, he most certainly will discover it. But if he simply wants to believe whatever he has come up with on his own, he will be, at best, "always learning and never able to come to the knowledge of the truth" (2 Tim. 3:7).

Summary Thoughts

Sometimes people make things harder than they really are—or harder than they need to be. This is true about the gospel of Christ and the entire NT pattern. The pattern is not terribly difficult to understand, but one does have to approach it with an open mind and a sincere heart. If one's objective is to defend, say, his own religious persuasion, then he will find himself cramming square pegs into round holes, so to speak. In other words, his present belief system will not correspond to what is written. To make it work—or *appear* to work—he must utilize some creative interpretation of the Scriptures. This has been going on for a long time, and it has been the source of much of the religious division among all those who identify as Christians.

There is, of course, a need for biblical interpretation, and there is a rather scientific approach to it. This does not mean only a few people are allowed to do the interpreting; it means that *whoever* is doing the interpreting needs to do so according to the rules and principles *of* interpretation. These involve word definitions, critical thinking, objective analysis, contextual study, etc. The objective must never be to defend one's previously chosen belief system but just the opposite: to discover what his belief system *should* be as determined by whatever God declared through His written word.

God did not provide the NT pattern for every version of "Christian" or every flavor of "Christianity" to dissect, overanalyze, and variously interpret it. Rather, He gave us a pattern that is easy to understand and relatively easy to implement. The hierarchical, bureaucratic, highly politicized, and often fiercely protected modern denomination, for example, has drifted so far away from the NT pattern that the *pattern itself* is what seems foreign, not the departure from it. People may believe that whatever their denomination teaches *is* "the pattern" because this is what they have been repeatedly told, and because relatively few people take the time to study God's pattern for themselves.

Hopefully, your desire—since you have read this far—is not to defend one human belief system or another, but to "read and understand" what has been preserved for the last nearly 2,000 years in Scripture (2 Cor. 1:13). The NT pattern was not written for seminary graduates and theologians; it was written for *all* people. This does not mean you are allowed to understand it however you choose (or however *I* choose) but that you *can* understand it in the way that God meant for you to understand it. The truth always has a singular conclusion, never many.

Chapter Twelve: Departures from the Pattern

If I program my truck's navigation system to take me to a certain destination, the system wants me to stay on the course that it has determined is best. If I veer away from that course, even by a little bit (say, to pull into a coffee shop drive-thru), the voice of the navigation system keeps insisting that I "proceed to the route, proceed to the route, proceed to the route."

The navigation system, through its lightning-fast algorithms and calculations, knows how to get me to where I'm going better than I do (at least, regarding a destination to which I've never been). Of course, it does not care about me personally; it's not even a living being that is doing the talking, but an impressive, computerized version of a human voice. So then, whether I stay on the "route" or go rogue and find my own way, it really does not matter to the computer. Its job is to provide information, not save my life—or my soul.

It is amazing to me that so many people put great confidence in a humanly programmed computerized navigation system but feel free to defy or ignore God's spiritual navigation of the human soul. God knows where our soul needs to go; He knows the best—in fact, the *only*—way in which to get there. If we veer off course, He gives us warnings to "proceed to the route." The first warning is our conscience, which serves as a moral compass for determining how close to or far away from God we are. The second is His revealed word, which spells out the directions for finding and remaining on the "narrow" path that leads to God (Mat. 7:13–14). The third (for those who are Christians) is God's own discipline, which may be painful to experience but is meant to correct our wayward steps and get us back on course (Heb. 12:4–13).

All this means that God is not unconcerned if we depart from the path of truth and righteousness. His care for us is not expressed through a dispassionate, computer-generated voice intoning a purely informational message. Instead, He speaks to us through the voice of His prophets, His apostles, and most importantly His own Son (Heb. 1:1–2). He pleads with us to find the way that leads to life, and then to stay on that course without turning to the right or to the left (Joshua 1:7, in principle). He has not hidden this "way" from us but has made it more knowable and accessible than ever before in all human history.

Despite this, *most* people in the world turn a blind eye to His Son, turn a deaf ear to His word, and turn *away* from Him in disappointment (to their expectations), disinterest (because they seek other pursuits), or contempt (because they imagine themselves smarter than God).

All this is very sad, especially for those of us who know how awful things will go for such people in the hereafter.[134] But what is also sad is when those who claim to "know God" and "love Jesus" also go their own way, yet project themselves as "faithful believers" and "good Christians." In other words, it is not just the atheists, agnostics, and irreligious that have rejected the route that their souls ought to have taken. It is also those who ought to *know better* what that route is, how to stay on it, and how perilous it is to depart from it—even a little bit. There are millions of people posing as "Christians"—I use quotation marks here since their actions betray a sincere identity with God—who have indeed departed from the NT pattern but act like everything is all right. Atheists (for example) aren't the only ones who can be blinded by human pride and false appraisals. Those who sit in pews on Sunday mornings in church buildings across the country can be equally deceived.

At least the atheist is being honest about who he is: he admits to being an unbeliever. Yet, when those who profess to be Christians depart from the God-given pattern for His churches, they *act* like unbelievers.

- First, they **do not believe** (for whatever reason) that God is serious about following the pattern. If they did, then they would learn the pattern in detail and abide by it.
- Second, they **do not believe** that they are *bound* to the pattern. They think the pattern is provided only as a general guide for following Christ. All that matters is that one worships God, loves Jesus, and loves his fellow human being in whatever way seems right to him.
- Third, they **do not believe** that the pattern will lead them to where they want to go. If they did, then they would follow it without hesitancy or deviation. Instead, they feel comfortable improvising, modifying, and sometimes even completely revising the pattern to accommodate their expectations, modern times, or social pressures.
- Fourth, they **do not believe** that a departure from the pattern has any moral consequence. They see their actions as being principle-driven rather than doctrinally defined. In other words, they justify

themselves on loosely defined Christian principles without feeling the need to be obedient to every single apostolic instruction. And, because "God knows [their] heart" (a popular defense), He will allegedly understand and be pleased with their customized version of honoring Him.

As stated earlier in this book, if God's NT pattern was in any way expendable, then why did He bother giving it to us in the first place? If it is only a moral guide but not a prescription that needs to be adhered to, then why didn't He just say so *in* the pattern? As it is, such language is conspicuously absent from the NT Scriptures. It is contradictory to honor Christ as the "head" of His own church (Col. 1:18) but then to think we can do whatever we feel is right and good *for* His church. This devalues Christ's headship; it relegates His role to that of a mere figurehead without any meaningful power or authority. Sadly, this is what a lot of "Christian" churches have done today. In essence, they profess their allegiance to Christ, yet their actions follow their collective heart, appetite for entertainment, and/or social causes.

Apostasy Defined

In 1 Tim. 4:1–3, the apostle Paul was warned by the Holy Spirit that, in due time, "some will fall away from the faith." Someone cannot "fall" from something he never once stood upon, so this must refer to genuine Christians *falling from* what it means to be a genuine Christian. The immediate question is: why would a person who once believed in the gospel, obeyed the gospel, and committed himself to live by the gospel, then *fall away* from it? It must take a persuasive influence to con someone into doing this.

Paul provides the answer: such people will "[pay] attention to deceitful spirits and doctrines of demons" (1 Tim. 4:1). While many "Christian" churchgoers and church leaders today feel fully justified in honoring not *all* the NT pattern, but only the parts they choose to honor, the apostle Paul reveals the satanic spirit behind this. We are warned elsewhere that we are not to believe in every "spirit" that masquerades as being righteous. Instead, we are told to "test the spirits to see whether they are from God because many false prophets have gone out into the world" (1 John 4:1). The standard by which to "test the spirits"—or even to test our *own* spirit (2 Cor. 13:5)—is the NT pattern (word of God).

"Doctrines of demons" is a heavy description for a departure that seems so right, feels so good, and appeals to so many people. This tells us that the incentive *to* depart from God's standard comes not only from within (i.e., our human desires and appetites) but also from without ("the world forces of [the] darkness" and "spiritual forces of wickedness"—Eph. 6:12). Any willful departure from Christ's blueprint for Christians and their churches does not come from Him, but from demonic entities that would love nothing more than to see His people fail. Thus, instead of listening only to Christ and His apostles, many Christians have chosen to listen to the soothing, persuasive, and seductive words of demons. Christians and their churches cannot follow Christ *and* demons all at once (1 Cor. 10:21). Absolute decisions must be made, and absolute loyalties must be chosen (see 2 Cor. 6:14 – 7:1).

Paul goes on to say that people who depart from the God-given pattern and then repeatedly—and often very defensively—attempt to justify themselves are "liars," not seekers or proclaimers of divine truth. He speaks of them as having their conscience seared, as with a hot iron. (This alludes to the branding of slaves or cattle, or the cauterizing of a wound.) Such searing removes all sensation of God's word *and* one's own conscience. In effect, his heart becomes insensitive toward (or unfeeling of) the influence of God's warnings, and he veers off course without concern or cause for alarm. Keep in mind that Paul is talking about *Christians* who once committed themselves to Christ but then submitted to a different lord instead—one that seeks only their destruction. This can be applied to many Christians today who began as genuine, sincere, and truth-seeking believers but then were seduced by persuasive preachers, false religion, and deceitful spirits to abandon the very pattern that made them Christians in the first place.

Paul also gives a couple of manifestations of this "falling away" (or apostasy). Citing the Spirit's prophetic utterance, he cites the forbiddance of marriage (i.e., celibacy) and an abstaining from foods (i.e., the imposition of a strict diet as a means of achieving righteousness; see Mark 7:18–19 and Col. 2:20–23). Historically, the Roman (Catholic) Church did enforce these two practices centuries later, yet Paul's warnings are hardly limited to any one church or religion. He is not really talking about "a" church (as if one among many) but speaks to those who were once part of *Christ's* church who nonetheless will turn away from God's Spirit to follow "deceitful spirits."

Later, Paul comments again on this departure/apostasy: "For the time will come when they will not endure sound doctrine; but wanting to have their ears tickled, they will accumulate for themselves teachers in accordance to their own desires, and will turn away their ears from the truth and will turn aside to myths" (2 Tim. 4:3–4). The rejection of "sound doctrine"—revealed heavenly truths that comprise a blueprint for establishing fellowship with God—leads to myths, false teaching, and useless information. "Sound" here means healthy, whole, and complete; whatever is less than this is unsound, unhealthy, and incomplete. What God has revealed to us is superior to whatever we come up with on our own. In turning *away* from His pattern, people must turn *toward* something else, because no one can go in two opposite directions at once. Whatever people turn *toward* in this case will always be inferior to what they turn *from*. Human nature, once it abandons divine influence, always degrades over time: it never improves, never remains unchanged, and never pleases God.

Departing from "the faith"—the revealed gospel of Christ—is not a harmless or benign decision. Those who depart are no longer in fellowship with Christ; therefore, they cannot be in fellowship with God's people. The two groups cannot simply "agree to disagree, but we're all still brothers in Christ," because one group follows Christ and the other group has *departed* from following Him and is now following something else.[135] The departing group cannot argue that "Christ meant well by giving the church a 'pattern' to follow at first, but things have changed," because Christ never said that His pattern has changed, needed to be changed, or that anyone has permission to change it. This assumes, too, that He never saw the change in "things" coming, or that His revealed word could not have dealt with these changes.

A System of Departure

We have already examined specific actions that "Christian" churches practice (recall the substantial list given in chapter four). Now, we will examine the overall *system* of departure that provides for these specific actions. A *system* of departure begins with a collective mindset that:

- Does not believe that it *is* departing or turning away from the truth (even though it cannot justify what it is doing *by* the truth).
- Does not see anything wrong with what it is doing (even though it is different—and sometimes radically so—from what Christians are

instructed to do in the NT).
- Believes that changing times, social perspectives, and cultural influences give permission to change the teachings, practices, and structure of Christ's churches (even though this permission is nowhere granted in the NT pattern).
- Believes itself to be acting in good faith, in Christian love, and with the best of intentions (even though these motives are defined subjectively rather than by God's word).
- Believes that as long as we show godly love and Christian fellowship to one another, God approves of its actions, and all will be well. (The huge problem with this is that the NT pattern defines godly love and Christian fellowship by an unchanging doctrine which this mindset has already deemed changeable.)[136]
- Justifies its changes—not "departures," but allegedly harmless modifications—to the NT pattern based on human emotions, opinions, and a consensus of the group.
- Does not condemn other groups from doing what it is doing (because to do so would be self-incriminating).

If one person did all this, then the problem would be isolated and easily excised from the rest of the group (meaning: any given church). What has happened, though, is that many people have come together to make the departure from the pattern seem like a widely acceptable thing, implying that it is a universal consensus of the entire brotherhood. The more people that do this, the better it feels, and the more popular it becomes. Soon, it is the NT pattern itself that sounds foreign to the modern churchgoer, rather than the wayward churchgoer himself being so foreign to the pattern. The pattern, rather than the one who has departed from it, is put on trial and found guilty (so to speak).

According to Paul's prophesy (in 1 Tim. 4:1–2), this departure would begin from those who once knew the truth, believed in the truth, and were saved by the truth (1 Cor. 15:1–2). However, as the movement outlives this initial group of Christians, those who continue in it are not even taught to *become* Christians but are taught to be followers of the dogma and system of the departure itself. Any doctrine that has departed from the NT pattern cannot produce what the NT pattern alone was designed to produce. **False teaching and false religion can never produce true Christians.** Put another way: if the NT pattern is the only means by which Christians can be made, then it stands to reason that anything *different* from this will produce something other than Christians.[137] To argue otherwise—or, to claim that this is not true—assumes without legitimate authority that *people* can come up with a plan of salvation equal to and (because it supersedes the original) superior to what God's *Holy Spirit* revealed in the first place.

Some examples of what this looks like include:

- Being made a "Christian" by simply "asking Jesus into your heart to be your personal Savior." This is perhaps the most popular method used today, made hugely popular in the United States through the "Jesus crusades" of the 1960s and 1970s. Particularly, it removes the need for water baptism in the process of one's conversion to Christ. Its appeal is based on convenience, popularity, and human emotions. Yet, nowhere in the NT is this method taught, practiced, or even hinted at.[138]
- Being baptized into a church system rather than into Christ. Some denominational churches will teach "Just ask Jesus to be your personal Savior" and assume that this is sufficient for a person to become a Christian. After the conversion is allegedly complete, *then* they require these "Christians" to be baptized to identify with their denomination (or congregation). While the NT pattern requires baptism to identity with Christ (Rom. 6:3–7, Gal. 3:26–27, etc.), they make it apply instead to church membership. This is not a minor disagreement with the NT pattern but a revision of it.
- Joining a church (or church system) based on family, cultural, or traditional premises rather than becoming a member of Christ's church based upon His revealed truth. Many people identify (even proudly) with one "Christian" religion or another because their family has been doing so for generations. This creates an *inherited* faith rather than a *chosen* one as defined by Christ and His apostles.
- Participating in a church system because of familiarity, tradition, or personal preferences, particularly at the expense of biblical doctrine, apostolic authority, and discipleship to Christ. It is popular for people to "go to church" or become members of a church because they like what a church has to *offer* (in the form of amenities or assistances) rather than what it teaches or how its practices measure up to the NT pattern.[139] This focuses on consumerism rather than discipleship to Christ.
- Participating in a church system only to showcase one's talents or advance one's personal status. In this category are the celebrity

preachers, singers, musicians, church growth specialists, etc., that enjoy a rewarding and perhaps lucrative career in church work. While this "work" is often foreign to what Christ's churches are told to do in the NT, it is enough (for such people) that they find personal fulfillment in what they do. Typically, they are offended if you dare to challenge the selfish imposition of their "God-given talent" as if you were denying God Himself the opportunity to express His gospel.

- Unwilling to deny a person's "faith in Jesus" or "love for the Lord," even when their "faith" or "love" is inconsistent with what Jesus taught. The reasoning here is that if we deny someone's personal versions of these things, they will "fall away" from the church. Yet, this fear presupposes that those people belonged to the church in the first place. They might belong to "a" church, but to belong to *the* church (Christ's body), one's faith and love must be defined by Christ, not each person. One's claim to have "faith in God" cannot be unchallengeable; claiming a "love for the Lord" cannot trump doctrine. Otherwise, this renders the need for doctrine useless: if a person can determine his own faith and love, then there is no need for Christ to define these (or any other divine requirement) for him.

- Unwilling to say or teach anything that sounds unpleasant or violates modern sensitivities. Many contemporary, mainstream, and "progressive" churchgoers are unwilling to say or hear anything that sounds even remotely critical, especially when it is directed at themselves. As a result, "Many churches are attempting to create an atmosphere of non-qualifying acceptance by avoiding anything negative and remaining strictly positive. ... People are then attracted by the positive atmosphere and promise of acceptance and not by truth."[140] Today, positivity has been elevated above biblical doctrine, the teachings of Jesus, and even common sense.

- Unwilling to "judge" anyone, because "judging" sounds bad, harsh, and unchristian.[141] With this mindset, many people today are more terrified of offending sinners than they are of offending Christ. The "Don't judge!" doctrine allegedly welcomes people into Christ's church whom Christ Himself would never admit. In sharp contrast, Jesus spoke openly about the need to identify people for *who they really are* rather than how churchgoers decide to treat them. People who repeatedly reject what God said is holy make themselves out to be "dogs" and "swine"—this is what *Jesus* said (Mat. 7:6). Others are wolves in sheep's clothing—again, what *Jesus* said (Mat.

7:15–20). Still others are "false apostles," "deceitful workers," and "enemies of the cross of Christ"—this is what Jesus' *apostle* said (2 Cor. 11:13, Phil. 3:18). We cannot tell who truly belongs to God and who simply masquerades as a believer unless we use "righteous judgment" (John 7:24), exercise discernment (Heb. 5:14), and "test all spirits" (1 John 4:1).

It is very likely that most Christians—both real and imagined—have little knowledge of what the NT teaches concerning Christians and their churches. While some of this fault lies with those who unquestioningly swallow human opinions that pose as the truth, the greater fault lies with the teachers and preachers of this mass deception. For this reason, these latter people will receive "stricter judgment" (James 3:1).[142] "When those in the pew are ignorant of the Word, it should not be surprising that those in the pulpit can wander from the Word unchallenged and unchecked."[143]

It is popular today to do "fact-checking" regarding political statements, financial issues, social media, and even celebrity gossip, but very little fact-checking is being done toward what church leaders are teaching. The apostle Paul referred to this when he wrote, "For we are not like many, peddling the word of God, but as from sincerity, but as from God, we speak in Christ in the sight of God" (2 Cor. 2:17). The word "peddling" here implies corruption and deception; historically, it applied to merchants and tavern owners who watered-down their wine and drinks to increase profits.[144] The ultimate discernment between those doing the "peddling" and those who speak the truth falls upon the ones who accept false information without making the effort to examine it closely (1 Thess. 5:21–22).

Any deliberate departure from Christ's pattern for Christians and their churches rebels against the One who gave the pattern in the first place. This rebellion may be quiet and subtle, but it is rebellion all the same. Apostasy—which is any departure from God's truth—listens to the doctrines of demons *rather than* the revealed instructions of the Holy Spirit. No one who follows demons will be justified by God, no matter how spiritual, religious, church-attending, or well-versed in the Bible they claim to be. (Even Satan quoted Scripture when it served his purpose—Mat. 4:6. Yet, he took it out of context and misapplied it—something many religious people commonly do today.) On the other hand, everyone who follows the leadership of Christ, and the teachings of the Holy Spirit, will most certainly be with God in the hereafter. It is these very people whom God seeks to be His worshipers (John 4:23–24).

Knowingly departing from the NT pattern is a serious moral crime. It is not an innocent mistake; it is a sin against Christ and God's Spirit. No one can claim to be a genuine Christian—a Christ-follower—who refuses to follow Christ's pattern. The pattern was not given as a nice gesture, a mere suggestion, or a good rule of thumb to follow. Rather, it was given so that we can know how to become Christians, how to live like Christians, and how to form and govern congregations of Christians. We do not own the church, but Christ does. We do not tell Christ how we are going to follow Him, but He has the right to tell us how this is to be done.

Summary Thoughts

Recall my opening illustration about a vehicle's navigation system. If you input the destination, then the system plots a course and expects you to remain on it. If you depart from the course, then it will remind you (insistently) to "proceed to the route." If your destination is to be with Christ in the hereafter, then you need to let Christ plot your course, because "apart from [Him] you can do nothing" toward accomplishing this (John 15:5). If you depart from this course, the word of God will insist that you "proceed to the route," because your departure will lead you to spiritual ruin, not a heavenly home.

Of course, you could simply ignore your truck's navigation system and do whatever you want to do—forge your own path, so to speak. Or you can simply turn off this navigation system so that you do not have to hear its warnings and pleadings any longer. People do both with reference to the NT pattern: some just ignore it and forge their own path, thinking it will lead to their desired destination. Others just close the Bible and set it aside, silencing the Holy Spirit's instructions, yet assume that all will be well. Both actions are disastrous, but this does not stop many people from pursuing them.

When we are honest and sincere, our ambition is to do everything in our power to follow the heavenly blueprint. There are many great rewards for obedience and compliance; there are many warnings against and awful consequences for disobedience and rebellion. Though Christ is not going to twist anyone's arm into obeying Him, He is not indifferent to the spiritual peril of those who will not listen to His instructions. It may even be that He has used this book as a means of getting the attention of some who read it. But my book is merely a giant arrow that points to *His* book (the Bible) for true direction.

So then, what is your desired destination? What path have you taken to get there? Who came up with that path—was it you, your family and friends, your church, or your church leadership? Or was it Jesus Christ, the only One with the credentials and authority to bring you home to God? I will let the apostle John finish this out: "As for you, let that abide in you which you heard from the beginning. If what you heard from the beginning abides in you, you also will abide in the Son and in the Father" (1 John 2:24). Amen!

Chapter Thirteen: Denominationalism

The previous chapter examined the general description of departing from the NT pattern. Now we will turn our attention to a specific church system that by its very design exhibits this departure: denominationalism. Modern denominations portray themselves as being synonymous with the Christian church of the NT, and many people make no distinction between the two. Yet, the concept of a "Christian denomination" is an oxymoron—a self-refuting or -contradicting phrase—because there is nothing truly Christian about separating into different groups, camps, sects, beliefs, systems, or organizations under Christ's name.

For the record, the focus here is on the *system* or *structure* of denominationalism (as an "-ism" of human design) rather than all the *people* involved in it. This means that no attempt is being made here to categorically evaluate every *person* who is a member of a denominational church. (Likewise, it is not true that every "non-denominational" church is automatically sound or justified based only on its avoidance of denominationalism.) On the other hand, just because hundreds of millions of people believe something to be true is, by itself, no measure of its actual worth. Many more hundreds of millions refuse to believe that Jesus is the Son of God, and God says that they are *all wrong* (John 8:24, 1 John 2:22–23, 4:2–3, 2 John 1:7, etc.).

The Definition of a "Denomination"

A dictionary definition of "denomination" is an "identifying word or words by which someone or something is called and classified or distinguished from others."[145] It is derived from a Latin word which basically means "of a name," or, the act of having named something as a class or category within the scope of a much larger context. This concept is hardly limited to religion. For example, a nickel is a denomination of United States coinage; a $5 bill is a denomination of United States currency; the Marines are a denomination of the United States military; pine trees are a denomination of all trees worldwide; etc.

With reference to religion, a denomination is a sect, faith, or group with a specific identity, doctrine, and/or practice within an overall religious context.[146] The overall context, in this case, is claimed to be "the

Christian faith" or "all religions that name Christ as their head." This is contrived, of course, because Christ approves of only *one* religion: the one that abides by His authority and the NT pattern. Furthermore, He approves of only one church in that religion: His church, which is defined by this same pattern. Even so, for the sake of understanding the concept, denominationalism will be explained by how it is used popularly, not as it claims to be used biblically.

Denominations are said to be subsets of the entire body of Christ. Supposedly, Christ's body has been divided up into numerous faiths, religions, and doctrines that are all a part of the Christian religion. Instead of creating one body with one faith (Eph. 4:4–5), Christ has allegedly created one body with many faiths. These faiths may share some common beliefs but are purposely and distinctly different from each other. For example, they all believe in God as the supreme head of the godhead; they all claim allegiance to Christ; they all claim to use the Bible as the basis for their existence. After this (and a few other basic shared beliefs), things quickly begin to go in multiple directions.

This means that Christ's church—the spiritual fellowship of all believers worldwide—is said to be comprised of many different varieties of believers. Denominations often cite John 15:1–5 in support of this: Jesus is the "true vine," denominations are allegedly the "branches." Because all these "branches" are connected to Jesus, therefore they are all legitimate. The insurmountable problem with this interpretation is that Jesus was not talking about denominations, religions, or churches; He was talking to His disciples *about* disciples—individual believers. In the context of His own words, it is not denominations that are connected to Him (an idea nowhere found in the NT), but believers are connected to Him (which has substantial support).

A denomination, by design, is a recognizable system, pattern, or organization which is used to differentiate itself from all other faiths or groups within the general context of "Christianity." It rests upon human authority to do something that Christ never said to do yet assumes that it has Christ's approval. Something is catastrophically wrong with this kind of reasoning. The NT alone defines both Christians *and* their churches, and this authority comes from heaven, not people. Even so, denominationalism has become such a fixture in modern culture that to even question it (like what I am daring to do here) seems unwarranted or even hostile.

The concept of denominationalism began barely one hundred years after the apostolic age. Instead of maintaining the NT pattern of elders (bishops) governing one church, they were appointed to oversee groups of churches, then geographical regions of churches. As questions arose concerning doctrine or procedure, these men came together to discuss them, producing the primitive form of local church councils that would later give rise to (allegedly) universal church councils, such as the Council in Nicaea (AD 325) overseen by the Roman Emperor Constantine.[147] These councils produced creeds, and these creeds designated *human-determined* conditions of fellowship among those claiming to be God's people.

> By the fourth century, the metropolitans of the four leading cities of the Roman Empire (Rome, Constantinople, Antioch, and Alexandria) competed for oversight of the universal collection of congregations. At the end of the sixth century, Gregory the Great, Bishop of Rome, denounced John the Faster (Patriarch of Constantinople) for his assumed title of "Universal Patriarch." In 606 A.D., Boniface III was proclaimed "Universal Bishop" [or Pope] over all the churches.
>
> In only five centuries, men completed the transition from the simple organization of the autonomous local church to the universal coalition of local churches now seen in Roman Catholicism. *Rather than the body of Christ that consists of Christians, the concept now was the body of Christ that consisted of churches, which themselves consisted of Christians. This is the essence of denominationalism.*[148]

In the NT, churches were never addressed by any denominational names familiar to us today. Paul, the author of most of the letters to the NT churches, never used such names. Christ, in His dictated letters to the seven churches of Asia Minor (Rev. 2 – 3), never addressed them denominationally. In fact, He never even hinted that they *were* denominational in any respect. Most of our modern denominations did not even exist until during or after the 16th century Reformation—over 1,500 years *after* Christ established His church. The absence of names, descriptions, specific teachings, offices, and practices of modern denominations in the NT is more than conspicuous: it exposes them as being something *other than* what the NT sought to identify.

Additionally, if denominations really are "branches" from the vine (Christ), then for some inexplicable reason it took 1,500 years for most of them to sprout. And "if these organizations are the branches, then it follows that the church was a branchless, fruitless, lifeless thing until they came into being."[149] Not only this, but each of these alleged "branches" operates by different rules, exercises different practices and offices, and produces different fruit. Thus, one vine provides many kinds of fruit—something foreign to nature *and* the NT.[150] Yet, Jesus did not draw on nature (vines, branches, and fruit) to illustrate a monstrosity of His church in contrast to it, but to show the *parallel characteristics* between the two things being compared. This would be like comparing His church to the human body (as Paul did in 1 Cor. 12) but coming up with a Frankenstein monster rather than a fitting spiritual comparison. There is something terribly wrong with this kind of thinking.

The Characteristics of Denominations

Modern denominational systems share several common features. Every "Christian" denomination can be identified *as* a denomination by these features. They include:

- **A distinct name by which its church system is known or identified.** The "-ism" suffix reveals its source since all "-isms" are of human origin and design. Christ did not give us an "-ism" to participate in but a message to believe in and proclaim. The idea of "Christianism" is foreign to the NT pattern.
- **A distinct identity by which each member is known.** Members of denominational religions rarely identify themselves with "I am a Christian." Quite frequently, they will cite the party name to which they have given their allegiance ("I am a [insert a denominational name]") as though this was equal to or even superior to the seemingly bland "Christian" designation. Yet, the modern party names of "Christian" denominations are found nowhere in the NT pattern.[151] Again, historically, almost none of them even existed until over 1,500 years *after* Christ established His church.[152]
- **A central headquarters, office, board of directors, or individual person which serves as the source of final authority and legitimacy for the group.**[153] Most denominations today operate under the authority of some governing agency that determines their curriculum, public image, appointment of ministers, and oversight

of their churches. In contrast, the NT pattern allows for no larger collective entity than that of an individual congregation, and each of these are overseen only by their own appointed elders (shepherds) and no one else. According to the pattern, there is no interconnection between congregations except by way of teaching (doctrine) and a common fellowship in Christ (1 Cor. 10:16–17, in principle; see 1 Cor. 12:12–13, Eph. 3:6, and 1 John 1:7).

- **A hierarchal chain of command which oversees entire geographical regions, entire nations' churches, or multiple churches that adhere to its denomination.** Through this hierarchy, the local churches must be granted permission to make any major decisions, since they (the churches) cannot act independently. All of this exceeds the church organization as defined in the NT. The only men who had oversight of multiple churches in multiple cities were Christ's hand-picked apostles, and there are no such men alive today. The pattern calls for each church to honor Christ's doctrine independent of any other church, and there is no governing authority that presides over collections of churches.

- **Positions, offices, and titles within each denomination foreign to anything described in the NT.** In fact, some of these titles are even condemned *in* the NT (Mat. 23:9–10). Officials like titles and positions of authority because they provide a point of reference for who they are, what they do, and the security (it is assumed) of their own souls. *People* like titles because it separates such men from the rest of the people, often by elevating them *above* everyone else, and confers upon them certain privileges, status, and financial gains that are not available to the masses. In several denominational systems, there is a complete separation between the "clergy" (in essence, the church authorities) and the "laity" (the "lay" or common people). The NT pattern does have certain responsibilities within the churches (elders, preachers, deacons, teachers, etc.) but assigns no titles or intended separations of these people from the rest of the group. All groups need leadership, so leaders are essential to the organization of every congregation; however, these leaders are known only for what they *do*, not who they *are* (as a means of elevated status).

- **Specific doctrines, beliefs, creeds, and practices that must be consistent with its central government.**[154] This is necessary because denominationalism is all about the *separation* of one group of "Christians" from all others. It is true that, according to the

NT pattern, each congregation has its own distinct membership (for the purpose of autonomy and shepherding). It is *not* true that each congregation is to have its own statement of beliefs, doctrinal teachings, and unique practices. Yet, denominationalism is predicated upon intentional division: every denomination *must* look different than any other denomination, otherwise, it defeats the purpose of "denominating" one from the other. Allegedly, all of this has Christ's approval, as though He is happy with His people separating themselves into different camps according to beliefs and practices that they have chosen for themselves. This is the exact opposite of what He called for (John 17:20–22; see 1 Cor. 1:10, Phil. 1:27, and 2:1–2). Unity, not division, is the hallmark of Christ's church.[155]

- **Often, money from individual congregations of each denomination is funneled toward the central authority** (which usually operates in comfortable offices, completely detached from the actual work that is expected of church members). These central authorities do not have the means to generate revenue on their own; this all comes through the donations of members in their churches. This money pays for the headquarters' offices, top leadership, staff positions, programs, advertising, curriculum, and whatever else the central authority wants to spend it on. (Sometimes, this includes legal fees, tort payments, damage control to its public image, and services that have little or nothing to do with the biblical work of Christians.)
- **Approval from the central authority to identify with its denomination.** This may be done indirectly (through the authority imparted to its pastors and church leadership), but it is critical all the same. No one can become a member of a denomination who does not conform to its conversion policy. (Why this is not honored in the case of *Christ's* requirement for membership in *His* church apparently escapes their notice.) If this were not true, then it undermines the entire premise of having a denomination in the first place. In other words, if a distinct method of conversion and membership were not required by each denomination, then the distinction *between* denominations is no longer needed. This is the case in Christ's church: the same method is required of *every person* and is taught universally in *every one of His congregations*. The conversion process does not result in a unique party name for each church, but every person is made a Christian—nothing more, but nothing less, either.

"Has Christ been divided?" Paul asked rhetorically (1 Cor. 1:13). It was inconceivable to Paul even to imagine Christ's holy and united body (church) being carved up for any reason. Instead of being shocked and repulsed by such divisive action, as Paul was, the modern religious world seems perfectly content with this. In fact, it tends to glory in it, as though this is what Christ wanted all along. Yet, it remains true, given Paul's words here and elsewhere, that the only time denominationalism is even mentioned in the NT is when it is being condemned. This fact has not changed in 2,000 years.

"Has Christ been divided?" If He has, then Paul was mistaken. Also, the Holy Spirit who inspired Paul to write these words was mistaken. Not only this, but Christ—the founder of His own church—was also mistaken, since men *have* (in their own eyes) divided His church into numerous denominations and assume that He is very pleased with this. Allegedly, human authority can actually—and successfully—supersede heavenly authority, and there is nothing Christ can do about this but accept it as the modern way of "honoring" Him.[156]

But if Christ *cannot* be divided, then this means He *has not* been divided, and all divisions that have been done are without authority, even though they invoke His name. This has several significant implications. First, all divisions of Christ's body have come from people rather than from Christ. Second, all the pastorships, priesthoods, and positions that are involved in these divisions are also human-made and have no biblical authority to exist. Third, those who are made "Christians" by the authority of any human-made organization do not understand that these organizations *have* no such authority.[157] Christ will not recognize anyone as a member of His body who has not done what *He* said in *His* gospel to become a member of *His* church. Fourth, all denominations are mere followers of people and not "branches" of Christ. Their misapplication of Christ's words may seem to work for now but will be useless in the life to come.

Denominational Christianity?

Denominational leaders are never going to insist on following the NT pattern in its entirety simply because it will expose their own inconsistency toward it. This would be like cutting one's own throat. This is very similar to what the Roman Church did for centuries when it kept printed Bibles from the masses and only allowed them to be translated into a dead language (Latin) that only their trained priests could read. They did not want the people to discover how far away from the Scriptures that Church had strayed.

Today, however, anyone can obtain a Bible in virtually any language, so access to information is no longer the issue. Instead, the issue is a widespread failure (or refusal) to study the revealed word of God for the purpose in which it was intended (2 Tim. 2:15). Like the denominational leaders themselves, many people who are members of denominations are unwilling to allow the light of the gospel to expose their churches for what they really are. In my experience, such members are far quicker (and more zealous) to defend their denominations than they are the Scriptures.

On the other hand, denominational Christianity—a contradictory phrase, but this is what people call it—has been very successful in overseas missionary work. This sounds noble, of course, and is admittedly the result of great effort and expense on their part. The problem here is not their zealous effort to bring a message to those who need it. Rather, it is the content of that message. Bringing a good message that has been corrupted with human motives, emphasizes human division, and approves of human ideas posing as the gospel truth must never be called "good." Many of these missionaries are not proclaiming the pure, unadulterated gospel of Christ but are instead peddling their own version of that message. In the process, they are claiming to be "making Christians" according to a method that suits their denominational creed but is foreign to the NT pattern. Paul's words to the Corinthians' misuse of the Lord's Supper apply here: "Shall I praise you? In this I will not praise you" (1 Cor. 11:22).

Jesus said to the Jewish leaders, "Woe to you, scribes and Pharisees, hypocrites, because you travel around on sea and land to make one proselyte; and when he becomes one, you make him twice as much a son of hell as yourselves" (Mat. 23:15). This scathing rebuke—from no less than the Lord Himself—rightly applies in principle to anyone who converts someone to a mere *form* of the Christian faith rather than "the simplicity and purity of devotion to Christ" (2 Cor. 11:3). "It is one thing to teach the Bible; it is quite another to teach psychology and denominational theology."[158]

If you read the Quran, it leads you to become a Muslim. If you read the Book of Mormon, it leads you to become a Mormon. If you read the NT, it leads you to become a *Christian*—not one version, brand, type, flavor, or kind of Christian, but a Christian in the truest sense of the word: a *Christ-follower*. All religions that invoke Christ's name for their own agendas, borrow from His word, hijack His church system, and turn discipleship to Him into a form of entertainment "did not learn Christ in [that] way" (Eph. 4:20). All of this came from people, not the Lord; the word of God did not lead them to do any of this.[159] No apostle of Christ, if he were still alive today, would have taught or sanctioned any of this. The Holy Spirit did not reveal any of this, except as a manifestation of apostasy (2 Tim. 4:3–4).

This is strong language, to be sure, but it is not new. Two thousand years ago, Christ said that all "worship" under the pretense of man-made religion is "vain" (Mat. 15:9). The apostle Paul said that "if any man is preaching to you a gospel contrary to what you have received [from him and the other apostles—MY WORDS], he is to be accursed!" (Gal. 1:9). What does denominationalism promote, but human-manufactured worship and a gospel contrary to what was revealed from heaven? This brings with it nothing less than a divine curse. It is amazing—and terribly sad—that there is such a widespread acceptance of a religious system that God says pointedly is wrong. Where is the outcry? If denominational church leaders started killing puppies, you can only imagine the outrage that would ensue, both from their own memberships and the public. But leading human souls astray barely receives a raised eyebrow, then a shrug of resignation.

Confronting Church Leadership

If what has just been described is the church system that *you*, dear reader, are engaged in, what is *your* response? Now that you know what the Bible teaches, will you continue in a denominational system that contradicts this? If you know *the truth*, then will you continue in a direction that opposes that truth?

If I were you, the first thing I would do is: pray to God for help, courage, and a better understanding of His word. Then, I would call for a meeting with my church leadership and confront them with the passages that have been cited in this chapter and ask them to defend their denominational system *from the Scriptures*. If they refused to conform to the NT pattern but wished to keep doing what they have been doing, I would leave that church and find a group of people that will honor the word of God fully, even to its own hurt.

If you are willing to confront your denominational church leadership, do not expect a warm reception. Most likely they will respond in one of the following ways:

- They will attempt to discredit *me* rather than respond to your questions. In our modern "cancel culture" of shutting down, dismissing, or demonizing anyone that disagrees with the common narrative, this is to be expected. Yet, it fails to justify their position.
- They will claim that I am just "mincing words," "nitpicking," or being "legalistic"—another attempt to discredit me rather than address the problem. (Recall what was said earlier: it is not "legalistic" to defer to *God's law* for Christians and their churches.)
- They will claim that it is just a difference in "interpretation," even though it does not take a seminary degree to understand clearly what Jesus, the Holy Spirit, and Paul have said. God's law to His people (i.e., His gospel) is something we all can "read and understand" (Eph. 3:4). Think of what Jesus said, when questioned by a scribe: "What is written in the Law [of Moses]? How does it read to you?" (Luke 10:26). The principle here is timeless. Read the Scriptures yourself: what do they say to you?
- Instead of attempting to discredit me, they will try to discredit you. They will use their position, status, degrees, or personality to intimidate you and, essentially, tell you that you are not knowledgeable enough *in* the Scriptures to (dare!) question them *about* the Scriptures. They are the authorities; you are just, well, someone who is underqualified.
- They will tell you that their denomination has been around for a very long time and that you are calling into question the many, many people that have supported it. Yet, it is not *you* who calls those people into question; it is the *Scriptures that you are citing* that call the ones you are talking to into question. You would do well to insist on a biblical answer from them. Let God deal with all the others; that is not your business. You are looking after your own soul, and your church leadership ought to be helping you with this rather than standing in your way.
- It is possible that, if you are insistent on biblical answers and they are unable to provide them, they will tell you to leave their

congregation/denomination. Instead of offering a "ready defense to everyone who asks you to give an account for the hope that lies within [them]" (1 Peter 3:15), they will simply paint you as an uncooperative, nonconforming dissident and get rid of you. Be prepared for this upfront.

- In a rare but hopeful instance, they will say, "We cannot argue with Scripture. We have been doing it wrong all this time, but we are going to change that. From now on, we will let the NT pattern dictate all our beliefs, our teaching, and our practices. Thank you *so much* for bringing this to our attention!" I do not mean to be pessimistic here, but do not hold your breath in expectation of hearing this. Such people have far too much to lose to walk away from their positions so quickly. Even so, this is the best response you could receive.

Suppose in response to all that has been said about denominationalism, you say, "I go to a *non*-denominational (or the increasingly popular *un*-denominational) church, so therefore we are legitimate." The legitimacy of a congregation is not determined by how you or I describe it, but how the NT pattern does. It may well be that your church is following the pattern as best as it can; if so, then give it your full support. On the other hand, it is possible for any church to have the right organizational structure and still be promoting wrong teachings and unbiblical

practices. Focusing on only one aspect of a congregation does not adequately assess its fellowship with Christ. A house that is structurally sound but filled with black mold is still a problem. Citing the good framework will not fix this.

The fact is: *any* church—regardless of its professed status—can succumb to what might be called the spirit of denominationalism. This "spirit" claims that the only way you can be right with God is to be right with *that church* (or its system of churches). To get to God, so to speak, you must go through them (the church's leadership and its supporters)—their beliefs, their doctrine, their dogma, their traditions, their method of becoming a Christian, and their decisions.

So then, while a church's structure or design may technically adhere to the biblical pattern, its attitude and theology may not. No person, church, or religion has the right to serve as the mediator between you and God. Only Christ has this right: "I am the way, and the truth, and the life; no one comes to the Father but through Me" (John 14:6). Consider all that I have written here: I am not asking you to conform to me or my congregation; I am constantly telling you to *follow Christ* and *His pattern*. Gaining my approval will not help you; gaining Christ's approval, however, leads to the salvation of your soul.

Summary Thoughts

A lot of attention has been devoted here to one specific form of departure from the NT pattern (denominationalism) only because so many people have readily and unhesitatingly accepted it. This system poses as something good, sound, biblical, and God-approved. Its preachers, pastors, and priests remind its members constantly of all the "good works" that it is carrying out in God's name. So, on the surface, this seems positive and honorable. Sadly, very few people are holding this system up to the actual NT pattern to see if the two match. If they did this, glaring inconsistencies would suddenly be evident.

Calling into question centuries of church tradition is never popular, and it is even hard to have a civil dialogue on the subject. The "arguments" in support of denominational churches often begin as biblical, citing NT Christianity in the most basic sense. However, they quickly descend into emotional appeals: "Look at all the good our church is doing!"; "Many people's lives are being touched because of our church's efforts!"; "Our church has a loving passion for serving the Lord and

His people!"; etc. Such appeals assume much yet prove nothing. Emotional appeals must never be held on par with NT instruction. Christ never told us to invoke emotionalism to defend His gospel, but God's recorded truth (2 Tim. 3:16–17, in principle). This is what we should expect from any group that claims to identify as the Lord's people.

It should not be too much to ask for denominations to defend themselves from the Scriptures if indeed they are legitimate church systems. After all, every denomination claims to "follow the Bible" and "obey the Lord Jesus." If this is true, then church leadership should do the right thing and educate all their members—and everyone else—on why they promote a system of Christian religion that looks very different from what anyone can read about in the NT. They should stop citing historic edicts, synods, councils, and ecclesiastic decisions rendered from their own denomination's church leadership and focus only on the NT pattern. They should stop putting all their energy into trying to discredit those who call them into question and provide instead an intelligent, biblical, and convincing defense for who they are and what they are doing.

Denominational church leadership does not have to answer to me; *no* church is required to answer to me. But I am not the one that they should be concerned about. Rather, it is the Lord Jesus Christ to whom they will give an answer, and this ought to give them serious concern. It was He who said, "Every plant which My heavenly Father did not plant shall be uprooted" (Mat. 15:13). If God did not "plant" denominational church systems, then these will be "uprooted," despite claims of incidental good works that they may be accomplishing (Mat. 7:21–23, in principle). Instead of trusting in centuries of man-made religion and man-rendered decisions, one should listen to what Jesus said about any "plant" that He did not authorize.

All those who are involved in denominational religion have access to the same Scriptures that I do. They can read what Christ and His apostles said just like I can. They can understand the NT pattern as easily as I or anyone else can. One does not need a seminary education or a Doctor of Divinity (DD) degree to "read and understand" (Eph. 3:4) what has been written, recorded, and preserved for the last 2,000 years. The NT was not written for preachers, seminary students, theologians, or what is often called "clergy." It was written for *all* people and *any* person who wishes to "be saved and to come to the knowledge of the truth" (1 Tim. 2:4).

You do not need me, preachers, or any denominational teacher to tell you how to be in fellowship with God. All you need, when everything is said and done, is what God has revealed in His word. This is true for the individual believer as it is for the collective groups (churches) of believers.

Endnotes

1   R. K. Harrison, "Bible," *International Standard Bible Encyclopedia*, electronic edition (© 1979 Wm. B. Eerdmans Publishing Co.; database © 2013 WORDsearch Corp.).

2   This does not mean that there was no death involved, however, in establishing a covenant between God and people. The first covenant, between God and Israel, required the sprinkling of blood from those animals slain to ratify that covenant (Exod. 24:1–8, Heb. 9:15–22). The second covenant, between God and Christians, required the death of the Son of God to ratify it. We obtain fellowship with God because of Christ's sacrificial death, and those who enter a covenant with God are "sprinkled with [Christ's] blood" (1 Peter 1:2).

3   In a parallel example, see Jer. 11:1–8, where God curses any Israelite who "does not heed the words of this covenant"—i.e., the covenant that God had made with the nation of Israel. While we are not bound to that covenant today, the principle still applies. God still condemns all forms of covenant-breaking, regardless of the alleged good intentions of those who do this.

4   The citation is from 2 Tim. 3:16–17; bracketed words are mine.

5   "Legalism" has nothing to do with obeying God's laws but seeks to impose one's *own expectations* upon others as though this were necessary for salvation. Legalists are not monsters; many of them truly believe that they are honorable and justified in what they are doing. However, they see fit to qualify one's fellowship with God based on their own standard of righteousness. One ought never to conclude that, because legal*ism* is condemned, conforming to God's laws is also condemned. This is untrue: to pursue fellowship with God, we are committed to keeping His commandments (1 John 5:2–3). More will be said on this later in this book.

6   "They who boast of their liberality are, many times, the most narrow and unreasonable bigots. They are liberal while they differ from the old church authorities and are perfectly willing that you should join them in their new view of inspiration, or [their new view of] obedience to Christ, but they are unwilling that you should differ from them. Hence it is plain that they have reached their views without the tedium of the introduction of facts and the uncompromising use of logic, but have simply jumped to their conclusions without any such examination, and are determined that the rest of the world shall adopt their views of liberality" (D. R. Dungan, *Hermeneutics: A Text-book* [Delight, AR:

Gospel Light Publishing Co., no date (orig. 1888)], 79; bracketed words are mine). In other words, such people proudly claim to be "tolerant" and "open-minded," but only if you agree with them. If you do not, they brand you a "legalist" and level all kinds of accusations against you, instead of providing a biblical defense of their beliefs.

7   "Reformation" refers to the reforming of the Roman (Catholic) Church, which had a great deal of unbiblical teachings, papal and clerical abuses, and a heavy-handed imposition upon the religious, social, and political realms of all those under its power. Officially, the Reformation is said to begin with Martin Luther (1483 – 1546), who, in 1517, nailed a list of 95 charges against the Roman Church on the door of the church in Wittenberg, Germany. These are historically referred to as the "95 Theses." Luther's posting of these charges was not thought to be a break from the Roman Church, but a call for dialogue, explanation, and (as needed) reform. However, this posting set in motion a great movement which quickly *did* break from the Roman Church, then quickly splintered into several other religious groups.

8   "As I read human history, I find that every movement to break the shackles of ignorance and superstition and to make way for the entrance of the pure radiance of Heaven-born light has been the work of individual men and women, looking for help to no sort of organic control or indorsement [sic]. Their first step has been to break away from every entanglement of ecclesiastic mesh work and recognize themselves as directly responsible to God for the use they make of the provisions of divine grace. This whole idea of waiting for some human sanction and committing the grand question, 'What shall I do?' to the decision of any sort of corporate existence, no matter how nicely adjusted and officiated, is most ruinous and destructive of vigor and energy in the Master's service" (W. Lipscomb, "God's Means of Work," *Restoration Ideas on Church Organization,* compiled by J. Ridley Stoop [Nashville, TN: David Lipscomb College, no date], 33).

9   James Strong, *Strong's Talking Greek-Hebrew Dictionary,* electronic edition (database © 2003 by WORDsearch Corp.; orig. published 1890), G5546.

10   *Ibid.,* G5547. Some think "Jesus Christ" is the first and last name of God's Son. This is not true. "Jesus" is His given name for His human form ("in the flesh"—John 1:14), in which He identifies with those whom He seeks to save (Rom. 8:3–4). This earthly designation was determined by God, not by His mother (Mat. 1:21, 25, Luke 1:26–33).

"Christ" identifies Jesus' mission as the divinely anointed Savior of all of humankind: "the Lamb of God who takes away the sin of the world" (John 1:29). "Jesus Christ" indicates that the Man *Jesus* and the Savior *Christ* are one and the same person. An "antichrist" [lit., against Christ] is one who denies that Jesus *the Man* is the Christ *the Son of God* (i.e., a divine being), as the apostle John says: "Who is the liar but the one who denies that Jesus is the Christ? This is the antichrist, the one who denies the Father and the Son" (1 John 2:22).

11 All Christians are moralists; not all moralists are Christians. A "moralist" is one who upholds the ideal morals, virtues, and principles of what it means to be a decent human being. This requires, of course, an authoritative standard by which to make such a decision, and the NT is often the de facto source for this. While moralists who are not Christians will agree with the moral value system of the NT, they have not committed themselves to be followers of the source of that system, which is Jesus Christ. Christians, on the other hand, have made themselves followers of Christ and thus agree to the moral value system which He has revealed in His gospel.

12 F. LaGard Smith, *Who Is My Brother?* (Nashville, TN: Cotswold Publishing, 1997), 120.

13 Calvinism, a man-made doctrine that misrepresents the gospel of Christ, teaches that "the called" are those who are already saved by God before they were even born. Not only is this unbiblical, but it has also misled an untold number of people into believing that they are "saved" or "lost" simply because of this belief.

14 Strong, *Dictionary* (electronic), G1577. "In the time of Thucydides, about four hundred years before Christ, the Greek historians used the word 'ekklesia,' of which 'church' is the representative in the English Scriptures, in the sense of an assembly. Composed of 'ek,' meaning 'out,' and 'kaleo,' 'to call,' it literally meant a called-out assembly" (M. C. Kurfees, "The Church Revealed in the Bible," *Restoration Ideas*, 12. "[This 'called-out' phrase] does not mean that they [believers] were thus called into an ecclesiastical or legislative institution; it only means that they were called out from the world into a new relationship with Christ, or, in other words, were called into the spiritual body of Christ, of which He is the spiritual head" (E. G. Sewell, "The Church of Christ and of God—What Is It?", *Restoration Ideas*, 8; bracketed words are mine).

15 This is expressed *generally* throughout all of Jesus' teachings concerning entrance into the kingdom of God. Certain requirements

must be met: humility of spirit, belief in God and His Son, faithful submission, obedience to the gospel, and commitment to following Jesus. This is expressed graphically in, for example, the parable of the wedding feast (Mat. 22:1–14), where a man is forcibly removed from the feast because he refused to dress properly for the occasion. (According to Oriental tradition, if a man was invited to such a feast and could not afford the proper clothing, the king would provide these at his own expense. The implication, then, is that the man in the parable *refused* the king's offer, yet thought he was still welcome to participate.)

16 I have written considerably on this subject before. I recommend my book, *The Gospel of Saving Grace* (Spiritbuilding Publishers, 2020); go to www.spiritbuilding.com/chad.

17 To clarify, there is no man-made linking of churches in the NT. At best, the only grouping of churches we see is based upon geography, not human decisions, dogma, or distinctive practices. For example, Paul wrote to "the churches of Galatia" (Gal. 1:2), a region in the middle of modern-day Turkey, and Jesus dictated letters to "the seven churches" of Asia Minor, a Roman province (Rev. 1:11). Yet, in both cases, each church addressed was held responsible to apostolic teaching rather than told to unite as one conglomerate of churches. Notice, too, that in both cases, there was not a so-called "mother church" that answered for or gave directions to all the others.

18 "The word 'congregation' is from the two Latin words *con* and *grex*. *Con* means 'together' and *grex* means 'a flock.' Hence, a congregation means a flock together or a flock assembled. To take the word literally, therefore, Christians compose a congregation only when they are congregated or assembled. But we use the word to mean those in a town or community who meet together for worship at a stated place and at appointed times" (G. C. Brewer, *The Model Church*, quoted in *The Restoration Reader and Review,* electronic edition, ed. Kevin L. Greer [vol. 4, no. 3: March, 2022], 8).

19 Dave Miller, quoting Michael Casey from *Restoration Quarterly* (1989), in Piloting the Strait (Pulaski, TN: Sain Publications, 1996), 152.

20 There are three such journeys recorded in the book of Acts: Paul's first journey, with Barnabas (Acts 13 – 14); his second journey, with Silas (Acts 15:36 – 18:22), and his third journey, with various men (Acts 18:23 – 21:17).

21 Smith, *Who Is My Brother?*, 168.

22 By "gifts," there is no need to assume that miraculous ability is meant, although it is true that the apostle Paul wrote at a time when such abilities were imparted by the Holy Spirit to certain Christians. He also provided direction for the use of these gifts in the assemblies, to avoid mishandling, confusion, or chaos (see 1 Cor. 14, in particular). However, the miracles and miraculous gifts of the very early church were necessary to provide confirmation and direction in a time when no written record yet existed to cite or provide instruction. Now that we have this instruction in the form of the NT, we are no longer in need of such verification or revelations. While miraculous gifts have ceased, God's many other kinds of gifts to His people have not. For further reading on the work of the Holy Spirit, His miraculous gifts, and why these gifts are no longer necessary, I strongly recommend my book, *The Holy Spirit of God: A Biblical Perspective* (Spiritbuilding Publishers, 2010); go to www.spiritbuilding.com/chad.

23 Edward C. Wharton, *The Church of Christ* (Nashville, TN: Gospel Advocate Co., 1997), 121.

24 *Ibid.,* 124.

25 *Ibid.,* 121.

26 Recall what I wrote in this book's "Introduction." In all "restoration" efforts, we need to be careful what, exactly, we are seeking to restore. A wayward Christian can be restored to his original pledge of fidelity to Christ; a church system can be restored to the NT pattern. But *the church*—the spiritual body of Christ—has no need of our restoration efforts since it has never fallen away from Christ Himself.

27 One of the greatest known patterns is that of human DNA. Within each human cell is a blueprint to recreate *the entire human body,* not to mention the specialized pattern for individual organs, the greatest of which is the human brain. It is illogical and entirely unscientific to assume that a complex and sophisticated blueprint created itself over time apart from a Creator. It is literally impossible for organized, intelligent, and recorded information to just "happen" or evolve into existence—no matter how much time is assumed for this.

28 Miller, *Piloting the Strait,* 131–132.

29 Wharton, *The Church of Christ,* 14.

30 Wharton, *Ibid.,* 14–15.

31 For a much fuller description of God (and why He must be "God"), I recommend my book, *Seeking the Sacred* (Spiritbuilding Publishers, 2009); go to www.spiritbuilding.com/chad.

32 If we *are* justified by sincerity and good intentions, then the gospel would just say so, and would be rather brief ("Just be sincere and have good intentions, and you will be saved!—The End"). But the gospel does not say this, and all the instructions for Christians and their churches indicate that we are to conform to God's plan rather than Him simply accepting whatever we deem "good" and "sincere." In fact, it is impossible for one to claim to be good or sincere if he has access to this information but simply refuses, for any reason, to abide by it.

33 For a much fuller discussion on the afterlife, I recommend my book, *This World Is Not Your Home* (Spiritbuilding Publishers, 2021); go to www.spiritbuilding.com/chad.

34 Adapted from Dungan, *Hermeneutics*, 48–58.

35 Miller, *Piloting the Strait*, 62.

36 A "tabernacle" is a portable and temporary unit; a "temple" is a stationary and permanent structure. Our physical body is referred to as an "earthly tent [or, tabernacle]" (2 Cor. 5:1); likewise, when the Son of God "became flesh," He "dwelt among us"—literally, "He tabernacled among us" (John 1:14). Our earthly lives are finite, temporary, and not permanently tethered to this world. But the church is never referred to as a tabernacle, but a temple, since it is a fixed, unmovable, and permanent structure built upon an eternal and unchanging foundation. Likewise, a Christian—in the spiritual context—is also a temple, since his place in the Presence of God is (ideally) fixed and permanent, extending beyond this life and into the eternity to come.

37 A Levitical priest who refused to wash would be condemned to death (Exod. 30:18–21). God will not allow men to serve Him who are unprepared or unfit to do so. Similarly, refusing to be "washed" through baptism yet assuming permission to enter holy communion with God does not remove one's condemnation but only compounds it. Baptism is as much an act of faith as is any other form of obedience to God's word (Gal. 3:26–27). A refusal to obey can never be reconciled with "faithfulness," despite many people being seemingly oblivious to this most basic understanding.

38 The Israelite men were commanded to wear blue cords or tassels on the "corners of their garments" to outwardly identify them as belonging to God (Num. 15:38–41). This also reminded the men to think twice before carelessly engaging in any immoral activity. Incidentally, blue is a color often associated in Scripture with holiness and was used in the curtain fabric of the tabernacle (Exod. 26:1), the garments of the priests (Exod. 28:2–6), and the covering for the ark of the covenant and other

furniture in the transport of the tabernacle (Num. 4:6–12.)

39 Wharton, *Ibid.*, 15.

40 The citation is from 1 Sam. 2:30, but the entire context (1 Sam. 2:12–30) ought to be considered to appreciate the full force of God's judgment here.

41 See also Mat. 12:25, where Jesus said, "Any kingdom divided against itself is laid waste; and any city or house divided against itself will not stand." If Christ *was* divided (among hundreds of competing and contradicting faiths), then He and His church is certain to fail.

42 There are several passages where Christians in a particular church are told to be united, of the same mind, and "that there be no divisions among you"—see Rom. 12:16, 1 Cor. 1:10, Phil. 1:27, 2:1–5, etc. These passages can be extended to the entire brotherhood of believers since we all belong to the same body of Christ as "one new man" (Eph. 2:13–16). This "new man" cannot be divided up into many different parts but must remain entire and complete.

43 This is reminiscent of Luke 16:16, where Jesus said that many Jews were "forcing" their way into the kingdom—in essence, trying to enter the kingdom of God by means (deceptively, doctrinally, militarily, or otherwise) that God never approved of. So it is today: many people have, in essence, "forced" their way into Christ's church through a means by which Christ never approved. This does not mean that Christ just shrugs in resignation and allows them to enter anyway; it means that they really are not whom they think they are.

44 Paul refers to "those who are baptized for the dead" (1 Cor. 15:29) in his lengthy discourse on the resurrection. This has since been construed to mean that a living believer can be baptized *in place of* one who has died outside of Christ, thus saving that dead person's soul in the hereafter. Think about what this teaches: baptism by proxy; substitutionary baptism; salvation (in the hereafter) without faith, obedience, or sacrifice (in one's earthly life); a salvation that is dependent upon the decision of a person other than the one being saved; a different method of salvation than is given to everyone else; etc. None of these teachings are part of the NT pattern. Whatever Paul meant in his reference could not have been any of these things. A full reading of the context reveals that most likely Paul referred to those Christians who were baptized *with a view toward* the resurrection of the dead.

45 This necessarily implies: if one has not been *made* a Christian according to Christ's authority, then that person must rectify that

situation and become a Christian as outlined in Christ's pattern.

46 I have written on the subject of "miracles" and modern so-called miracle-workers in my book, *The Holy Spirit: A Biblical Perspective* (Spiritbuilding Publishers, 2010); go to www.spiritbuilding.com/chad.

47 The word "pastor" (only used in Eph. 4:11 in the NASB) is from the Greek word *poimen,* which means "shepherd," and is nearly always translated as such (Strong, *Dictionary* [electronic], G4166). A shepherd, in the context of the NT church, is an elder or overseer. It is the only official position described in the church beyond the apostleship itself, which is no longer an active role. Thus, when people call their preacher a "pastor" and put him in a role above that of church-appointed elders, they are doing something for which there is no NT teaching or practice. Likewise, when they use "pastor" as a title ("Pastor So-and-So"), they elevate him above everyone else.

48 Someone might argue, "But there are several positions in the church that contribute to the overall function of the group but are not mentioned in Scripture, such as treasurer; secretary; youth (or seniors) ministers; etc." The difference here in my "pastor" example is the *kind* of role people have assigned to him. These other roles are expedient and thus expendable in nature; they are descriptive, not "official" (i.e., office-holding). The modern pastor, however, is deemed an office-holding role, and he officiates or exercises authority that is nowhere in the NT given to him. In being set above even the church elders, he usurps *their* roles as shepherds over the flock (1 Pet. 5:1–3). Typically, these other descriptive roles do not do this, nor are they intended to do this.

49 This quote is from Thomas Scirghi, *Everything Is Sacred: An Introduction to the Sacrament of Baptism* (Orleans, MA: Paraclete Press, 2012), 108.

50 I do not believe Jesus is speaking of His Second Coming in this context, but most likely His judgment against the Roman Empire. Churches that did not remain faithful to Him would be swept up in that judgment and face severe consequences or even be destroyed. In any case, Jesus speaks of a (then) future time when His patience and mercy for these churches will have been exhausted.

51 On a related note, amid a multicultural community we should not have a Korean church, a Hispanic church, a black church, a Ukrainian church, etc. We should have *Christ's* churches that do not cater to one culture, color of skin, or ethnicity. Christ's blood has brought us all together into "one new man" (Eph. 2:13–18); it is not right that we

should once again divide ourselves according to earthly distinctions. I have yet to hear a justifiable and biblical reason why we should *segregate* when Christ has called us to be *united*.

52 This happens, for example, with Rom. 10:9–10, where many claim that "all you need to do" is believe in God and confess Christ, "and you will be saved." While belief and confession are required *for* salvation, these two things by themselves necessarily imply that whatever is *involved* in "belief" and "confession" are also required. Yet, we could cite 1 Peter 3:15, where Peter makes it sound like "all you need to do" is to be baptized, but the same people who rest solely upon the "believe and confess" method will balk at this. Clearly, neither Paul nor Peter are being *exclusive* in their instruction (as in, "Only this thing and no other!"); they are simply speaking about what must be *included* in one's salvation. Thus, to confess that Christ came from God and believe that He was raised from the dead is just as important as being baptized into Christ in an appeal to God for a good conscience.

53 Smith, *Who Is My Brother?*, 122. He also says: "When one starts with Scripture and stays with Scripture, the texts pertaining to Christian birth are clear and unequivocal: baptism is an essential prerequisite to forgiveness, salvation, and kingdom fellowship. At that point Christian unity finds its natural boundary around all those who have been immersed in faith into the family of God. By contrast, when one goes about it backwards—starting, instead, with subjective feelings about where the boundaries of Christian unity ought to be—the inevitable result is an end run around the many texts which speak so clearly about how we come into a saved, forgiven relationship with God" (ibid., 41–42).

54 The biblical teaching on the necessity of baptism for salvation is strong and consistent: John 3:5, Mat. 28:19, Acts 2:38, 8:12, 8:35–39, 9:18, 10:47–48, 16:14–15, 16:31–33, 18:8, 19:1–5, 22:16, Rom. 6:3–7, 1 Cor. 12:12–13, Gal. 3:26–27, Col. 2:9–12, Titus 3:5, Heb. 10:22, and 1 Pet. 3:21–22. For a further study on baptism, I strongly recommend my book, *Being Born of God: The Role and Significance of Baptism in Becoming a Christian* (Spiritbuilding Publishers, 2014); go to www.spiritbuilding.com/chad.

55 Smith, *Ibid.*, 47.

56 Only those who repented and were baptized received "the gift of the Holy Spirit" (Acts 2:38). Many today think that this "gift" was the ability to perform miracles, but the text does not support this. The

context here has nothing to do with performing miracles, but with *salvation* in the name of Jesus Christ—a new and unprecedented means of obtaining fellowship with God the Father. Later, the apostles will lay their hands upon believers for the purpose of miracles (Acts 8:12–17). The phrase, "receive the Holy Spirit" has different meanings, depending upon the context. For a much more in-depth study on this subject, I recommend my book, *The Holy Spirit of God: A Biblical Perspective* (Spiritbuilding Publishers, 2010); go to www.spiritbuilding.com/chad.

57 Many denominationalists reject baptism as a "work," claiming that we are not "saved by works"—citing Eph. 2:8–9—but then require a person to repent, confess the name of Jesus, recite a scripted "sinners" prayer, etc. The fact is: anything that we must do as an act of faith is also a work of faith. Such works do not save us by themselves (which is Paul's point in Eph. 2:8–9), but this does not mean they are not required of us (Rom. 5:1–2).

58 This speaks to the collective work of Christians, not to *everything* or *every assembly* of Christians. "We can meet as Christians, and do all that the word of the Lord requires us to do without organizing" (E. G. Sewell, "Organization," *Restoration Ideas,* 51). This is true regarding worship and Christian fellowship, but it cannot be true regarding *getting things done* over an extended period. Christians can assemble in any building and carry out the functions of worship, but they need to be organized to be identified as a known and deliberate group of workers. All such organization requires leadership, and leadership of any kind implies some form of organization, however basic this might be. We cannot act as an organized body without different *organs* working *together* to fulfill different *functions,* as Paul illustrated in 1 Cor. 12:12–21.

59 Some are critical of the word "organize" because it is not in the New Testament. "The word 'organization' is not found in the Bible and has introduced much confusion. In using the words 'organization' and 'organize' which are not found in the Bible, we are almost sure to present ideas not found there" (David Lipscomb, "Questions Answered by Restoration Scribes," *Restoration Ideas,* 195). Yet, neither is "song leader," "baptistery," "pulpit," "collection tray," and even "Bible" in the New Testament, but no one seems to have a problem with using these words. "Organization" is being used very generally here. It does not refer to individual Christians coming together to create a congregation according to their own design. This thought violates the premise of this book as well as the entire New Testament pattern.

Rather, it speaks to those who *use* the God-given pattern to carry out Christians' collective and God-given work. It should not be construed to mean anything more than this.

60 This passage is not cited to support the idea of miracle-working among Christians today but does show that whatever God gave the early church (in lieu of the written record) was for its stability, structure, and organization.

61 A good analogy here is that of building a large structure. Early on, scaffolding is needed to put it together. Once the building is completed, however, the scaffolding is removed, since its purpose has been served. So it is with apostles and miracles: the blueprint (or pattern) for Christ's church has been fully revealed (or "once for all handed down to the saints"—Jude 1:3). Now that the "building" is complete, there is no longer a need for the scaffolding. Having more apostles and more miracles does not change what has already been fully established.

62 "Teaching the word of God, and exhorting men to obey it, needs no official authority" (E. G. Sewell, "The Tract on Church Organization Again," *Restoration Ideas,* 89). This is true, as regards an official capacity for preachers. But the role of the preacher is not an "office," and therefore he is not an "officer" of the church, nor does he have any authority outside of the word of God. On the other hand, Paul's point (in Eph. 4:11) is not to name "officials" of Christ's church but *functions* or *responsibilities* that certain men will need to fulfill. Thus, while a preacher is not an officer of the church, he does commit to a specific responsibility *of* the church, and in this way, he is considered a Christ-given "gift" to the church. This is because of the work he does, not because of any individual merit or special recognition of him personally.

63 This "love" must be defined by Christ since He is the head of the body of those who are to love one another (John 13:34–35). To "hate" one's brother, in the context of John's letter, means to withhold godly love from him for any reason (see 1 John 3:11–18).

64 The Greek word for "church" *(ekklesia)* is also used with no reference to Christ or His redeemed people. In Acts 19:39, 41, the town clerk of Ephesus refers to the mob of people who had gathered in the city as "the assembly"—lit., the *ekklesia,* elsewhere translated "church."

65 Right here is one of the great errors of Catholicism: the idea that a man (along with an ecclesiastic body of men—the Vatican) can oversee the entire brotherhood of Christ on earth. While it is true that the Pope

and his magisterial priests do rule over the Catholic Church, they have no authority to rule over all of Christ's people. Likewise, no man (or woman) can appoint himself, or be appointed, to this role, since this authority belongs to Christ and Him alone.

66 "Although no congregation is to be a watchdog over any other local congregation or group of congregations, individually and collectively we are still our brothers' keepers. We owe it to each other to contend for the faith in both our immediate and extended families. What we must be careful never to cross is the line between mutual edification, on one hand, and usurping the responsibility given to local churches and their spiritual leaders, on the other" (Smith, *Ibid.*, 172).

67 This word "autonomous" comes from a Greek compound word, *auto-* ("self") and *nomos* ("law" or "rule"). It is not a biblical word, but most certainly identifies biblical teaching on the nature of church organization.

68 The fact that elders are appointed necessarily implies that they are not *recognized* as a given congregation's leaders *until* they are appointed or inducted into that role. They ought to have already been doing "elder work," as is sometimes said, but they are *not* elders in the biblical capacity until *appointed* as such. While no elaborate ceremony or formal ordination is necessary for this appointment, it needs to be an appointment all the same. Prior to this, these men were not elders; after their appointment, they *are*. This is like becoming a Christian: prior to one's baptism into Christ, even if a person was very devout in his pursuit of God, he is not a Christian; after his baptism, he is recognized as a Christian (as in the case of Cornelius in Acts 10, for example).

69 Management and leadership are not the same thing. Management has to do with sorting, organizing, classifying, etc.—i.e., giving a certain order to things that otherwise are disorderly or chaotic. Leadership has to do with *leading* people in a certain direction, for a certain reason, and with an appropriate means of guidance. True leaders know the way in which to go, are going that way themselves in all sincerity, and are actively inspiring others to follow them. Leading is far more difficult than managing. For this reason, in my multi-decade observation, many church elders are good organizers and decision-makers, but few provide quality leadership for their churches.

70 For further study on "elders," their work, and their appointment, I recommend my *1 & 2 Timothy Study Workbook and Titus and James Study Workbook* (Spiritbuilding Publishers); go to www.spiritbuilding.com/chad.

71 Bruce A. Ware, "Believer's Baptism View," *Baptism: Three Views,* David F. Wright, ed. (Downer's Grove, IL: InterVarsity Press, 2009), 70–71.

72 The idea of a "rogue" Christian—or, more often, a "floating" Christian that bounces from one church to another without ever committing to any of them—is foreign to the NT. This refers, for example, to Christians who demand such perfection of churches that no single church can satisfy their expectations; have such stringent beliefs that no church will welcome them; are retired and want to be on permanent vacation from all church responsibilities; or are running from a shameful past and do not want this to be discovered. Such people cherry-pick the teaching, efforts, and sacrifices of every group without contributing to any of it. They take advantage of established groups and what they offer for their (the floaters') own personal gain, but if everyone did what they did, there could be no established groups. This scenario defies the NT model; it is selfish and unproductive.

73 This does not mean, and never has meant, that members must agree with everything the elders say or decide. Even godly men can make poor judgments at times or overlook critical information—and so can members that disagree with them. Submission to the elders does not mean 100% surrender of one's will to them. It means to voluntarily subject oneself to another, out of respect for that person's position, rank, or authority. Both parties—the elders who lead and the members who submit to them—are in pursuit of something greater and more important than their own personal interests (Phil. 2:3–4).

74 "Abuses and imperfections in membership and leadership are not valid reasons for indicting this New Testament plan as unworkable. The local church must struggle to attain the ideal as revealed in the word of God. In such a conscientious effort the church can attain a happy degree of mission accomplishment. The by-product will be peace, unity, spiritual growth, and congregational stability" (Wharton, *Ibid.*, 130).

75 This has traditionally been the case with those who are baptized and made Christians. It is almost always assumed that if a person is baptized by the congregation's preacher, elder, or member, and especially has been baptized in that congregation's baptistery, then the new Christian is automatically made a "member" of that same group. Yet, the believer's baptism is into *Christ,* not the congregation's membership. The elders would do well to talk with the newly baptized believer about his (or her) membership with the congregation, to establish the expectations of both parties. He should be given the right

to ask questions, ask for clarifications, and make a personal agreement to this. Too many Christians have been made "members" without their knowledge, consent, or understanding of what is required of them. If a Christian cannot be assumed a member by simply showing up to a church service, then a Christian should not be assumed a member simply by having been taught by an existing member—or worse, by being baptized in a church's baptistery. Baptism must *never* be the sole means of becoming a member of a known and identifiable congregation.

76 "Church membership does not consist in having [one's] name enrolled on a list; it consists in obedience to the Lord Jesus" (David Lipscomb, "Church Membership," *Restoration Ideas*, 31). If we are talking about membership in Christ, then yes. If we are talking about membership in a specific *congregation,* then obedience to Christ is necessary as well as submission to that congregation's elders (as a specific manifestation of obedience to Christ).

77 In 1 Tim. 3:1, "office of overseer" (NASB) comes from a single Greek word, *episkope;* it can also be translated "bishopric," or "office of a bishop" (KJV) (Strong, *Dictionary* [electronic], G1984). An *episkopos* (the person who holds the office; see Phil. 1:1) is a superintendent over a particular work, realm of authority, or people; he is over (*epi-*) those whom he sees, inspects, or visits (-*skopos,* from which we get "scope"). In no other place is an "office" associated with anyone in the churches, except for that of an apostle (Acts 1:20, with reference to the replacement of Judas Iscariot).

78 It has long been assumed that deacons hold an "official" position in the churches, and therefore are, by implication, officers, office-holders, or officiants. In his seminal book, *Scriptural Elders and Deacons* (Marion, IN: Cogdill Foundation Publications, 1959), for example, H. E. Phillips adamantly maintains that this is an office, entirely based upon the word "deacons" in 1 Tim. 3:13 (255), and the original KJV translation there as "office of a deacon." Yet, the Greek word used in this passage (*diakoneo*) is used 45 times in the NT, and never as an "office" or in an official (office-holding) capacity (Strong, *Dictionary,* G1247). William Hendriksen concurs: "Nowhere else in the New Testament does *diakoneo* mean serve as *deacon*. It means to serve, to minister, to care for one's needs (Matt. 20:28; Mark 10:45; Luke 10:40; 22:26; John 12:2; 2 Tim. 1:18; 1 Peter 4:11; etc.), or to *supply by ministering* (1 Peter 1:12; 4:20). The mere fact that Paul has just been speaking about deacons would seem to be hardly sufficient

to ascribe to the verb a technical sense which it has nowhere else in Scripture" ("1 Timothy," *New Testament Commentary: Thessalonians, the Pastorals, and Hebrews* [Grand Rapids: Baker Books, 1996], 135, fn. 67). In any case, based on this assumption, women have been denied being appointed as deaconesses because it has been argued, they cannot usurp the authority of men in any "official" role. This is tradition speaking, not the Bible: deacons are servants, not officeholders, and not officials. While a congregation may refuse to appoint its women as deacons for other reasons, citing the "official" argument is inconsistent with what the NT teaches. For further study on this (and women's roles in general), I recommend my *1 & 2 Timothy Study Workbook* (Spiritbuilding Publishers, 2019); go to www.spiritbuilding.com/chad.

79 Referring to Mat. 20:25-28, where Jesus taught that the route to greatness is through servitude, Sewell says, "The whole work of the church is a system of service and not a matter of official authority. The Savior never did teach anything more plainly than He teaches this lesson in the above passage. He also gives Himself as an example. He was not an official over the people, simply to be respected for His official position; He came not to be ministered unto, but to minister, to serve, and was, without doubt, the greatest servant this world ever saw" ("Official Authority in the Church," *Restoration Ideas*, 91–92).

80 Cited from etymology.com. The NT often uses the Greek word *proskuneo*, which literally refers to kissing the ground (as in bowing prostrate) or licking the hand (like a dog would do to its master), both as a means of humility and submission (Strong, *Dictionary* [electronic], G4352).

81 Strong, *Dictionary* (electronic), G3619.

82 For a much fuller treatment of this subject, I recommend my *Galatians and Ephesians Study Workbook* (Spiritbuilding Publishers, 2011), especially the comments on Eph. 5:19; go to www.spiritbuilding.com/chad.

83 "Pentecost" means "fiftieth," as it was the fiftieth day after the Sabbath that was on or immediately followed Passover (Lev. 23:15–16). Thus, it was always on the first day of the week.

84 God commanded that the Sabbath ("rest") was to be observed by Israel as a part of His covenant with them (Exod. 20:8–11). Christians are never told to observe the Sabbath, a "sign" of the old covenant, but to come together on the "first day of the week," a day on which the *new* covenant is to be honored. To cling to Sabbath-keeping (as some denominations do today) is to honor that which has been superseded in

Christ—an "old" or "first" covenant made obsolete because it has been completely fulfilled (Heb. 8:1–6). Wherever the priesthood has changed, so has the law (Heb. 7:12); since Christ is now our High Priest, we are under a *new* law as part of a *new* covenant with God through Jesus Christ. It is impossible to marry the "signs" of the old covenant with those of the new since this ignores Christ's supremacy over Moses, the Law of Moses, and God's covenant with Israel.

85 Those who "assemble" by way of a screen, instead of in person, do not "participate" in the service any more than one participates in an actual football game by watching it on television in his own home. This reduces fellowship to a mere spectator event as if watching the service through the window of a church building, rather than personal human interaction. We cannot serve people remotely, sing together remotely, or carry out our discipleship to Christ remotely. People's rebuttal to all I have just said will be based on opinionated or emotional responses. Yet, no one can provide any biblical justification for why some can choose—for *any* reason—to remain at home and "assemble" with the congregation, while others are expected to literally assemble and carry out the actual work of such an assembly.

86 We are to "come together" to observe the Lord's Supper, not elect to take it in the privacy of our own homes—again, under the pretense of virtual assemblies. If you asked me to "come together" to have dinner with you, I could hardly do this remotely. Imagine you inviting me over for dinner, but me electing to eat my *own* dinner at my *own* house while videoconferencing with you! We would hardly be "together," and you would surely be offended.

87 To "break bread" in this context does not mean "eat a meal" but to partake of the memorial. In Acts 2:42, we see this as part of the spiritual fellowship among believers; in Acts 2:46, the same "breaking bread" phrase is used in a completely different context, as a means of social fellowship "from house to house" rather than in one assembly.

88 In some denominational churches, "tithing" is required, even to the point where one's income is disclosed to the church and his "tithe" is determined by the church. This sounds a lot like "under compulsion." Instead, one's offering to God ought to be a freewill offering—one that he decides, not his church or anyone else.

89 I say, "in principle," because Paul's instructions to the Corinthians were offered for a specific need and under specific circumstances. Paul himself was going to visit Corinth and collect the money; he did not want to have to wait for the money to be collected once he arrived. This

money was to be given to "the poor among the saints in Jerusalem" (Rom. 15:25–27). None of these factors have to do with why Christians *today* are collecting money: we are not waiting for Paul to arrive; we are not putting money together for a single donation to another church; we are not aiding the church in Jerusalem. However, the *principle* of this collection is the same: we collect money for Christians, particularly for those Christians of our own congregations *first*. The Corinthians would be wrong to collect money for a need in Jerusalem while ignoring the needs of their own members, and Paul never would have told them to do this.

90 Sadly, the world—and especially the religious world—has been so conditioned by denominationalism regarding the subject of money that an actual appeal to Scripture (like what is being done here) may come across as unfamiliar and unnatural. Yet, the authority for the collection of money in Christ's churches does not come from the churches themselves or from social expectations, but from Christ.

91 Miraculous gifts were given to early Christians because they did not (yet) have the written word to guide them; they needed to know, in the absence of the written word *or* access to apostolic teaching, what was revealed by God and what was not; and they needed miracles to underscore or confirm the gospel, as it was a new message to the world (Mark 16:16, Heb. 2:3–4). These scenarios no longer exist; the purpose for miracles has been fulfilled. Recall my scaffolding analogy in an earlier footnote. There is no longer a need to keep re-proving God's gospel over and over. It has been "once for all handed down to the saints" (Jude 1:3); the verdict is in; the confirmation of the gospel as God's message from heaven is completed; miracles are no longer necessary.

92 There are many Christians who think that God's *kingdom* and Christ's *church* are synonymous, and therefore interchangeable. This is not biblically supported. God's kingdom, in its full sense, refers to His rule over all that has been created—whether those of the Creation submit to Him or not. It is this authority over this kingdom that was imparted to Jesus, as He Himself said (Mat. 28:18). Christ's church, however, describes a specific people within this far larger domain, a people that have voluntarily given their full allegiance to Christ the King. After declaring Christ's supremacy over all kingdoms and authorities, Paul *then* specifically designates Christ as "head" over His church, "which is His body" (Col. 1:15–18). Christ is never called the "head" of the Creation, and He is never called the King of His church.

A far different—and more intimate—relationship exists between Him and His "body" than exists between Him and the rest of Creation. It is true that "the kingdom of God [or, heaven]" in Jesus' ministry did have reference to those who give their submission to the One whom God would appoint as King over all things; it is not true that this equates "the kingdom" with "the church." It is context that tells us what is being meant, not merely the description of the word itself. "The idea that church and kingdom are synonymous is of Catholic origin" (Lee Jackson, "Questions Answered by Restoration Scribes," *Restoration Ideas,* 200).

93 The word "tradition" in Scripture needs to be defined by its context. For example, the "tradition of the elders" is a man-made one (Mat. 15:1–6; see Gal. 1:14); it is subordinate to God's law and therefore expendable. "Tradition" in the context of apostolic teaching, however, refers to instructions, doctrines, and procedures dictated by the Holy Spirit (see 1 Cor. 11:2, 2 Thess. 2:15, and 3:6). These things communicated to the churches constitute church law, not mere ceremony, optional practices, or expendable teachings. The word "tradition" comes from the Greek word *paradosis,* which refers to something committed, transmitted, or handed over (as teaching, precept, or instruction) (Strong, *Dictionary* [electronic], G3862). "Paul draws here no distinction between oral tradition and written tradition as was done later. The worth of the tradition lies not in the form but in the source and the quality of the content. Paul in 1 Cor. 11:23 says: 'I received from the Lord what I also handed over *[paradoka]* unto you'" (A. T. Robertson, *Word Pictures in the New Testament,* electronic edition [© 1932, 1960 by the Sunday School Board of the Southern Baptist Convention; database © 2007 by WORDsearch Corp.], on 2 Thess. 2:15).

94 Cited from etymology.com.

95 Cited from https://www.merriam-webster.com/dictionary/policy.

96 A similar situation occurs in Acts 10:28, where Peter tells Cornelius that it was "unlawful" for "a Jew to associate with a foreigner or to visit him," and yet Peter had been sent by God to Cornelius' house. The fact is, there was nothing in the Law of Moses that forbade an Israelite from being in a Gentile's home for any reason. The Law only forbade any Israelite from adopting the religion, cultic lifestyle, and heathen practices of such people, and especially intermarriage with them (Lev. 18:24–30, Deut. 7:3–12). What Peter called "unlawful" was technically a policy, not a God-given commandment; otherwise, God commanded

Peter to break His own law! Likewise, it was the Jews' policy not to have men talk to women in public, and yet Jesus violated this policy (not divine law) by talking with the Samaritan woman at the well (John 4:9, 27).

97 Again, this involves personal choices, not actions that are expected of Christians. If my giving prayerful thanks to God for a meal in my own house offends a dinner guest, I am not at fault. However, if my dinner guest is a new Christian whose conscience is offended by drinking coffee, but (knowing this) I serve him coffee anyway and he feels obligated to drink it, I am the one at fault. I should have had enough spiritual maturity to forego my coffee for the evening on behalf of my fellow believer, rather than force my personal choices upon his tender conscience. In a parallel example, Paul said, "Therefore, if food [i.e., meat] causes my brother to stumble, I will never eat meat again [in the presence of that brother], so that I will not cause my brother to stumble" (1 Cor. 8:13, bracketed words are mine). Paul had every right to "eat meat," but he had no right to carelessly cause his brother to sin against his own conscience.

98 Chad Sychtysz, *1 Corinthians Study Workbook, revised edition* (Waynesville, OH: Spiritbuilding Publishers, 2020), 39; bracketed words are added here.

99 This list adapted from Sychtysz, *1 Corinthians Study Workbook,* 67.

100 This example does not negate the use of modern technology in this process, at least *to a point*. In other words, many Christians and churches use social media or the Internet to cast a wide net of information to whoever would respond to it. Ultimately, however, sharing the gospel should not be replaced by technology but thrives in a person-to-person exchange, just as we see in the book of Acts.

101 Many will point to Acts 6:1–4 as an approved example of the church being involved in the distribution of food. Yet, this is not an apples-to-apples comparison to the modern food bank or soup kitchen situation. In Acts 6, all the food was donated *by* the church (Acts 4:32–35) and was only *for* the church (i.e., Christians, not unbelievers). Also, the ministry of the word was said to be of far greater importance than even this. The NT offers no example or teaching of *the church* collecting and/or distributing food to those who are not Christians.

102 Some might add a third thing here: necessary implications. For example, in taking the Lord's Supper, it is necessarily implied that there must be some means by which to distribute or serve the bread and fruit

of the vine, even though these means are not literally spelled out in the instructions given to us. In my opinion, necessary implications are not a third category to consider but are simply a part of "godly wisdom." It stands to reason that things necessarily implied in carrying out God's word are already approved by it.

103   Often cited in support of this is 1 Cor. 11:22, where Paul states that we "have houses in which to eat and drink." But Paul was not forbidding *any* eating in a place that was also used for the regular assembly of Christians. The idea of a church-bought "church building" did not even come to his mind; he made zero reference to buildings, or the protocol expected within them. Instead, he addressed the abuses of the Corinthians in putting more emphasis on eating meals (and getting full and even drunk) than the sacred memorial for Christ's death: "the Lord's Supper" (11:20). This verse, then, proves nothing regarding whether a person can have a meal in a church building at a time other than the assembly.

104   This follows the pattern of what the Jews did in collecting revenue for their temple; see Mark 12:41–44.

105   My opinion, for what it is worth: if video conferencing is offered at all, it should be a temporary measure due to extraordinary circumstances, never an indefinite practice under normal circumstances. We are not allowed to redefine the "assembly" by allowing people who are *not assembling* to be treated as though they were, or for the church to be divided between those who literally do assemble and those who choose not to assemble. Extraordinary circumstances may require special responses, to be sure, but we cannot perpetuate an "extraordinary circumstance" into a regular way of doing business, so to speak, because this contradicts the very definition of what "extraordinary" means in the first place.

106   Some church leaders have been accused of being "unloving" and "uncaring" to their members for not providing them with video conferencing, brushing aside all the discerning reasons for this decision. In this case, a "loving" action is being subjectively defined, and one who violates this expectation is being charged with sin. In other words, a personal expectation is put on par with divine law, and (allegedly) church leaders will lose their souls because they did not conform to it. Instead of citing the biblical pattern for how assemblies ought to be done, this kind of thinking cites a different pattern altogether and then condemns those who will not conform to it. Such condemnation manifests neither godly love nor godly wisdom but is unchristian to its

core.

107   Paul wrote, "Do not tear down the work of God for the sake of food" (Rom. 14:20). While his statement has a specific context (i.e., food dedicated to an idol), it also has broad application. When we put food and meals ahead of what we are commanded to do in our assemblies, we are putting these ahead of God's work.

108   This refers to unnecessary food and drink—things that can wait until after the assembly is over. It does not have to do with what one might require for simple hydration or food intake for medical conditions.

109   See 1 Cor. 8:9–13 for a good explanation of what it means to offend another brother's conscience.

110   I read and use these people's works all the time in my own studies. Most of my own books stand on the shoulders of those who are far more brilliant, educated, and insightful than I am. I depend upon such resources to help my own navigation through the complexities of God's word. At the same time, it is not uncommon for these men to make mountains out of molehills—in other words, to spend a great deal of time (and pages of seminary-level prose) on a nuance of Scripture that, in the end, doesn't really change the outcome. Sometimes they do this because they feel that it needs to be done; other times, it seems, they do this to justify their credentials. In any case, the bottom line is that the world needs sincere, Christ-following theologians. On the other hand, one does not need to be a theologian to know exactly what God wants from him or her.

111   The context here refers to doctrinal teachings, not to any biblical subject. The doctrine has to do with what is required by God to enter *and* continue in fellowship with Him through His Son, Jesus Christ.

112   What Jesus *did* mean, in the context of Mat. 12:1–7 (and 9:9–13, a parallel passage), is that conformity to religious rites, including the general business of sacrifice, is not to be upheld at the expense of someone's spiritual well-being. God wants humble hearts and seeks the salvation of human souls before the rituals of worship. This does not render such rituals expendable or optional but simply puts human souls as more important than all else. Albert Barnes, in paraphrasing Jesus' words, says it well: "You Pharisees are exceedingly tenacious of the external duties of religion; but God has declared that he prefers benevolence or mercy to those external duties. It is proper, therefore, that I should associate with sinners for the purpose of doing

them good" (*Barnes' Notes,* electronic edition [database © 2014 by WORDsearch Corp.], on Mat. 9:13). It should be noted, too, that Jesus was dealing with religious rituals, not moral issues. Morality never changes, no matter what the situation. Jesus never would have said, for example, "God desires your compassion over telling the truth," because lying is a violation of God's holy nature and is therefore never permissible.

113   This word comes to us from secular usage. It is derived from Hermes, the alleged interpreter of the Roman god Jupiter; thus, it has come to be known as "the science of interpretation," and specifically the science of interpreting the Bible (Dungan, *Hermeneutics,* 1). In the book you are reading, I am purposely avoiding getting too deep into the science of interpretation simply because it does get very involved, and I do not want that discussion to take away from the subject at hand. I am using this science in the background, so to speak, but I am not wanting to take the time to develop it. If you wish to do this, however, I recommend some of the books from which I am citing (see the bibliography in the back of this book).

114   For further exploration of subjects like biblical criticism, canonicity, divine inspiration, and how what we know as "the Bible" came to be, I recommend *The Origin of the Bible* by Philip W. Comfort, who is that book's editor and a contributing author (Wheaton, IL: Tyndale House Publishers, Inc., 1992).

115   Carl F. H. Henry, "The Authority of the Bible," *The Origin of the Bible,* 13–14.

116   Ibid., 14.

117   The apostles were recipients of the Lord's in-person teaching; witnesses of His resurrection (Acts 1:21–22); given power to perform miracles (2 Cor. 12:12); entrusted with preaching the gospel accurately and entirely (Acts 20:26–27, Eph. 3:4–7, Col. 1:25–26, etc.); and enforcers of that gospel (2 Cor. 10:5–6). To support teachings, doctrines, lifestyles, and specific behaviors that have been condemned by the apostles, one must first discredit or ignore the apostles themselves. Once this is done, all restraints are seemingly lifted, and people can read *into* the NT whatever they want to believe, having robbed the apostles of their authority, and assumed it within themselves.

118   Strong, *Dictionary* (electronic), G3948.

119   This is called "presentism," when we read ancient literature or biblical texts from a purely modern perspective, imposing our present

context over the teop of the ancient one. For example, some think that the way our modern society looks upon women today is how the ancient world viewed women—or should have viewed them—then. Or some think that because our modern culture gratifies, caters to, and idolizes children today, therefore this has always been—or should have always been—the case. None of this is true, of course, but it will seem true to those who refuse to view texts according to their original source context. In studying ancient literature, just as with studying history, it is not necessary that it conforms to one's contemporary beliefs or preferences; we are simply to read it for what it is and let it draw its own conclusions—which may, in fact, be superior to our own.

120   A good example of this is 1 Cor. 1:17: "For Christ did not send me to baptize…" Many interpreters have cited this statement as proof positive that baptism is not necessary for salvation, arguing that it was not part of what Paul was "sent" to do. Yet, this ignores the immediate context (*why* Paul said this) as well as the larger context (*all* the passages that teach on baptism in the NT). The result is a teaching on conversion that is squarely at odds with the NT gospel—a most serious offense.

121   The technical word for this process is exegesis, a Greek word that means, basically, "to draw out of the text." This allows the Bible text to make its own conclusions, rather than forcing our conclusions into the text (which is called eisegesis). Exegesis is not interchangeable with hermeneutics but is a process within it.

122   One scholar says it well: "Almost anything that men want to do, they can find some text of Scripture that will sound like giving it support. And it is exceedingly difficult to make any man see that he has been preaching that which is not true. … **The Bible is not a book with which to prove doctrines; it is the doctrine itself.** Almost anything can be proven to the man who wants to find the proof. It leads to a wrong use of the Scriptures, so that, instead of searching them for whatever they may contain, the doctrines have been first assumed, and then the Bible is compelled into some sort of recognition of the position" (Dungan, Hermeneutics, 39, 43; emphasis added).

123   "The simplest and most natural interpretation of a passage must be preferred" over any other interpretation method" (Clinton Lockhart, *Principles of Interpretation* [Delight, AR: Gospel Light Publishing Co., no date (orig. 1915)], 81). Yet, the "that's your interpretation" crowd seems always to be after something different than the clear understanding of what God has said, in pursuit of something that He

did not say. For many, a conclusion has already been reached, and now an "interpretation" must be sought that justifies this predetermined conclusion. To prove this, all one needs to do is study what the Bible says about the method of conversion, church organization, homosexuality, women's roles in the assembly, and the music of God's people (to name a few of today's hot-button subjects) and compare these to what is being hailed today as "progressive," "mainstream," and "contemporary" Christianity. That person will discover a gaping chasm between these two things.

124   Lockhart, *Principles of Interpretation*, 105.

125   Dungan, *Hermeneutics*, 17.

126   Miller, *Piloting the Strait*, 157–158; emphasis is his.

127   The reason why Jesus was a worthy sacrifice for our sins is because of His perfect obedience to the Law of Moses. He was "born under the Law [of Moses]" (Gal. 4:4), and therefore had to be subject to that Law all His life. He could not be obedient to a Law that He had purposely changed; any change to the Law would have been a violation of it (see Deut. 17:19–20, in principle).

128   There are times when Jesus spoke in anticipation of His church (such as in Mat. 18:18–20, John 3:3–5, 4:21–24, 7:37–39, etc.), but such instruction did not become binding until He had fulfilled all the work that His Father had given Him to do on earth (John 17:4–5), culminating in His ascension to heaven (Luke 24:50–51, Acts 1:9–11).

129   The most common (alleged) explanation is Jesus' "vine" analogy (John 15:1–9). Jesus is the vine, and every denomination is a "branch"—or so we are told. Thus, one vine produces numerous different kinds of branches, all producing "fruit" of their own making, rather than the "fruit of the Spirit" (Gal. 5:22–23). Somehow, not only did Christ allegedly authorize this, but all such self-made "branches" are supposed to honor Him through their own particular *version* of "unity." Yet, anyone who reads the NT pattern will find zero justification for any of this, apart from subjective interpretations that completely abandon the basic rules of interpretation.

130   Such voting is often defended by citing the so-called council in Jerusalem (Acts 15), and thus we can allegedly use "councils" today to define or redefine church doctrine. Yet, the apostles in Jerusalem were only seeking to be unified on what had already been defined, based on what had already been revealed to them (Acts 15:7–12). Furthermore, morality is never and has never been decided by men, but only by God Himself, since He is the source of all moral instruction.

131   The Greek word here *(malakos)* means "soft," "luxurious," or "dainty," which refers to one's clothing. But, as Vincent says, "The word was used in a darker and more horrible sense," namely, that of a man acting like a woman in order to pursue sexual activity with another man (Marvin Vincent, *Vincent's Word Studies,* electronic edition [database © 2014 by WORDsearch Corp.], on 1 Cor. 6:9); see also Joseph Thayer's *Greek-English Lexicon* (database © 2014 by WORDsearch Corp.), G3120.

132   The Greek word here is *arsenokoites,* lit. a sodomite (Strong, *Dictionary,* G733a); also used in 1 Tim. 1:10. In 1 Cor. 6:9, Paul lists several sexual sins: fornicators, idolators (which often involved sexual promiscuity and temple prostitution), effeminacy, and homosexuality. Whatever is negatively said about fornicators and idolators must be equally applied to the other two listings, since they are all in the same category; see also Rom. 1:24–27. Sexual crimes are moral issues, not ritualistic or ceremonial teachings. Thus, sexual crimes in the Law of Moses are still crimes today (see Lev. 18:22 and 20:13) since they are timeless and changeless.

133   Indeed, even Paul has been accused of being a misogynist [lit., a hater of women] because of his teachings on male leadership and headship both in marriage and the church. It has always been amazing to me that the same people who hold Paul in contempt for his "sexist" comments on men or women will then embrace Paul's teachings elsewhere on subjects with which they agree with him. This begs the question: does Paul have the authority to speak as an apostle of Jesus Christ or doesn't he? And: are Paul's words only to be accepted if he conforms to the modern worldview (toward women, marriage, etc.), or are we to obey his apostolic authority regardless?

134   I have written on this subject (the hereafter) in considerable detail in my book, *This World Is Not Your Home* (Waynesville, OH: Spiritbuilding Publishers, 2022); go to www.spiritbuilding.com/chad.

135   Denominationalists and even liberal non-denominationalists have argued that we (allegedly, Christians) can all come together in unity and fellowship in Christ based on what they have dubbed a "core gospel." This means that, instead of treating all the apostolic teachings as necessary for such fellowship, only "core" teachings need to be considered (Miller, *Piloting the Strait,* 135). For example, the death, burial, and resurrection of Christ are of "first importance" in teaching the gospel (1 Cor. 2:2, 15:1–4). Therefore, all who teach this must be in spiritual fellowship with one another. But "first importance"

does not make all other teachings unimportant, and even Paul himself taught many other things to the churches and regarded them as "commandments" (1 Cor. 14:37). Naturally, proponents of "core gospel" unity are always the ones who decide which teachings are "core" and which are expendable or simply irrelevant. This is always the hallmark of departure from the pattern: those doing the departing are the self-appointed authorities to decide when to depart, how to depart, and what this departure will look like. (They do not, of course, use the word "depart," but this is what it is.) Also, the "core gospel" approach defines "unity" and "fellowship in Christ" differently than how Christ and His apostles defined it. Christ made His word the foundation of these things—not just selective excerpts from His word, but all of it (John 14:15). The apostles not only agreed with this but made it a test of fellowship (Gal. 1:8–11, 1 Tim. 6:3–4, 2 Tim. 1:13, 2 Peter 3:1–2, 1 John 2:3–6, etc.).

136   Many modern churchgoers have a "feeling of indifference as to what God may have said on [a given] subject. Men are ready to conclude that it matters little whether they do God's way or not. In their opinion, it will do well enough to obey the Lord in His commands, but this is not essential. If they do not prefer to do the Lord's way, He will accept them while they do their way. These persons may believe that there is a God; they may believe that He is the author of the Bible; but it has not entered their minds that it makes any particular difference whether they do His will or not. This is practical atheism. Like the Samaritans of old, they fear the Lord and serve other gods [see 2 Kings 17:24–33]. With such views of the authority of Jehovah [God], it is not possible to have any correct understanding of the Scriptures" (Dungan, *Hermeneutics,* 45; bracketed words are mine).

137   As an analogy: only a human male and a human female can, through procreation, produce a human child. If a human man mates with anything other than a human female, this will not produce a human child; likewise, if a human female mates with anything other than a human male, this will not produce a human child. Desire, good intentions, popular consensus, "God knows my heart," etc., will not change this situation. So it is with producing a Christian: only when the "seed" of the "living and enduring word of God" (1 Peter 1:23) is implanted in a sincere and obedient human heart will a "new creature" be produced (2 Cor. 5:17). A child of God cannot be produced in any other way, regardless of desire, good intentions, popular consensus, etc. Only one kind of union brings about the intended result; all other

unions will fail in this.

138   "Apostasy happens when we pervert the idea of accommodation. Are we accommodating people for the sake of truth, or are we accommodating truth for the sake of people? When numerical growth becomes more important than faithfulness to the Word, you can be sure that it is no longer God who is adding souls to the church. It is not church growth like Pentecost, but church growth at any cost" (Smith, *Who Is My Brother?*, 54).

139   "No man, who has looked with philosophic care upon the present state of denominationalism, can have failed to notice that parties aggregate largely upon the single point of taste. Nine-tenths of those who are Presbyterians are so, not because they appreciate the distinctive doctrines of that sect, or really care anything about them, but because they like the Presbyterian way of doing things. Others, whose tastes, feelings, habits, and preferences are different, go to the Methodists, for a similar reason. Others of a different type still become Episcopalians. And so, through the whole round. It is only the few who are actuated by consideration of doctrine and creed; for, whether true or false, it is beyond doubt that the prevailing opinion is that in these respects one church is about as good as another. But, aside from these, every man has his preference, and takes position as it leads him" (J. S. Lamar, "The Essential, the Important, and the Indifferent," quoted in *The Restoration Reader and Review,* electronic edition [vol. 4, no. 1, Jan: 2022], 37).

140   Miller, *Piloting the Strait*, 73–74.

141   Private condemnation of someone based on one's own standard is wrong, which is what Jesus was talking about in Mat. 7:1–2. Jesus did not say, "Do not ever criticize or disagree with anyone's beliefs or behavior." He said, in so many words, "Do not condemn anyone by your own standard of determining righteousness, otherwise God will use that standard against you, and you will certainly fail to measure up to it." The unchristian world has taken a fragment of Jesus' words and exploited them to serve its own self-serving purpose rather than to uphold biblical teaching. But discernment and decision-making are essential for upholding what is right as well as refuting what is wrong (cf. Titus 1:9). Drawing a conclusion about a person's true identity (i.e., whether he is a genuine Christian or something else) is necessary and expected. Exposing spiritual error and those who practice it is required of Christians (Eph. 5:5–12). This means Christians are *wrong* to embrace doctrinal error and other people's ungodly behavior. Instead,

they are to speak out—tactfully, and "in love" (Eph. 4:15)—against such things.

142   Compare this to what Jesus said about the scribes and Pharisees who used their positions of trust and authority to mislead the people (Mat. 23:1–15). The greater condemnation is always upon those who lay out the stumbling blocks rather than those who, through their own lack of discernment and discretion, allowed themselves to stumble over them. Even worse is causing those to stumble who are *unable* to know the truth on their own—especially, young children—an act that Jesus strongly and graphically condemns (Mat. 18:7–10).

143   Smith, *Who Is My Brother?*, 53.

144   Vincent, *Word Studies* (electronic), on 2 Cor. 2:17. Incidentally, a synonym for a "peddler" here is "huckster."

145   "Terminology" app, version 4.6.0.4, © 2010–2021 by Agile Tortoise, Inc.

146   Technically speaking, "a denomination is a collective of congregations. When congregations function as a unit, they function denominationally" (Samuel Dawson, *Denominational Doctrines* [Sumner, WA: Gospel Themes Press, 1990], 23). The collective function to which Dawson refers is most often given a name, and all the members of those congregations subscribe to that name. Historically, this is how "denominationalism" has been defined.

147   Many claim that all these men did was imitate what the apostles themselves did in the council at Jerusalem (Acts 15). Yet, this is hardly an apples-to-apples comparison. The apostles convened (along with the elders of the church at Jerusalem) to address, for the first time publicly, the issue of how to respond to Jewish Christians who mandated that all Gentile Christians keep the Law of Moses (Acts 15:1, 5). This was at a time when there was no written gospel, and therefore no final conclusions had been established. The Holy Spirit oversaw this council (Acts 15:28), since it produced a doctrinal teaching (what has been called the NT canon) that would be permanently recognized by the entire church. By the time of the later councils, however, doctrinal teaching had been clearly established, and there was no need for any new decisions concerning it.

148   Dawson, *Denominational Doctrines*, 25; italics are his; bracketed words are mine.

149   T. W. Brents, *The Gospel Plan of Salvation* (Nashville, TN: Gospel Advocate Co., 1973), 170.

150   Someone might cite Rev. 22:2, where the "tree of life" in the

vision of the church's future glory will be "bearing twelve {kinds of} fruit, yielding its fruit every month." (The words "kinds of" are inserted by the translators in the NASB.) This makes it look, at first glance, as though one tree will produce twelve different fruits. Closer examination proves otherwise, however. The Greek text here speaks of "twelve fruit harvests" or a new crop of the same fruit every month. The meaning here is that the tree of life will always be fruitful, no matter what time of year it is (Barnes, *Barnes' Notes* [electronic], on Rev. 22:2; cf. Ezek. 47:12). Of course, the tree, its fruit, any reference to months or years, etc., are all within a highly symbolic vision; they are not to be taken literally.

151   This does not mean that some modern denominational names have not been drawn from NT words, however. For example, the Baptist Church obviously draws its name from the NT practice of baptism, even though it exercises this practice differently than how the NT teaches it. The Presbyterian Church draws its name from the presbytery (or, office of the eldership) defined in the NT; however, it has one board of elders presiding over the entire denomination, which is a radical departure from the pattern. Similarly, the Episcopalian Church also draws its name from another word for elders (*episkope*, "overseers") even though it also does not follow the NT application of this word. In other words, just because names sound legitimate does not mean that the group associated with them is immediately justified.

152   As of 1990, over 700 denominations existed in the United States, all claiming allegiance to God, Christ, and the NT gospel (Dawson, *Denominational Doctrines*, 341–356). A quick Google search will probably reveal a higher number today, but some of these numbers are redundant entries, as one denomination may have several (or many) different cultural or regional names.

153   Entire denominations have been historically founded by one individual: John Knox (who studied under John Calvin), Presbyterianism; Joseph Smith, Mormonism; Ellen G. White, Seventh Day Adventists; Charles T. Russell, Jehovah Witnesses; etc. Catholicism is said to be founded upon Peter, who allegedly was its first Pope, but nowhere in the NT does it teach, say, or practice this. Christ would never have founded *His own spiritual church* upon a sinful, mortal man who needed His salvation as much as anyone else.

154   A "creed" here refers to an organizational (or collective) and binding statement of belief. Denominational creeds are not about personal statements of belief, but "state what someone says you

must believe to be in fellowship with them. It follows from this that a denominational creed must be a condition of communion in a specific coalition of congregations. This idea did not exist among New Testament Christians" (Dawson, *Denominational Doctrines*, 19). If the NT cannot produce the unity that Christ intended among His people, then a man-made creed implies that it must do what Christ failed to do.

155   "'Thank God,' they [supporters of denominationalism] say, 'that there are so many different denominations, each holding a different doctrine, that all can be suited. If *our* church doesn't suit you, in the multitude of others you can find one suited to your fancy; so you cannot fail to be suited.' ... [Yet] we see that Jesus considered divisions among those claiming to be His people as a most fruitful source of infidelity [see John 17:20–22], and He was not mistaken" (Brents, *The Gospel Plan*, 173; bracketed words are mine).

156   A "militant atheist" once argued: "Common sense tells us that atheism is a much more rational stand in the face of the conflicting claims of the world's religions than fleeing to the Bible. ... The fact that there are so many religions [that all claim to be "of Jesus"] shows, at best, that human beings have a weakness for irrational beliefs" (quoted in Dawson, *Denominational Doctrines*, 12; bracketed words are mine). The sad truth is this "militant atheist" agreed with Jesus regarding the destructive element of religious division. "In fact, he preached more like Christ on this subject than many preachers do" (*Ibid.*).

157   Those in the NT who were baptized into Christ in obedience to His gospel were not identified with any party (or denominational) name. When the Corinthians started down that road, the apostle Paul soundly condemned such separations or partyism (1 Cor. 1:11–13). Today, however, when someone becomes a member of a denomination, then he is identified from that point forward *by* his denomination.

158   Miller, *Piloting the Strait*, 69.

159   "The organic law of the church of God is the New Covenant [i.e., the gospel of Christ, which spells out the terms of salvation in His name] dedicated with the blood of Jesus; hence, any church having any other organic law than this covenant cannot be the church of God" (Brents, *The Gospel Plan*, 185; bracketed words are mine).

Sources Used for This Study

Barnes, Albert. *Barnes' Notes on the New Testament* (electronic edition). Database © 2014 by WORDsearch Corp.

Brents, T. W. *The Gospel Plan of Salvation.* Nashville, TN: Gospel Advocate Co., 1973.

Comfort, Philip W. (ed.). *The Origin of the Bible.* Wheaton, IL: Tyndale House Publishers, Inc., 1992.

Dawson, Samuel. *Denominational Doctrines.* Sumner, WA: Gospel Themes Press, 1990.

Dungan, D. R. *Hermeneutics: A Text-book.* Delight, AR: Gospel Light Publishing Co., no date (orig. 1888).

Hendricksen, William. "1 Timothy." *New Testament Commentary: Thessalonians, the Pastorals, and Hebrews.* Grand Rapids: Baker Books, 1996.

International Standard Bible Encyclopedia (electronic edition). © 1979 Wm. B. Eerdmans Publishing Co.; database © 2013 WORDsearch Corp.

Lockhart, Clinton. *Principles of Interpretation.* Delight, AR: Gospel Light Publishing Co., no date (orig. 1915).

Miller, Dave. *Piloting the Strait.* Pulaski, TN: Sain Publications, 1996.

Phillips, H. E. *Scriptural Elders and Deacons.* Marion, IN: Cogdill Foundation Publications, 1959.

The Restoration Reader and Review (electronic edition). Kevin L. Greer, ed. Leitchfield, KY: MilePost 12 Publishing & Project New Antioch, 2022.

Robertson, A. T. *Word Pictures in the New Testament* (electronic edition). © 1932, 1960 by the Sunday School Board of the Southern Baptist Convention; database © 2007 by WORDsearch Corp.

Scirghi, Thomas. *Everything Is Sacred: An Introduction to the Sacrament of Baptism.* Orleans, MA: Paraclete Press, 2012.

Smith, F. LaGard. *Who Is My Brother?* Nashville, TN: Cotswold Publishing, 1997.

Stoop, J. Ridley (ed.). *Restoration Ideas on Church Organization.* Nashville, TN: David Lipscomb College, no date.

Strong, James. *Strong's Talking Greek-Hebrew Dictionary.* Database © 2003 by WORDsearch Corp. (orig. published 1890).

Sychtysz, Chad. (All works are published by Spiritbuilding Publishers in Waynesville, OH.)

- *1 Corinthians Study Workbook*, revised edition (2020).
- *1 & 2 Timothy Study Workbook* (2019).
- *Being Born of God: The Role and Significance of Baptism in Becoming a Christian* (2014).
- *Seeking the Sacred* (2009).
- *The Gospel of Saving Grace* (2020).
- *The Holy Spirit of God: A Biblical Perspective* (2010).
- *This World Is Not Your Home* (2022).

Thayer, Joseph. *Greek-English Lexicon* (electronic edition). Database © 2014 by WORDsearch Corp.

Vincent, Marvin. *Vincent's Word Studies* (electronic edition). Database © 2014 by WORDsearch Corp.

Ware, Bruce A. "Believer's Baptism View," *Baptism: Three Views*, ed. David F. Wright. Downer's Grove, IL: InterVarsity Press, 2009.

Wharton, Edward C. *The Church of Christ.* Nashville, TN: Gospel Advocate Co., 1997.

www.ingramcontent.com/pod-product-compliance
Lightning Source LLC
LaVergne TN
LVHW051116080426
835510LV00018B/2068